Rucks, Mauls
& Gaelic Football

Billy Keane is a sports journalist with the *Irish Independent* and published his acclaimed first novel, *The Last of the Heroes* in 2005. He lives in Listowel where he runs the family pub, John B Keane's.

Moss Keane

"The phrase is overused but Moss Keane defines it – he is a living legend. Funny and wise, he is admired throughout the rugby world for his determination as a player, and for his decency as a man."

— ALAN ENGLISH, *THE SUNDAY TIMES*

"Moss writes as he played – with total honesty. I can still see him breaking away from a loose scrum under the West Stand and surging towards the Havelock Square end. [As] the Evening Press said: 'He handed off two Scots and left them spinning in the turf, rolling stones that gathered no Moss'. His book will keep you up beyond your normal bedtime. How would I sum up my old neighbour across the Brown Flesk? He is a man of few airs and many graces."

— CON HOULIHAN

"...the father figure of the second row after the retirement of Willie John McBride his record speaks for itself...in his first year on the Irish team he helped the country to their first International Championship success since 1951, and the only one in 30 years."

— *IRISH INDEPENDENT*

"Moss just go out and cause mayhem. Disrupt their lineout. Stop them getting quick ball. Stand up for yourself and your team. Kerrymen have more All-Irelands than anyone else – you're afraid of no one. Kerry are the All Blacks of Ireland. That's why we picked you."

— NOEL MURPHY, MUNSTER COACH

Rucks Mauls
& Gaelic Football

MOSS KEANE

with

Billy Keane

WOLFHOUND PRESS

First published in 2005
This paperback edition published in 2010 by
Wolfhound Press
33 Fitzwilliam Place
Dublin 2
Tel: +353 1 278 5090
Fax: +353 1 278 4800
sales@blackhallpublishing.com

ISBN 978-0-86327-970-6

Typeset by Gough Typesetting Services, Dublin
Cover design by Graham Thew Design
Printed and bound in Ireland by Colour Books Ltd

To my wife Anne and daughters, Sarah and Anne Marie,
whose love and support have provided
the inspiration for this book

and

To my late parents, Cassie and Willie,
without whose sacrifices, in tough times,
I would never have had the opportunities I did.

Contents

	Acknowledgements	ix
	Foreword	xi
	Prologue	1
One	The Very Beginning	7
Two	The Sem	21
Three	UCC	41
Four	Doctor Keane	59
Five	Picked for Ireland	75
Six	International Championship	89
Seven	Tough Times	103
Eight	The Lions	121
Nine	Munster and the All Blacks 1978	145
Ten	Winning Down Under	159

Eleven   Scoring for Ireland   173

Twelve   The Triple Crown 1982   185

Thirteen   Moving On   203

Fourteen   Mugged   217

Fifteen   Parties, Presidents and Doyler   235

Acknowledgements

To Edmund Van Esbeck for his invaluable assistance.

To Padraig Slattery for recommending Billy Keane to me.

To Billy's wife Elaine and Mick Kearney's wife Eugenie, for their wonderful hospitality and patience.

To Roger Downer, President of the University of Limerick, for facilitating our meetings from time to time.

To Mick Kearney, without whose motivation, encouragement and peace-keeping ability this book might never have been published.

To Peter Malone for his help in editing the manuscript.

To my great friend Con Houlihan for honouring me with the introduction.

To Merlin Publishing, and in particular Chenile and Aoife, for their persistence and advice.

To Mick Daly of Lansdowne, for providing valuable assistance with dates and logistics.

Finally, to Billy Keane for his patience, good humour and help in producing this book.

One particularly fond memory is myself and Mick trying to locate a B&B in Listowel at 2.30 in the morning and trying the key in a number of doors before eventually hitting pay dirt!

Foreword

by Con Houlihan

Some people, God love them, cannot accept that there is such a species as a Kerry Rugby player. The game is deeply rooted in the South West; the game called Cad was widespread there until Michael Cusack invented Gaelic Football. The new game took over because it was much safer to play.

Cad in various forms was played, if that is the word, in many parts of Britain and Ireland. It is still resurrected in parts of England, but not seriously, it is more a kind of museum piece on local holidays.

It was a good game for doctors and bonesetters; invariably it caused broken bones and cracked skulls.

The last recorded "game" took place between the sub-parishes of Cordal and Scartaglen. The occasion was sometime in the last decade of the nineteenth century.

Folklore tells us that the final score was twenty-one broken collar bones and fifteen broken legs.

Cad could not go on indefinitely – it was too costly in terms of days lost at work. In Britain a new game, Soccer, was taking root so much so that it spread all over these islands.

Cad was mainly a working class game; the public schools distilled it until it eventually became a form of Rugby.

Cusack was a genius: he could see around corners – he sensed that the time had come for an Irish game to replace Cad.

He took, what he deemed the better elements of Soccer and Rugby, and turned them into a game that he shrewdly called Gaelic Football.

The game grew like potato stalks in a moist May – because it wasn't too difficult to play and also easy to understand.

In many parts of this island it took over from Rugby. This was especially true in Kerry. Rugby was strong in Killorglin, Tralee and Killarney. Incidentally there wasn't a great difference between Gaelic and Rugby in those early years. Here is an extract from a newspaper account of an early All-Ireland final…

> "Masses of men drove into each other while the
> fleeter afoot waited in the outskirts".

In 1905 when Kerry first reached the All-Ireland final, we were represented by Laune Rangers – they had changed over from being a Rugby club.

Cad was the obvious precursor of Rugby in Kerry. Rockwell College and Blackrock College helped to nurture the game. Soldiers back from the wars played their part. This was especially true in my home town, Castle Island. Our locality was a hotbed of Rugby even though the club was only officially formed in 1925.

Castle Island RFC hadn't too long to wait for a smidgen of fame; Joe O'Connor was picked to play against Scotland in 1933. Our little community was in ferment; excitement tended to burst its bounds as the big day approached. Wireless sets were as rare then as the corncrake is now. Times were bad; people couldn't afford them.

There were however two men who could more or less; Tommy Casey was a famous tailor; Danny Sheehy was a shopkeeper who doubled as a photographer. They lived in Chapel Lane, now gone up market to Church Street. Tommy's house was in the western side of the little street and Danny's house was directly across the road.

The third figure in this story was Bill Harrington, a butcher, but a marvellously innocent man. Both Tommy and Danny had full houses. It would have been all ticket but this was unknown at the time.

Scotland were leading by two points with five minutes to go. Bill Harrington could bear it no longer – and to ease the pain he went across to Tommy's house – and was just in time to hear Joe O'Connor to score the winning try.

That night in "the parliament" at Molly's Corner, he said, "Tommy Casey has a great wireless – Danny Sheehy's is no good at all".

When Moss Keane got his first cap for Ireland, my father took a day off work to watch television. He joined many of his bosom pals in Myra McCarthy's pub in our town. There wasn't a dog to be seen in the streets. He said, "it would be a bad day for a man's cow to fall into a drain".

Moss is a native of Currow parish but we claim him as a Castle Island man. It is his family's shopping town.

I have a vested interest in Currow: I taught in two schools in the parish – Currans and Kilsarcon. For good measure – indeed for great measure – I love Currow village.

It has two very good public houses; a famous creamery; a lovely church; and the Brown Flesk. The Brown Flesk is one of the finest fishing rivers in this island – or in any island.

I love to stand on the bridge and watch it flow past the creamery, where my father spent most of his working life, and where my brother served for many years as assistant manager.

Moss Keane was lucky in his birth place. He grew up in a very lively community, where sport is a big part of the culture.

When Castle Island won their first county championship, seven of the team were from Currow. The captain Tom Shanahan, a great friend of mine, lived on the verge of the village. And the parish produced many outstanding players in Rugby. Bill Dennehy was a star mid-field back in the 1930's/40's.

Later generations included, Eamonn O'Mahony, Mickey O'Donohue, Tom Dennehy, Sunny and Martin Culloty and of course Mick Galwey.

Mick Doyle liked to pretend he was a Currow man too. His mother was a native of the village, a sister of Bill Dennehy. Mick spent most of his holidays in the famous village – but, like his brother Tom, he was as much a part of Castle Island as the Market House and the Nun's Pool and The Fountain.

I was privileged to play with them both. Mick, alas is no more.

Moss Keane had a long, and honoured, and honourable, career. There was one flaw: he was one of the best second row forwards ever capped for Ireland, but he was never capped for Castle Island.

The greatest day in his career was surely the occasion when Ireland won the Triple Crown for the first time in a generation.

Moss was at the heart of a powerful pack that slowly ground down their Scottish counterparts.

It was a wonderful day for Ollie Campbell; he got all our scores – six penalties and a drop goal.

I can still see the headline in the *Evening Press* on the Monday, "Ollie Campbell, Crown Prince".

Moss has another special memory of a game against Scotland at Lansdowne Road. I can still see him breaking away from a loose scrum under the West Stand and surging towards the Havelock square end.

The *Evening Press* said: "He handed off two Scots and left them spinning on the turf, rolling stones that gathered no Moss."

His partnership in the second row with Willie McBride, was a symbol of Ireland united in the only real way – in hearts and minds.

This book goes outside Rugby, especially in telling us about his boyhood in Currow, his beloved heartland.

Moss writes as he played – with total honesty. His book will keep you up beyond your normal bedtime. How would I sum up my old neighbour across the Brown Flesk? He is a man of few airs and many graces. Flow on lovely river.

Prologue

It was January 1974 – my first cap for Ireland.

I'd been picked to play against the French at Parc des Princes in Paris in the opening game of the Five Nations. I'd been warned by some of the old hands that this would be bloody and brutal. More bloody and brutal than anything I had ever encountered before. The French would go for us from the off.

I could do with all the advice I could get. It was only two years since my first game of rugby and here I was, a rookie as green as my jersey, in the dressing room of one of the most famous sports arenas in the world.

Ray McLoughlin the legendary Irish prop forward pulled me into a corner just a few minutes before the kick-off.

'They'll target you because it's your first cap. You must give no quarter or you'll never wear the green jersey again.'

In a way the warnings helped to take away the pre-match nerves. The forecast of a dirty game didn't bother me in the least. I was much more afraid of making an absolute donkey out of myself in front of 60,000 people and the many hundreds of thousands more watching the game on television – especially at home.

The French National anthem boomed out from the brass band just in front of us. The sound waves seemed to thump against my chest. Their fans joined in and sang with verve. There's something about *The Marseillaise* that stirs the heart. It got us going as much as it did the French. When the anthem finished private bands started up all over the place. I remember thinking it was a bit like The Rose of Tralee festival back home in Kerry and the beating of the drums brought me back to Sunday afternoons watching cowboy pictures in the cinema in Castle Island near my village of Currow.

The party atmosphere didn't last too long. I was punched three or four times in the early stages. Even though I had been warned by the old hands the savagery of the first few minutes was something I never experienced before. I threw three or four back. There was no time to think. It was just unbelievably brutal and fast. The game flew. I found the pace was on a different level to anything I had ever encountered before. I gasped for breath and for a minute thought I would never breathe again. I didn't so much breathe as swallow the air in big gulps.

But I began to adjust to the speed and intensity of the game. The punches were still flying and you could never be sure where they were coming from. Twenty-five minutes into the match, Ray McLoughlin had his ankle reefed by a French forward and was shouldered off with his bad leg dangling, like an apple ready to fall off a tree. The French were always braver in Paris than they were in Dublin, but we had a tough pack of forwards. Willie John McBride, our world-class captain, led and we followed. It was time for an 'evening up'. We started a few fights ourselves. Up to then if you were punched you just belted someone back even if he wasn't the man who'd hit you in the first place. Someone called it 'cluster punching'. There was no standing back.

I knew I would be finished with international rugby if I didn't have a cut. You might be able to hide from the crowd but your teammates would know if you opted out.

I couldn't believe it when the half-time whistle sounded. It was as if the half lasted five minutes. We gathered round our captain Willie John McBride. He was furious.

'Come on,' he roared, 'are we going to let this crowd beat us again? Look what they did to Ray. We can beat them. We are a better team – tougher, stronger and we will win. But only if we continue to stand up to them.' He seemed to look each one of us in the eye as he spoke. The second half couldn't come soon enough.

Later on in the half, I found myself at the bottom of a ruck with my hands trapped in the jumble of bodies, my head sticking out on the French side. I had no way of protecting myself. I was not in an offside position, unless you could reason my head was offside, but big and all as my mouth is there was no way I could swallow the ball. I had no chance of getting my hands on the ball either as they were trapped as well. All I could do was just lie there and wait for the fellas on top to get off. It's just something you have to put up with in rugby.

A French forward spotted me. Probably the worst thing was I could see him coming and could do nothing about it. It was like watching a scene in slow motion. He looked to see where I was lying, looked away almost nonchalantly, as if he was looking for his mammy in the stands, and then deliberately drove his studs into the side of my head with the full force of his boot. He ran off without looking down, but he knew he was on target. He must have felt the crunch of flesh and bone under the sole of his boot.

This was in the era of the long studs. Back then steel studs were long and jagged as a saw. The laws of the game were later changed, largely as a result of the match that day I'd say. The International Rugby Board brought in a specially designed gauge to measure players' studs. But the Frenchman was a practised stamper and the attack was totally premeditated. Fair enough if I threw a dig at him and he threw one back. That was spur of the moment and was acceptable. This wasn't – he was out to do me for no reason at all. But for the fact that I moved my head a fraction just as the boot came down, he could have blinded me.

The blood poured out of the gash in the side of my head between my eye and my ear. And right there in the middle of Parc des Princes, Paris, a very strange thought went through my mind. I thought it would be handy if someone had a bucket so we could have made a few black-puddings. We used to kill a pig twice a year at home in Currow and the blood was mixed with bread, barley, onion and spices to make up the black-puddings. I got a fit of laughing. It was a surreal thing to be thinking. Maybe it was the kick that triggered it. I was definitely a bit groggy.

I was still sort of smiling to myself as I was helped off the pitch, the blood getting in my eyes. I thought of my mother and father at home and I hoped the camera wasn't on me. My eyes were closed to keep the blood out and I felt the depth of the cut with my fingers. I said a prayer on the sideline as I started to come around that I wouldn't have to be taken off on my first cap.

I couldn't get it out of my head though that my mother would be in a terrible state watching this back home. Why would anyone do such a thing?

Ken Kennedy strapped up the head. Ken was our hooker and doubled up as the team doctor on the field. 'Moss. Maybe you better come off. It's a nasty wound.' But I wouldn't have it said that the Frenchman did for me.

'How much do I owe you, Ken?' I asked as we ran back on to the pitch together laughing. My head was turbaned with a yard of bandage. I was still a bit groggy but the temper and the thirst for revenge kept me going.

The French were watching. The stamper was watching. The best I could do was scowl at him. I swore revenge, of course, but I couldn't catch him before the end of the game, he was too cute. And referee Alan Hosie and his touch judges never took their eyes off me, even though all of them missed the original incident.

The battle raged on but the shoeing I'd taken seemed to concentrate everyone's minds on actually playing the game as it should be played. It was still ferocious stuff. The game went down to the wire.

There was nothing in it as the play ebbed and flowed but we were the better team. We just ground them down. McBride was right at half-time. We were the better team, but moral victories are of no use. We lost narrowly after the referee disallowed what we considered to be a valid try.

The retreat from the pitch at the end of the game was as slow as a funeral party walking behind a hearse. I wasn't sure how I'd played. I thought I did fine but I just wasn't sure. I dropped my head and thought of what might have been. We'd been so close.

I walked off on my own. Had I let my country down? Would I ever get a chance again?

Our captain, Willie John McBride, my partner in the second row, put his arm round my shoulder as we crossed the touchline and said, 'Well done, wee Maurice.' That's a strange thing to say, I thought, seeing as I was a half an inch taller than he was, but I knew what he meant. I had been hoping he'd say something. The relief seeped through my tired body. It was if I was after getting into a hot bath. Up went the head as our captain and myself walked off the pitch, side by side.

After the match I shook hands with all the French except the coward who did me. I pointed my finger at him and in a mixture of Irish and English I made him a promise I very much intended to keep. 'Beidh lá eile, you French bollix.' I think he knew what I meant, even if he didn't speak either English or Irish.

'Beidh lá eile,' there will be another day.

In the dressing room Mr Jamesy Maher, the Irish team surgeon, stitched me up without anaesthetic. If I went into hospital there would be no post-match night out in Paris for me. Stewart McKinney, our tough, rough wing forward stood beside me and said I should consider myself 'extremely lucky'. I thought it a strange remark as Jamesy Maher's needle expertly sewed up the side of my head. But I didn't say too much. I was a new boy and thought it as well to keep my mouth shut in case I'd say something stupid. I learned afterwards Stewart was trying to distract me to take my mind off the stitching.

'Cheer up Moss,' he said consolingly, 'it could have been a lot worse. You would have suffered brain damage if you'd been kicked in the arse.'

ONE

The Very Beginning

My arrival in the world on July 27, 1948 was a lot more turbulent and punishing for my poor mother Cassie and myself than the raking in the Parc des Princes over 25 years and a half years later. I was a stone weight when I was born. My two brothers, Brian and Matt, who came along a few years later, were big babies as well – a stone a man at birth. The wonder was how my mother came through her ordeal in times when there was no epidural or the like. It must have been a great relief for my father that she did survive her three pregnancies – his own mother died in childbirth on Christmas Eve 1918, when he was only a small boy.

The Keanes were small; my brothers and myself got our size from our mother's people, the O' Mahonys from Bullockfield, or Lissanore to give it its post-colonial name, about five miles from our home in Currow. My mother's grandfather, Charlie O'Connor, was a sparring partner for the world heavyweight boxing champion, John L Sullivan. He emigrated to the USA when his older brother inherited the farm, but later, when his brother died suddenly, Charlie returned to Ireland with his wife and two daughters. Half of the population of Ireland was emigrating across the Atlantic in those years, just as my ancestors were coming in the opposite direction.

Although they were small the Keanes were strong and wiry. My father Willie was about five-foot-eight, an inch smaller than my mother. Height aside, they were a good match. They married in February 1947, during the worst winter anyone could remember. My mother was in her mid-thirties, my father a few years younger. We were never told how they met but I strongly suspect it was a match – matchmaking was common in those days. My mother probably brought a dowry with her to Currow, for that, too, was the custom. Whoever made the match did a good job. There wasn't much kissing or holding hands between them but they loved each other in a practical way. They worked as a team, running the farm, rearing their three sons, and they had a wonderful respect for each other. I think that was the key to their happiness.

My father had a good farm and milked 50 cows. Our farm had been in the Keane name for about 200 years. My ancestors were tenant farmers paying rent to the local landlords. They had no security of tenure and could be evicted at a moment's notice. The landlords, the Merediths, were of Welsh origin and were decent people, but still they were landlords. When I was young I heard stories about my grandfather having to bow and scrape before them at the annual garden parties and fêtes tenants were obliged to attend. Good landlords or not, they demanded homage. Stories of those years were handed down in the family. My father's grandmother could remember her childhood during the black years of the Great Famine and she'd tell him and his brother Matt stories about it. As a young girl, she remembered throwing heads of cabbage out of the back of a donkey and cart to a group of starving people, who ate the raw cabbage there and then. My grandmother and her father were afraid to get down from the cart because of the high risk of cholera.

It's strange that a man like me has a direct connection with the famine of the nineteenth-century. To this day it kills me to see food wasted. I get genuinely upset when someone sends back food in some expensive restaurant without even touching it. Poverty has not gone away.

The Merediths' house at Dicksgrove, just a few miles away from us near Castle Island, was burned to the ground in 1921, during the War of Independence. Our house was a safe house during those years, and there was a field on our land, the Fort Field, where the freedom fighters went for shooting practice. It was only half a mile from the house but it was wild country up there, on the side of the hill, full of rushes and wet in bad weather. It offered a good vantage point for lookouts, though, which my grandfather would organise when the volunteers were training. My uncle, Fr Matt, was up there with them as a boy and remembers the volunteers being fed in the house.

The War of Independence was a cruel time. Its savageness was brought home in a terrible incident which happened right outside our front door. Jack 'Cud' O'Connor, a neighbour and by all accounts a nice, quiet man, was on his way home from attending a Sinn Féin court, set up by the Republicans as a rival to the official courts. The courts were strictly illegal, but the people were happy to use them to resolve disputes. Just a few yards from our house, Jack Cud was stopped and searched by the Black and Tans. They found papers in his possession relating to the local Sinn Féin court. Jack Cud was not a Sinn Féin party activist, nor was he involved in any form of violent struggle, he was just using the court to sort out a problem. The Tans shot him and left him for dead.

Jack Cud was badly wounded but still alive. My grandfather and some neighbours took him by pony and cart to another house nearby – grandfather could not bring the man into his own house for fear of putting his children in danger – and a priest was sent for. When the Tans spotted the priest leaving the house, they went back for Jack and shot him through the head at close range. My grandfather was lucky not to have been shot as well.

Many years later Jack Cud's descendants erected a memorial to his father. It stands 50 yards from our house, in the exact spot where he was shot. You can see it from our lawn. After the Land Acts and the reforms following Independence, my grandfather bought the place out but all that was too late for poor Jack Cud.

My mother and father held the same views on everything except politics. They were from totally different political backgrounds and I often wondered why they bothered to vote at all. They just cancelled each other out. My mother was a Fianna Fáil woman, from a staunch Republican family. Her uncle, Father Martin O'Mahony, taught Irish at Blackrock College, the famous rugby school in Dublin. He was an ardent supporter and personal friend of Éamon de Valera, founder of Fianna Fáil, many times Taoiseach and later President of Ireland. Father Martin was up to his eyes in the struggle for Independence, so much so that his superiors shifted him to a sister school, Rockwell College, to keep him out of trouble. He died there in 1944. De Valera, who was Taoiseach at the time, attended his funeral.

My father was related to Marcus O'Sullivan, the first Minister for Education in the Free State Government, and naturally he drew all the Keanes to the Fine Gael party side of the political spectrum. My Grand-uncle Nicholas hated de Valera with a vengeance. Uncle Nicholas had a right of residence in our house for his lifetime, and spent his last years ensconced in our kitchen. My mother treated him with respect and kindness, and they never had a cross word about politics or anything else. Uncle Nicholas would read the *Irish*

Independent, the Fine Gael-friendly paper, and my mother would read de Valera's paper, the *Irish Press*. Occasionally when my mother was away shopping in Castle Island or Tralee, Uncle Nicholas would sneak a look at the *Irish Press* 'just to see what that gangster de Valera is up to'.

It's not surprising I became a keen student of history and have always taken a great interest in politics. It was in the family. But the important thing was that my parents were able to get on with their lives and separate politics from the work on the farm and rearing their family. They just agreed to differ.

I was four years old when I started at Currow National School, one of the youngest children in the place. On my first day, my father brought me on the bar of his bicycle, over potholes wide and deep enough to bathe a baby in – even a Keane baby. My arse was sore for a week afterwards. In time I made my own arrangements for getting to and from school. We lived only about a mile-and-a-half from the school but the journey each day was fraught with danger. First there was Bradley's red bull. I was terrified of him and skirted the ditches in case he attacked. I had little to fear. Bradley's bull was an amorous sort and only ever came to life when he was presented with the rear end of a cow. Tom Bradley's gander was another story. Every day he set out to ambush me. He and his gaggle of girlfriends waited until I passed by and then out they came from Bradley's yard. The gander, with his long neck stuck out, hissing and snapping, the geese following him, every bit as vicious. I used to run for my life. I had to stop my mother reading the nursery rhyme *Goosey Gander* and I eventually carried out an act of censorship by tearing the page out of our story book. Nothing ever scared me as much in later years as Bradley's gander. Even to this day when I'm walking down that road taking in the panoramic view, with the rivers and streams criss-crossing the fields across our valley, and on over to the Stack's Mountains in the beautiful beloved County of Kerry in the south-west of Ireland, I always keep an eye out for that gander.

Mrs Meredith was our teacher in national school. We got on very well from the start. There was something special about her. She controlled four classes, 35 boys in all, and did so without ever slapping any one of us. I was a bit of a pet. Even when I was kept back after class – and I often was – we used to chat about this and that. By that time most of the anti-landlord feeling was long gone and the Merediths had integrated and converted to Catholicism. Sure wasn't Mrs Meredith a cousin of my father.

Tim Keane, no relation, was in charge of my brains from third class to sixth class. He was strict, though if we got a few slaps from his cane they were usually well deserved. Caning was customary at that time and didn't do us any great harm.

When we weren't in school, and almost from the time we could walk, my brothers and I were involved in helping out on the farm. That was probably the way I built up my strength. New Zealander Colin Meads, who was possibly the greatest second row of all time, was reared on a farm too, and is convinced it gave him a huge advantage in terms of physical development.

But it wasn't all work. There was also sport. I remember as clear as crystal the radio commentary when Ronnie Delany won the gold medal for the 1500 metres at the Olympics in Melbourne, 1956. Dad was beside himself with excitement, jumping all over the kitchen. My mother, not realising the significance of the occasion, pointed her index finger to her temple, twisted it around and nodded knowingly to me. But Delany's win meant so much to the country. Ireland was a developing nation back then and his victory brought a sense that now we were able to compete with anyone, anywhere in the world. Even though I was only a young lad, Ronnie Delany had a huge effect on me. I imagined myself racing up the straight, winning a gold medal for Ireland, for days afterwards.

In Kerry, though, the sport of sports was Gaelic football and our daydreaming was inevitably a case of pretending to be a Kerry football great. Gaelic football is a religion in the county. On Sunday afternoons we would gather around the radio in the kitchen to listen to the big games. I was seven when Kerry beat Dublin in the All-Ireland final of 1955, led by my hero, captain John Dowling. Even when I met him in later years, I was still in awe of him.

My father was a staunch Gaelic football man. He never missed a match if he could help it. I remember when I was very young travelling to a Kerry game with him on the train from Farranfore to Caherciveen. The old line, which is now closed down, wound around the side of the mountains overlooking Dingle Bay. I could see little boats bobbing up and down on the white, curly waves of the Atlantic. I was thrilled by the huge skies and the steep cliffs falling headlong onto the rocky shore below, but then we crossed over a high viaduct and plunged into a dark tunnel cut into the mountain and I became frightened. I remember pushing into my father and he put his arm around me to calm my fears.

Every Sunday, Patsy Bradley, Timmy Hickey, Johnny Junior Brosnan and myself played our own All-Ireland in our own Croke Park, in the corner of a field where we'd put up goalposts for the match. It was two against two and sometimes tempers rose in the heat of the contest, but there were always a few adults present to ensure matters didn't get out of hand.

My father explained the rules. 'No cursing, kicking, scraping or biting. Get the ball in hand and then kick it. It's catch and kick, that's what it is. It's not soccer you're playing.

Hit hard with the shoulder, but hit fair. And let there be no pulling and dragging at jerseys or jumping up on fellas like in that oul' rugby. And no crying.'

Patsy has since passed away, but the three of us remaining are still the best of friends. In time Brian and Matt joined in. I was two years older than Brian and Brian was three years older than Matt, but we all got on well together. Even if we often beat the bejaysus out of each other as kids, to this day we are very close: my mother and father always emphasised that we should stick together.

We boys were all stone mad about football but we loved our horses almost as much. My father kept two giant Irish draughts, Nellie and Molly, and there was a pony too by the name of Gubby. Mollie was wild, Nellie tame, and Gubby and I were good pals, or so I thought until the day of my Confirmation. I was walking home from Mass in my shiny new suit, new shoes and white ankle-socks, with Sheila Bradley and Eileen Gorman, two girls my own age. There was Gubby standing in the muck and puddle at the gate. I hopped up on her back, showing off with no saddle or bridle, and off we galloped around the field. When we got back to the point of take-off, Gubby pulled up suddenly and I shot out over her head. My new suit was in shite, in every sense of the word. It was never worn again, though the plan in those days was for the Confirmation clothes to be handed down to the next in line. My mother burned my suit in the rubbish barrel in case my father got to see the state it was in. I'd discovered that showing off in front of girls could have serious repercussions.

Our farm lay on the banks of the Brown Flesk river, which rose not far from the source of the Blackwater across the border in Cork, then travelled westwards to join the River Maine before turning for Castlemaine Bay and the Atlantic. In my boyhood it was a fabulous river for fishing, and my brothers and I spent many an hour on the banks of the Brown Flesk, fishing for salmon and trout with bamboo rods.

Brian came up with a game that married fishing to Gaelic football. A trout was a goal or three points and an eel was one point. Eels were plentiful. I caught nineteen eels but Brian caught five brown trout and five eels. He won it 20 points to 19, one of my earliest GAA defeats.

Our life was a routine imposed by the needs of the farm. We had no electricity until the 1950s and no television until the '60s. Cows were milked early in the morning, so we went to bed early at night. Dinner was at 12 pm. I can still taste my mother's stew, which simmered on the range for hours filling up our kitchen with an aroma that would have you ravenous. There will never be a stew to beat it: our own beef, carrots, parsnips, and potatoes grown in the garden. There was more food at four and again at about nine after the cows were milked a second time.

Johnny Brosnan Senior, who worked for us on the farm, and his wife Maureen were very nearly part of our own family. Their son, Johnny Junior, was like the fourth brother. My father sent me working with Johnny Senior at every available opportunity and I got to know him well. He had no great education but he was one of the most brilliant men I ever met. Johnny was a man who seldom dished out advice, but I got in the habit of listening closely when he did.

Directly across the narrow river from us lay Bill Dennehy's farm. His nephews, Mick and Tommy Doyle, who went on to play rugby for Ireland, used to spend lots of time there. I met them from time to time, but they were a good bit older than me. Bill's cattle were staunch proponents of the maxim 'faraway hills are always greener' and often swam or paddled across the river to graze on our land. Sometimes my father sent me over to negotiate their return. We never fell out over it; indeed, my father always voted for Bill, the local Fine

Gael Councillor, even when his cattle were helping themselves to our grass.

Neighbours were neighbourly. They called in to chat in the evenings, and left early to get back to their own farms. There was great storytelling. I was often kept awake at night after listening to a ghost story or kept laughing at the funny things I'd heard. I was shy and never said a word, just took it all in.

Our area had been ravaged by emigration so it was not all that uncommon for a neighbour to have taken a trip to the States to visit some relative or other. One evening, a neighbour dropped in who had just come home from America, where he was visiting his son.

'What did you make of America Tom?' asked my father.

Back in those times there were still a good many outdoor toilets in our area and we'd never heard of such a thing as a barbecue.

Tom replied, 'William, it's a strange place America, very strange.'

'In what way Tom?' asked my father.

'Sure don't they go to ate out of doors and don't they go to the toilet indoors!'

Of course we said the family rosary every evening as well in those days, each of us kneeling at a chair in the kitchen, my mother leading and my father offering the second decade. I was a proud boy the night I led for the first time.

I felt closer to my mother than my father, which was the way of things in those days. I could tell her everything that was bothering me and she always seemed to have the right words to solve the problem. Every year she brought us to the beach in Ballybunion for a week's holidays. We splashed about in the sea but I never learned to swim. Even though I lived on the banks of the Brown Flesk I was afraid of my life of water. I still am. If I go in above my ankles I get a bit panicky.

My father was usually too busy to come for the full week but he might join us for a day or two – farming was too demanding a life to allow any time for holidays. As a young fellow, I grew up with the idea that I had better get used to it.

I always had great respect for my parents. We did as we were told, well most of the time anyway, and there was no backchat.

The first night we stayed in Currow as a married couple my wife Anne, and who could blame her, was feeling a bit amorous.

'Ah Anne will you stop!' I said to her.

'Why Moss?' she asked, knowing this wasn't my normal form.

'Ah Anne,' I replied, 'not under the same roof as my mother and father.'

My parents were decent, hard-working people and had no bit of malice or angst in them. It showed in the way they cared for us. We weren't pets, far from it, but we were petted if the need was there for petting.

And what a childhood I had – off all day around the fields with my friends and Rover Keane. All the dogs in our area were called Rover hence the need to add on the family name at the end. There was Rover Keane, Rover Bradley, Rover Brosnan and so on. They were funny times, innocent and carefree.

But nothing lasts forever. I had my first taste of reality during the Christmas holidays. It was my job to bring Uncle Nicholas his breakfast in bed. The first time I called up to his room I thought he was sleeping. I called back again at about 11 o'clock. I knew immediately he was dead. It was the first time the world intruded in my childhood.

I suppose that was the moment I discovered there were sad days and a whole process from the cradle to the grave.

Life changed a bit for me after that. I was due to take the primary certificate that summer, the final state exam in primary school, so I had to study more. My parents wanted me to try for the entrance exam to St Brendan's College in Killarney as well so I was kept hard at it.

On the day I did the primary cert I decided to carve my name on the desk. I reasoned there was no point in spending all those years in the place without leaving a mark, something to let future generations of schoolchildren know that a young lad by the name of Maurice Keane had sat at that desk, that day. I knew that Master Tim Keane would take a dim view of this, but I'd heard that I'd passed the entrance exam to St Brendan's and would be going there in the autumn, so I decided to award myself an early summer holiday while I was at it.

I planned to spend the days heading off to the bog where the men were cutting turf and helping out. I loved working in the bog during the summer time. The men worked as a *meitheal*, a group of neighbours who got together to help each other out in busy times or if someone was ill. There was a tremendous sense of community among the farmers in my area; they would go to the ends of the earth to help each other out. We children helped too. Any one of the three of us could be posted to neighbouring farms to give them a hand with gathering fodder for the winter or hauling turf home for the fire.

So it ended up that I left Currow National School before I was 12. My parents didn't mind as there were only a few weeks left in the term and I was handy enough around the farm by then.

I was bringing tea to the bog a few days later when a Garda stopped me and asked if I was the boy who was dodging school. 'Maybe,' I replied cautiously, anxious not to tell a lie to a policeman but at the same time not wanting to incriminate myself. Then I ran off before he could ask me any more. The Garda didn't give chase. It might have been a set-up to put manners on me, but I wasn't taking any chances.

Carving my name and the truancy may have seemed trivial enough but they were to have important repercussions. In my youthful innocence I considered myself a marked man, almost a criminal. I made up my mind I could never again return to the scene of the crime, Currow National School, even though Tim Keane wanted me to wait another year before going to secondary school. But there was no going back to Currow National School. Sure I thought I was practically on the run. I tried not to think too much about going off to boarding school that autumn and enjoyed an idyllic summer, working on the farm.

TWO

The Sem

As the day approached the idea of heading off to St Brendan's filled me full of excitement but I was fearful too: Johnny Senior had warned me it might not be all it was cracked up to be. I sensed Johnny might be right but my father had a different view. He was convinced St Brendan's was the place for me, and pointed out that I had been lucky to pass the entrance exam when many boys were denied a place due to the big demand to get into the school. And my uncle, Fr Matt, had gone to St Brendan's, so there was a precedent. The way my parents saw it, there was no other choice.

But the small boy who left Currow on that fine September morning in 1960 was not really ready for the rigours of boarding school. I was still convinced I couldn't return to school in Currow but I was so petrified when I saw the big grey limestone buildings looming over me, as Davie Fitz's Zephyr pulled up outside the college, that I was almost ready to ask Davie to turn for home. My mother said her goodbyes and told me to behave myself, to say my prayers and study hard. Then the car pulled away down the drive and out through the big wrought-iron gates, and I realised that I was on my own.

St Brendan's, or the Sem as it was known, was also a Diocesan seminary, charged with encouraging and preparing pupils for possible entry into the priesthood. I can say without fear of contradiction that my family never saw me as Fr Moss, although I must say it has a nice ring to it. Canon Moss would be even better, though my favourite title would have to be Monsignor Moss, for the alliteration alone. I'd have made a lovely priest, full of compassion and altar wine.

I was very shy that first term. All I wanted to do was keep my head down, but at study I was placed at a desk inside the door. When someone knocked I had to march all the way down the long study hall to inform the priest in charge that there was somebody asking for him. I tried to walk as quietly as I could but my shoes were too big, and as often as not I tripped over a bag or barged against a desk. I felt everyone was looking at me and my face would go a blotchy red. I would have covered my head with a blanket if I could.

The college authorities were well aware of young boys' loneliness and from time immemorial the Sem was 'regionalised' – boys were seconded to a group from their own area, which was called 'a column'. My group was the Firies Column which embraced an area from Milltown to Castle Island. The system meant you belonged to a group with links to your own place and ensured a certain amount of protection from the bigger lads in the school. Socialising outside the confines of the column was frowned upon, though it was all right to be friends with boys from your own class. As the years went by the divisions became blurred and I made friends from every column, even the Cork one!

I hated those first few months in the Sem. I found it impossible to talk to the other lads, and I would wander along the corridors hoping no one would talk to me, but wishing at the same time that they would. All I wanted to do was go home. I was only 12 miles from Currow, but it might as well have been a million. There wasn't much communication with home. We had no telephone and anyway the college authorities would not allow a call even if you had one. We did write and my parents always answered but that was that, until the end of term. Visits were allowed, two a term, but aside from that the regime seemed to go to great lengths to keep us incommunicado.

Then a few months in I got into a fierce row with one of my classmates. I have no idea what caused the fight but all at once fists were flying. We wrestled, broke loose, re-engaged, fell, got up and flaked away at each other again. The boys were delighted; they stood up on their seats and roared us on. We soon ran out of steam and the scrap fizzled out, but it was the best thing that ever happened. We combatants shook hands a few days later. The lads enjoyed the fight and talked about it for the rest of term. The flare-up brought us all closer together and I lost some of my shyness. I even made a few friends.

A few weeks later, just before Christmas, I was in trouble again. I threw a boot at one of my new friends, missed him and broke a window. The code of honour in the school ruled that if you broke something you had to own up. One of the bigger lads from the Firies Column advised me to go straight to the President, Fr Moynihan.

I knocked feebly on the door of his office and eventually he called out, 'Enter!'

I was hardly able to speak with fear and shame, but in the end I told him my story. I was sure I would be sent home or slapped until my fingers were red raw.

'I have no money to pay for it, Father,' I explained, almost in tears.

'Well isn't that a fright, Keane,' he said. 'That's the worst I ever heard of in all my years here.'

That was it: expelled after three months. I'd be shamed back home. The mother would be bawling and the father would get thick.

Fr Moynihan delivered his verdict. 'That boy you threw the boot at, was he so mean as to duck? Go on away and try to stop breaking things.'

I walked down the stairs to my class with the jaunty gait of a man reprieved from death row.

Fr Moynihan was a kind man but the regime in St Brendan's was as strict as any prison. The very building even looked like a prison. The inmates were housed in dormitories, or cells, of different sizes. In first year our sleeping accommodation consisted of box rooms, four boys to each room. We first years were at the bottom rung of the food chain. At the top were the priests.

The day was a carefully planned routine.

Wake-up bell 7.15 am
Mass 7.40 am
Breakfast 8.15 am
School 9.00 am
Lunch 1.00 pm
School 2.00 pm
Football 3.45 pm
Study 5.15 pm
Supper 8.00 pm
Bed 9.30 pm
Lights Out 10.00 pm

The fact that I was at the end of the chain of command didn't bother me as much as the confinement. We were prohibited under pain of expulsion from leaving the school grounds. I longed to run and run – I began to have nightmares about being tangled in barbed-wire, the thought of not being able to roam like I could at home cut through me. Even when we crossed the road to get to the Gaelic football pitch, the manoeuvre had to be carried out in a straight line, we schoolboys like ducks following the leader. It was humiliating for young adults to have to take their place in a chain-gang just to cross the road. I subsequently discovered the priests didn't have much freedom either, and it showed in many cases.

There was one priest in particular who inflicted more physical punishment on me than anyone else. In fairness to him he had no favourites. He beat everyone and anyone. I used to be terrified of him on Monday mornings when he came into class in the foulest of moods. The cane was hidden behind the black cloak, which all the teachers wore in those days. There were days when you would hope that maybe he'd forgotten it or that maybe it was broken. Then, without warning, out would come the stick, like a sword from a hidden scabbard, and the shouting and roaring would start. I can still hear the swish as it rained down us. And I can still feel the stinging on the tops of the fingers. He shouldn't have been there at all and maybe if he wasn't he could have been a decent man. The priests also had to donate half their salary to the college and make many other sacrifices.

The only other means of escape was through a visit to Mrs Carey, the dentist in High Street. Boys developed toothache just to get a glimpse of the outside world, but I was afraid of dentists, so that ploy was no good to me.

I was only back after Christmas when I was dying to go home again. I just couldn't get used to the regime at school after those first Christmas holidays. We had wonderful Christmases at home. Plenty to eat and drink and that year we'd a 20lb turkey stuffed front and back. I'd met up with my friends and we'd had the freedom of the farm. It had made going back to school a bit hard.

I was starting to wonder if I could stick it back in Killarney when I woke up one night in a terrible sweat, rambling and talking rubbish. The boys told me afterwards I was using bad language and calling the priests horrible names. I was mortified – and it was only towards the end of my final year in college that they finally relented and told me they had made all that up.

I was immediately transferred to an isolation hospital in Killarney and spent two weeks there, drifting in and out of fever. I was terrified and thought I was going to die. I kept saying Hail Marys and Our Fathers. I remember thinking, 'That's it now, Moss, you're a gonner, and you haven't had a proper kiss from a girl or won an All-Ireland medal.' All I wanted was my mother and father but I was kept in isolation. Whatever it was I was suffering from must have been very contagious. And I never knew what was wrong with me – I was never told. I was a tall, gangling lad, and my illness left me thin and miserable for months afterwards. When I got back to school I wanted to go home more than ever.

There were times, though, when God looks after his own. The lake known as the Devil's Punchbowl, which supplied water to the town, froze solid that winter and the school was closed for a week. The temporary reprieve saved me: I had been ready to ask to go home altogether.

But all the rest in the world wouldn't turn me into a top class Gaelic footballer. I just couldn't get onto any of the St Brendan's football teams. I was always strong for my age – even after my illness – but strength alone was not enough. The St Brendan's footballers were usually among the best in the county and in reality that meant in Ireland. If many mothers sent their boys to the Sem to be turned into priests, many fathers sent them to be trained as Kerry footballers. I was competing with lads like Mícheál Ó Sé, the excellent radio commentator from West Kerry who was as strong as me and a great deal faster. He was a superb footballer and went on to win two All-Ireland medals with the Kingdom. I could have no complaints about not getting onto any of the school teams; the side was picked on merit and I just wasn't good enough. But it left me disappointed. I wanted more than anything to be a football player. I remember thinking that maybe if I'd stayed put that extra year in Currow things might have been different. I would have been competing with lads of my own age.

Football always reigned supreme at the Sem. When I was in second year, St Brendan's reached the All-Ireland Colleges final and we were shipped to Dublin for the game. We might have been underfed in the refectory but the college authorities didn't spare money when it came to bringing us to matches. We headed off to the capital in our usual regimented style, warned by the prefects that anyone who strayed from the group could well be kidnapped and 'forced to eat mashed potato made from bananas and shovel coal in the hold of a ship for the rest of his days'. This communiqué was meant to keep us alert to the risk of getting lost, and it worked: we stuck so close together on the streets of the city that we were constantly bumping into each other.

When our bus pulled up outside Croke Park I was unable to speak. Our football ground at home in Currow was only the width of a farmer's gate compared to this stadium. I'll never forget those first impressions – the towering stands, the huge crowd, the shouting, the battalions in their colours, the sense of history and the realisation I was about to walk on holy ground. I swore I would die happy if I ever got to play there.

When the game started I wanted to tear off my street clothes and leap onto the field in the St Brendan's colours. Instead I said a few Hail Marys that the lads would win. I transferred that desire to the great rugby grounds of the world as I grew older, but it all started the day St Brendan's played St Mel's of Longford in the All-Ireland Colleges final in the early sixties.

Donncha Ó Corráin, a fellow pupil, and now Professor of History at University College Cork, was allegedly

responsible for penning a school song sung to the air of
O'Donnell Abú:

> Proudly the boys of St Brendan's are coming
> Loud rings the air with a cheer and hurrah
> Champions of Munster are bravely advancing
> To win with their valour, great victory today
> Onward the Green and Gold
> Forward the brave and bold
> Think of your glory, you fearless and true
> Proud of your name and fame
> Champions of every game
> Onward Killarney – St Brendan's Abú.

Lads who could never remember a line of poetry had the
song off by heart in minutes. We cheered our hearts out and
sang until we were hoarse but in the end the team lost.

I can still remember every bit of that game – it was one
of the best colleges' finals ever seen – and the sense of loss I
felt was overwhelming. On the way home I could hardly
raise my head out of my hands.

The excitement of the visit to Croke Park stayed with me
through the rest of second year and I took it home with me
to Currow at the end of the school year. That summer I
made my debut with the Currow under-14 team. I was
bursting with pride pulling on the jersey, no matter that it
smelled of stale sweat. Like most clubs, Currow could only
afford one set of jerseys, so you wore the shirt some lad had
worn the evening before, on another of the club's teams.
Those matches gave me my first real sense of the game,
playing for Currow in the Castle Island District League. It
was a long way from playing in the corner of a field with
Johnny Junior, Patsy and Timmy.

My father came to watch the match and at half-time he
didn't spare me.

'Stop running around like a headless chicken,' he said. 'Stay on your man. That's your job.' I was playing at wing half-back. 'You can't play in the backs and forwards at the same time,' he told me.

I had been so excited to get a game I wanted to be everywhere all the time, which of course meant I was nowhere at the right time – as soon as I got to the scene of the action the ball was already moving down the field. Even so, I loved every minute of the match and couldn't believe it when it was over. As we drove home afterwards, my father went back over my game and said he was pleased with my second-half performance. The football was the highlight of the summer and I improved as a player. I was delighted and thought that maybe third year would be my year to make it onto a school team.

It wasn't until then that I found my feet in Brendan's. At that stage I had moved up along the pecking order. Better again, on the first day back after the summer holidays we were met by the glorious sight of a new extension to the college. Not that we had any interest in this improvement to our educational facilities – what caught our eyes was the gap the builders knocked in the school wall. The shop was now only a 30-yard dash away. We set up teams of four, with lookouts, and took it in turns to race up the lane. We were never caught, even the slow coaches like me. By then I didn't care about the risk, I was hooked on cream crackers and Calvita cheese, which could be bought in little silver-wrapped triangles. I used to eat them in secret in case one of the bigger lads caught me and confiscated my supplies. My favourite place was in the toilet cubicles, which was about the nearest you could get to privacy in St Brendan's. For as long as supplies lasted, I slipped into the toilet every morning after breakfast for a feed. Every morning except Wednesday because the food on Tuesday was so good.

Our normal supper consisted of plain bread-and-butter and tea. Usually a second helping of butter would be provided halfway through the meal. As the maid approached the table there was a flash of steel and by the time she placed the butter tray on the table it was empty. There was never enough to eat except on Tuesdays, when we had sausages for lunch and cow pie – shepherd's pie – for tea. Years later one of my schoolmates, Paddy Kennelly from Ballylongford, a brother of the poet Brendan, wrote a hilarious book about St Brendan's, one roundly condemned by the school authorities and the clergy in general. He called his memoir of school life *Sausages for a Tuesday*.

I lived for Tuesdays. There were eight of us seated at each table and on average half the lads wouldn't touch the cow pie because there was a fair chance they would spend the next morning on the toilet bowl if they did. It never bothered me, but on Wednesdays I avoided the school toilets and took my cheese off to the shed near the football pitches.

I was luckier than most when it came to food. My Uncle Matt was a priest of the Diocese and as such was entitled to bring me out for something to eat once a month. Fr Matt never let me down, though I'm afraid I wasn't much company. All I did was eat.

'How are you finding the Latin, Moss?' he'd ask.

'Fine,' was as much as I'd answer, through a mouthful of spuds and meat.

On one occasion I ate so much the chef and kitchen staff in the Arbutus Hotel in Killarney came out to take a look at me.

Fr Matt was also good for a ten-shilling note about twice a term. I'd drop him a line and the red note would arrive by return post. I was grateful for the money and converted it immediately into little triangles of cheese and those square packets of Jacob's crackers.

But all the feeding in the world wouldn't get me onto the school team. I just wasn't good enough and that's what made it so hard to take.

Another school year passed, slowly, followed by a flying summer and it was back again for the annual student retreat which took place every September in St Brendan's. It ran from Friday night through to Sunday. It was meant to be a time of reflection, though how the powers-that-be expected young lads our age to reflect on anything other than food, football and girls was beyond me. I suspected that they had other motives. The Sunday of the retreat always coincided with the All-Ireland football final. My guess was that the timing was a crafty way of ensuring order in the school while half the priests went off to Dublin for the match.

There was a rule of silence during the retreat but an amnesty was declared from two o'clock until six on the day of the game. The whole school gathered around the radio as Kerry took the field to play Roscommon in the 1962 final. The game started with a bang – Gary MacMahon scored the cutest goal you could imagine inside the first few seconds. He just gave the ball a little flick of the wrist and it was in the back of the net. We went mad. Our excitement at the goal and our release from some 70 hours of silence came together – we nearly took the roof off the refectory. The priests threatened to turn off the radio if we didn't stop roaring. We calmed down as the game went on but at the end, when Kerry lifted the trophy, we let loose again. Then the priests rang a bell and the school returned to total silence.

Except for me. I couldn't keep my delight in – I just had to talk to someone. I was caught by one of the prefects, a vile-tempered, bullying boy who began to punch me hard with his fists. I was taking a terrible hiding when another boy stepped in. Normally senior students never interfered in an altercation between a prefect and a younger boy, but I was getting a bad beating. 'If you lay another hand on Keane,' my saviour said, ' I will whip you around the school for the rest of the year,' and he threw three or four rapid punches at my tormentor. Of course when someone his own size stood up to him, the bully slid away.

The boy who saved me is now a retired Garda Sergeant, Des Kidney. I met him many years later when he stood guard in front of Taoiseach Jack Lynch's house in Rathgar, Dublin. I never forgot his kindness and bravery that day; he had risked being expelled or ostracised from his own class for my sake. He got on fine, fortunately, because most of the big lads had the bully in their sights anyway.

Kerry contested three All-Ireland finals during my time in the Sem. When we lost to Galway and Down, the Cork lads gave us an unmerciful ribbing. All we could do was take it. We maintained that regal aloofness ingrained in the citizens of the Kingdom since the beginning of Gaelic football – say nothing, take your beating, for our day will surely come again. The 1964 final was another bad day for Kerry, though it was an incredible treat for us as the match was on television. We could hardly eat with excitement.

Galway got the better of Kerry by just three points that time.

After five years of trying I never did get onto a school team, but I finally beat Mícheál Ó Sé in the 12lbs shot at the Annual School Sports. The sports were held on St Brendan's Day, 16 May, a few weeks before exams. Maybe he wasn't trying his best, giving me a chance for friendship's sake. Still, it was a big day for me, in my final year in the school. I was the best at something there at last.

We were well-prepared for the exams. St Brendan's was an excellent school. I may have more marks on my hands from the slaps I took from some of the priests there than from all the blows I took on the rugby field, but I survived and I can honestly say the bad moments didn't leave any lasting affect on me. Those were different times, when corporal punishment was the norm, and the Sem was the same as any other boarding school. Even if some of the teachers went a bit too far at times, most of them were very decent, and by the time I left things were opening up a little. When Brian became a St Brendan's boy, the regime, if not quite liberal, was heading that way. I am proud to call myself a St Brendan's man: I always will be. I made many friends there, and the education we received meant we were able for anything that faced us in university.

I did a good Leaving Certificate and ended up with six honours, enough to get me into any university faculty I chose. I fancied my chances of becoming a primary school teacher, but when I was called for interview at St Patrick's training college in Dublin I failed the singing exam. I think I sang *Three Blind Mice* but obviously it was the wrong choice of song. Maybe the bit about running up the leg of the farmer's wife didn't impress the examiners too much. That was how that ambition ended.

I left St Brendan's on the final day of my Leaving Certificate in the same Zephyr that had brought me there five years earlier.

Davy asked me if I remembered the day he brought me and said, 'they must have fed you like one of your father's bullocks to get you into the size you are now.' If he only knew.

I decided to go to the Salesian Agricultural College in West Limerick, about 60 miles from Currow, to learn my trade as a farmer. The year I spent in Pallaskenry changed my life. We boarded, but it wasn't strict, and students were allowed home whenever they wanted. Fr Hannify, a noted Galway GAA player in his youth, took a special interest in me. He was an exceptional man who wanted the best for everyone in his care and he helped me to get the most out of my studies. Most of all, he instilled confidence in me.

I made the football team with ease and I was delighted with that. It was a great feeling to pull on a school jersey and if the standard wasn't quite as high as St Brendan's, it was still a good level of football with serious competition for places from players who hailed from all the Munster counties. I was involved in handball and basketball successes and I began to think more of myself. And then we won the Kerryman Cup, a junior Limerick Gaelic football competition, which was a first for the college. I was beginning to feel less awkward, too. It was a great relief that I had finally stopped growing. I felt more balanced and my fitness began to improve. Keeping fit was becoming part of my life. I loved taking long runs through the school's farm and I started at press-ups and sit-ups – before long I was into the hundreds.

At the end of my course I discovered I was to be Student of the Year for 1965-66. The Minister for Agriculture, Charles J Haughey, arrived for our graduation, and when I stepped up to be presented with my award I towered over him – the future Taoiseach was a small man. I felt embarrassed. He was the Minister and should have been bigger than me.

He beckoned me to lower my head as the photograph was being taken. I thought he was going to say something innocuous, maybe ask me how many acres we had at home. Instead he whispered in my ear: 'I hate big Kerrymen.'

'And I hate small Dubs,' was my hasty reply.

It was out of my mouth before I realised what I was saying, and in the same moment I realised that the man I was talking to could make or break careers in agriculture. But the Minister just laughed. He loved a bit of banter.

I headed for home at the end of a great year in Pallaskenry. It had done me good. I had matured and knew my own mind better which was just as well as I'd made a tough decision. My father felt I should help him in the farm but I wanted to go to university. It was a chance he'd never had – that was just the way it was when he was my age. There and then I dropped the bombshell – I did not want to take over the running of the family farm when the time came for him to sign it over. It was the custom for the eldest son to take over the farm, and my father asked me to think about it some more. I said I would. I knew he was disappointed, but there were two other sons and the land would remain in the family. My brothers were well capable of looking after it. Matt was the youngest but I think Brian and myself knew he would make the best farmer. Brian was still in the Sem. He was next in line to inherit but eventually he followed me to University College Cork, where he studied accountancy and excelled at boxing.

I also knew that if I stayed at home it would be several years before the place was signed over to me. I had seen very little of the world and wanted to experience a bit of life. I needed to cut loose. I was throwing up a lucrative business where I would be my own boss, on my own place, as we had a good-sized holding by the standards of the day, but I wanted a change.

There have been days since my bombshell when I'm sweating in the heat of the city and I think of Currow and how nice it would be to be up in The Field above the Top Field, looking down on the Brown Flesk River. I'm lucky that Matt and his wife Joan always treat me like royalty when I come home. I can walk in or out of my family home whenever I like, and that means a lot to me. And for that matter I can do the same with my other brother Brian and his wife Catherine, who live in Kilkenny.

But in the summer of '66 all those things were a distant prospect. England had won the World Cup and at just 18, I graduated to the Currow Senior Team. I played in goal in times when there was more violent action in the square than you'd get in a small war. Mick Galwey's uncle, Mick, was the leader of the team. A kind and gentle soul off the pitch, on it he was a man possessed. The old war-horse, Billy Walsh, was our full-back. Once – and only once – he shouted at me. 'If you let in another soft goal,' he roared, 'I will kick the shite out of you.' Or words to that effect.

Billy and Mick looked after me. Even though I was big, I was very green and still developing physically. The two made sure no one picked on me or hit me a dirty slap. I knew Mick and Billy would die for me but I was still more terrified of the two boys than the opposition. I was a happy man to be moved out towards mid-field and centre-back, well away from the front lines, where mistakes were more easily spotted and could lead to goals. They were tough times, those junior football matches, and Galwey always took the view that a pre-emptive strike worked well, from a tactical point of view.

The highlight of the football season was the game against our near neighbours, Castle Island Desmonds. Castle Island, a town of about 2,500 people, was situated just four miles from Currow, and it would not be an exaggeration to say that our rivalry was more intense than the competition between Celtic and Rangers – it was nothing short of bloody and brutal at times. I'm not quite sure why this should be. I have experienced nothing but kindness from Castle Island people in the years before and since. They always came to support me when I played for Ireland and I often travelled down to attend club functions. The cause of the friction might have something to do with some perceived slight at a cattle fair or a dirty dig thrown at a game years before. And we were always a bit in awe of the townies. They were snappier dressers, faster talkers, better at getting women – our women. Worse again, they usually beat us at football.

After several heavy defeats we did eventually master Castle

Island Desmonds, and made history in the next few years when we beat them all of four times. But that was when I was in my twenties. Now the big thing was that I was getting games and improving as a player. I was chosen to play in the full-back line for the Castle Island District minor team, the pick of all the clubs in the area. We trained every evening in the local field and disposed of Mid-Kerry and West Kerry in the County Minor Football Championship. We came up against Austin Stacks of Tralee in the final.

This was football of a high standard. There was a small, curly-haired lad, with incredible pace, playing on the Stacks team, even though he was only 14 at the time and shouldn't have been picked to play at all. At one moment in the match he stooped down somewhat naively to 'rise' the ball, and just then I could have sent him into the middle of next month. I left him be. He was fiery and fearless and I don't think he even saw me. He was Ger Power, who went on to captain Kerry and win eight All-Ireland medals.

That day, though, we beat the Stacks.

After the match there were objections against three of us. Our full-back line was big – the smallest was six-feet-two – and it was alleged we were over the age limit. I only discovered recently that we did in fact have an overage player, and of course he was the smallest man on the team. I didn't care. I had held my own against some really good players and won my first county medal.

The hard work around the farm also helped to keep me in shape. We had an old axle that was used to prop up the henhouse door and I could easily lift it over my head. My friends Johnny Junior and Patsy Bradley could only get it up to their waists. I built up stamina chasing calves and heifers in and out through gaps in the ditches and up the side of our hill. I never lifted a weight but five hours pikeing bales of hay on a humid August day built you up better than any gym. The work was backbreaking but still I loved life on the farm, even though I didn't want to run it. I just wanted a chance to go to university and maybe end up in some other type of agricultural career. I had been trying to decide what faculty to go to over the summer and I was close to settling on dairy and food science.

Johnny Junior and myself were keen scientists even back then. We were taking down an electric fence one morning to facilitate strip grazing, cordoning off a fresh section of grass to allow the cattle to graze. Bob Dick Twiss, who worked casually on the farm when extra help was needed, was gathering up the wire to move it to the next strip, wrapping the wire around his body to bring it along. I knew from my studies in St Brendan's that if you passed a current through a coil twirled around an iron rod, you magnetised the iron rod. I reconnected the electric fence.

He danced a jig, proof the experiment worked. We exploded into laughter but Bob Dick didn't quite see it that way. He didn't talk to me for weeks afterwards, but then he softened and we became the best of friends again.

Our Olympics that summer were Knocknagoshel Sports which were held every year on the Pattern Day or the Feast Day of Our Lady, August 15. We hit off across the valley early that morning. My mother prepared sandwiches and a flask of tea. They were gone before we reached Knocknagoshel. The sports went on all day and there was a huge crowd. It was good fun. There were egg and spoon races and throwing the wellington as well as the running and the field events. I was lucky enough to win some of the strength events. There was one I loved which involved throwing the 16lb weight. There was no doubt but that I was beginning to mature physically.

After the sports we went into Eddie Walsh's pub in Knocknagoshel for an orange. I didn't drink in those days.

Eddie was one of the greatest of all Kerry footballers and the pictures on the walls reflected his achievements. I was on a high after the day out at the sports. Maybe, I thought, just maybe I can still make it as a footballer. There had been many instances of late-maturing players making it onto the Kerry team and maybe UCC would bring it out in me.

It was a lovely summer's day just a few days after the sports in Knocknagoshel. Johnny and myself were working high up on the farm. We took off our jumpers and rested for a while. I knew from Johnny's manner that he had something he wanted to say to me. He told me I was unlikely to make it to the very highest level at Gaelic football. I might make a decent enough player but I would never be a Kerry senior. I was a bit too big for it, he said.

I knew once he said it that Johnny was right. There were times in tight situations when I felt like a man trying to turn an articulated lorry in a bathroom. He said that rugby might be the option. Johnny never gave you an opinion without having an explanation for it to hand. He explained that there was a game called Cad, which was very similar to rugby, and that it was in our genes. It had been played in Kerry since the Middle Ages. Cad was a kind of football played cross-country, scores of players on each side trying to carry a ball over a set boundary. Rules were few and far between and by all accounts it could be rough; it was not uncommon for the games to explode into faction fights between the opposing areas.

In the minutes it took Johnny to tell me about Cad, I felt something stir inside me. I started thinking maybe I could be a rugby player, even though there wasn't a team in the village. Worse still, GAA players were banned from playing it. But Castle Island had a team and I had seen the game on television. Below me was the farm where the Doyle boys were reared and they'd played rugby at their boarding school in Newbridge. And further on in front of me was our valley and my people had played Cad there in the big sweep of land before me. I was sure of that.

I have always felt some kind of connection to those who went before me. It is almost a spiritual thing. I loved Currow and wanted more than anything to put my own place on the map.

A few weeks later Galway went on to win the All-Ireland for the third year in a row and I headed off for University College Cork to study for a degree in dairy science. The plan was that I would eventually become a creamery manager, preferably somewhere in Kerry. I liked the idea of working in agriculture. More than that, this was a prestigious, well-paid job, and a secure one. The need for security was ingrained in us. The priority was to get a safe job rather than take the risk of going into business.

I said goodbye to my father at Farranfore train station and he wished me luck. My mother had repeated the advice she gave me on my first day in St Brendan's. I was excited, and a little wary, but I need not have worried. I would spend six of the happiest years of my life in University College Cork.

THREE

UCC

My mother organised digs for me for my first year at UCC. She wasn't taking any chances.

'The food is good,' she said, 'and it's just around the corner from the university and the chapel. The landlady will not tolerate any tomfoolery and you will have to keep your head down and study hard.'

My mother was right. My first landlady in Cork had a lodging house for students in Donovan's Road, just opposite the college. It was the most convenient digs you could hope for: a nice room in a comfortable home, with decent food. I think I scared her a bit when she saw the amount of food I was capable of consuming.

The fee for partial board, bed, breakfast and evening meals was £3, 17s and 6d – less than a fiver in today's money.

We were a lively bunch. I was just starting to come out of myself and soon joined in with the fun and games. One or two of the lads were wilder than the rest of us and loved to express their enjoyment of life by roaring out the window at night. They were ahead of their time: I read recently that screaming is now some kind of stress therapy. These young lunatics have since matured into solid citizens, but the landlady couldn't wait for that to happen – she threw us all out at Christmas. I told my mother that she was thinking of getting married again and wanted the house free for her new man.

When I got back I was left with the problem of finding new digs so I consulted Peter Cronin, a neighbour's son. He told me that when he was looking for digs he usually consulted with the local butchers to find out which of the landladies purchased the best meat. This was forward thinking at its best and when Peter recommended a Mrs Dorney I went to see her straight away. I was happy as her lodger for the rest of term and well fed too. A few years later another wonderful lady, Mrs Duggan, offered me accommodation for a week or two while I was relocating and I ended up staying with her for two years. I doubt if she ever risked having another student after me!

A few weeks after coming back to college in the New Year I took my first pint. It went straight to my head and I hardly took a drink again for the rest of term. The other lads were well ahead of me on that score.

I wasn't long in Cork when I headed for the Mardyke grounds along the banks of the River Lee. I stayed on the Gaelic side – there was a rugby side just over at the other end of the park. I fell in love with the place the first time I ever saw it. The facilities were far superior to anything I had seen before, with good showers and clean, well-maintained dressing rooms. The pitch was a joy; it had a perfect surface and a perimeter area outside the wire for running. There was a sloping bank on the south side facing the pitch and here I spied Billy Morgan, who was a famous goalkeeper for Cork even at that stage, practising his goal-keeping skills. Two other students were firing shots at him, and if this bombardment lasted a minute, it lasted at least an hour. The penny dropped as I watched Billy: the drive towards success depended on slogging it out on the training pitch, and here was a training ground available to everybody.

Here I am, I thought, with about 20 hours of lectures a week and maybe a few hours study a day. This left me a lot of time, if I chose to use it. I decided to set myself a training regime, and before I was very long at it I realised I had never been really, really fit in my life. I also joined the Fresher squad, the first year Gaelic Football Team in UCC. I wore the college's famous red-and-black jersey, with the skull and crossbones across the chest for the first time at an inter-varsity competition. I found a great camaraderie among the squad. There was no pecking order like we had in secondary school – you were made feel welcome even by the older lads, some of whom were almost qualified doctors. It was a perfect way of getting in with a crowd, though I didn't socialise too much then. I had no interest in drinking, and though I was fond of girls, I was very shy.

For recreation I went playing cards. Card-playing was the biggest pastime at home in Currow during the dark winter evenings. One night a neighbour lost 11 pence – all of eleven games – and in a temper he fired a shot at the crows in the rookery outside his house so that they shitted all over his fellow card-players as they made for home. Mind you, he didn't aim at the crows, which would have been bad luck.

We picked up the rudiments of whist, 45, 25 and 31 from an early age at home, and when I discovered there was a whist drive in St Augustine's Hall in Washington Street I went down there every Sunday night for a couple of months. It was hard going. The protagonists were mostly older ladies and if you made a mistake they put you through the mincer. When you won a game you moved on to another table; if not, you stayed where you were. There was a 'hatching hen's prize', the cards' equivalent of the wooden spoon, for those who didn't win enough games to move up a table. It was a great laugh, though some of the women played their hands with as much venom and ferocity as I ever encountered on the playing fields.

That Sunday night was the highlight of the week. I worked hard in first year. I had to; it was a tough year academically. I had studied what was called the 'old maths' in secondary school but 'new maths' were on the curriculum now. I didn't have a clue what they were about, and the lecturer was such a genius he assumed everyone was at his level, which was not at all the case. I took grinds from the late Freddie Holland, a maths teacher at a local school, and thanked God for having met a genius who knew how to impart his knowledge. The other three subjects were also new to me, as I had not studied physics, chemistry or applied maths for the Leaving Certificate, but things went well and I managed first-class honours in all four subjects. I won a scholarship for my second year, which eased the financial pressure on my parents.

At the start of my second year the hard graft I had put in on the training ground also paid off. I made the panel for the college team for the Cork County Championship final against Beara, which was played in early October 1967. We lost in a replay and I failed to get a game, but at least I was moving up the GAA ladder.

It wasn't long before I noticed a mysterious individual who always turned up to lend his support towards the penultimate stage of the championship. He was known as 'the Ghost'. He joined us for pre- and post-match food (he was no fool, there were no free lunches until the latter stages were reached) and freely offered his views as to how we should play the game that day. Curiously, he never appeared when the college was playing other universities, even in Sigerson Cup finals. Halfway through my time on the team he got cocky and brought along an accomplice, who we christened 'the Shadow'. They both appeared to bring us luck so nobody said anything to them as they sat devouring their after-match steak in the Victoria Hotel. No one asked them who they were or what they were doing there. It would have spoiled the fun, or even frightened them off.

The two big competitions in the college year were the Cork County Championship and the inter-varsity Sigerson Cup. I played my first Sigerson for UCC up in Santry in North Dublin when Trinity College hosted the competition in March 1968. The Sigerson is a life-changing experience. Holed up in a hotel with your friends for a weekend, playing two games on consecutive days to try to win the trophy – the friendship and the sense of belonging it creates last forever. The football is just short of inter-county standard and the competition is intense.

I played at full-back, facing Liam Sammon at full-forward for University College Galway, with Billy Morgan behind me in goals. I was well beaten by Sammon, who was an exceptional player and an All-Ireland winner, but I was standing in front of one of the greatest goalkeeper I have ever seen. Morgan was ahead of his time – he never stopped roaring instructions to his defence. I was establishing myself on a field which was to hold players like Morgan, Ray Cummins and the two Lynch brothers, Brendan and Paudie, Dan Kavanagh, Seamus Looney, the late Simon Murphy, Jim Coghlan and Mick Morris who were among the finest players ever to grace a Gaelic football field. Many of these men were, or were about to be, All-Ireland medal winners. I palled around with them too. But we were beaten that year.

My experience was widening all the time. I was very happy at my studies. The faculty was small and everyone knew everyone else. Most of the lecturers were either Gaelic or rugby fans and they went out of their way to be helpful and friendly. You were encouraged to call them by their first names. We did a lot of work in the lab and there were field trips as well as a fairly modest amount of lectures. I found the course very much to my liking and coming from a farming background was a huge advantage.

My shyness began to leave me and I was beginning to become a man about the campus. Aided and abetted by Jim Coghlan and Denis Coffey, I borrowed the silver inter-varsity trophy, the Embassy Cup, from the winners, Trinity College Dublin, at the annual post-tournament dinner. The Gardaí were all over the place as the cup was very valuable, but we managed to make our getaway to Cork.

We brought the trophy round to all the college pubs and we were treated like heroes. The cup was filled and pints were served up free of charge. We put down a great week of it before we returned the cup to Galway. The University College Galway boys were blamed for the theft and our standing among our fellow students, who were always on the lookout for free drink, was never higher.

We were often near starvation and desperate remedies were called for. Pat O'Meara, my flatmate, provided a tip for a dog at the Cork greyhound track, we invested our life savings on him. And when the useless hound was beaten out of sight, we lived on milk and turnips for weeks afterwards. The turnips we liberated from the back of a lorry; the milk we simply borrowed from neighbours' front doors. At least we fared better than the greyhound. We learned afterwards that he had to be put down and his skin was used to make a *bodhrán*, a type of drum. He was a lot more use dead than he ever was alive.

The exams went well and in July 1968 I received a call I had been waiting for since I was a small boy. My father answered and broke the news.

'Moss, you've been selected to play for Kerry in the All-Ireland under-21 Championship semi-final against Derry.'

I was stunned. I hadn't even been on the panel for the earlier rounds and now, all at once, I was on the team. The selectors had taken a look at me when I was playing for UCC, I supposed. I thought I'd never see the day; not so long ago I couldn't even get on a team in school now I'd be playing for Kerry, in the green-and-gold. But pleased as I was, there was no one more pleased than my father.

It took us about two days to get to Derry. We stayed overnight in Dublin and early the next morning we set out for Ballinascreen, a long drive up to the northern tip of the county, the bus vibrating with every pothole and bump along the way.

There was war when we reached the border. Our trainer, Joe Keohane, one of the greatest Kerry full-backs of all time, was also a fervent Nationalist. Intensely political throughout his life, Joe ran for the Dáil, just a few years after the Ballinascreen game. He called in to see his long-time friend, the writer John B Keane, during the course of the election campaign. John B was a staunch Fine Gael supporter, in the opposite camp politically, but as is the way in Kerry they remained close friends. Joe asked John B how he thought he'd do in the election. John B didn't want to insult his friend. Like everyone in Kerry he loved Joe, but he knew Joe had no chance of being elected.

'Joe,' replied John B, 'you will win provided you capture the Jewish vote in Knocknagoshel.'

We crossed the border July 13, the day after the famous 12th of July, when Orangemen marched in celebration of King William's crushing defeat of the Catholic forces at the Boyne in 1690. The streets were decorated in red, white and blue bunting and the Union Jack flew from every window. There were banners too, some sectarian, more merely proclaiming who had won the historic battle. At the sight of this display of Britishness, Joe began pacing up and down the bus. Normally he was a charming rogue but right now he was beside himself with temper.

'Look at that,' he said, pointing to an orange-painted telegraph pole. 'Do ye see what they're trying to do to the Kerry under-21s?'

This dastardly attempt to intimidate the cream of Kerry youth may have paid off in the end – we missed out on reaching the All-Ireland final by a couple of points. Keohane came into the dressing room after the match. We knew we had been expected to win and the trainer didn't have to ask for quiet. He thanked us for our display but said we had to improve and learn from today if we wanted to make it to the senior panel. Hard luck stories make no difference to Kerry fans and coaches.

When we were leaving the dressing room, Joe said. 'You played fairly well today, big fella.'

I was delighted. I couldn't wait to tell my father, who idolised Joe.

I was also picked for the Kerry Junior Panel in 1968, the county second team. I didn't get a game until we went over to Clare for a game at Miltown Malbay. My mother insisted I buy a new suit for that occasion. It had to be taken up so we dropped the suit into a tailor in Tralee. The tailor was an uncle of Mick Morris, a good friend and UCC man who won All-Irelands for Kerry and played golf for Ireland. In my hurry, I collected the wrong suit from Mick's uncle and the pants had to be trussed up by borrowed braces to keep them from falling down. I wore the suit on the day of the match as I had no change of clothes. I returned the suit to Mick's uncle the following Monday and kept my fingers crossed.

By the start of third year I was up to every trick in the book. We were never short of schemes. My favourite was a ruse to walk into any function or dance in the plush Imperial Hotel on the South Mall for free. We donned our white lab coats and carried a bucket and a mop in our hands as we

Johnny Brosnan Senior, Bob 'Dick' Twiss and myself, with my brothers
Brian and Matt. It looks like a back-row-forward had had a go at my jumper!

My Confirmation Day – before
Gubby the pony destroyed my new suit!

Mick Galwey's father's forge in Currow, where Currow GAA Club voted to retain
the Ban. We were one of only four or five clubs in Kerry to do so.
The GAA was later mandated to lift it anyway.

UCC's 1969 GAA football team – probably the best team that ever played for UCC. We won the double, the Sigerson Cup and the Cork County Championship, that year. Missing from the photo are coach, Denis Philpott and trainer, Denis Leahy – they were probably both barred from the grounds that day over a previous indiscretion! *(Courtesy of Irish Examiner)*

'Doctor' Keane – after six years at UCC.

One of the first rugby matches I ever played in the Mardyke. Billy Morgan, fourth from left at the back, went on to win an All-Ireland medal with Cork and then to coach the county to two more All-Ireland triumphs. Pat O'Meara, one of my greatest friends, is beside me in the white jersey. He made sure we didn't lose any lineouts that day.

Flanno', Tadgh and myself in 1974 at the Lansdowne Fashion Show to raise money for our Canada trip. We were enough to scare the real models away!
(© Irish Press)

1974: First cap in Paris before 'the stamper' got me.
(© George Herringshaw/Sporting-heroes.net)

A great night out at the Kerry All-Stars awards night in 1978. *Back:* Neilly O'Sullivan, John O'Grady, myself, Mick Morris. *Front:* Paudie Lynch, Dr Paddy Fitzgerald (who was Chairman of the UCC GAA club for years, including during my time there), Andy Molyneaux and Dr Brendan Lynch. Most of them have won wagonloads of All-Ireland Senior Football titles.
(© J Cleary & Ml O'Meara photographers, Tralee)

Lansdowne League team 1976/77 after winning the Leinster Senior League – it was obviously 14-aside back then! Con Murphy, my mentor, is at the back on the left. Donal Canniffe was captain and he subsequently captained Munster to beat the All Blacks in '78. The small fellow in the middle is Paddy Berkery, who succeeded Con Murphy as Irish full back a few years later. At the back on the back is my good friend John Driscoll – it beats me to this day how he got into the photograph!

(© Liam G Kennedy Ltd, Dublin)

June 18, 1977, on the Lions Tour of New Zealand. I was fighting a lineout with Ian Kirkpatrick during my first and only Test match in Wellington. For the life of me I don't know what he was doing at the front of the lineout because he was a back-row-forward! The All Blacks won 16-12.

(© Adrian Murrell/Allsport/gettyimages)

Myself, Fran Cotton and someone who looks a bit like Bobby Windsor, playing a match against the NZ Juniors in Wellington. We won that day, 22-19, but it never stopped raining for a second.

(© Adrian Murrell/Allsport/gettyimages)

Munster v All Blacks, Thomond Park October 31, 1978. It looks like Donal Spring was getting ready to put the boot in. I was in the back taking a breather!
(Courtesy of Irish Examiner)

All Blacks v Munster. A perfect example of disruption. New Zealand had won the lineout and Springer, Whelan and Ginger were moving in for the kill. It was this type of tactic that kept the All Blacks at nought throughout the game.
(Courtesy of Irish Examiner)

Ireland v Australia, First Test, 1979 – the Australians thought we'd hoodwinked them. They'd beaten Wales, the Grand Slam winners, the year before and they'd just come back from beating the All Blacks in Auckland. They thought they were in for an easy ride with us but we proved them wrong and won, 27-12.

The Ireland team in Australia – we were the first and only team on tour from the Northern Hemisphere to win two Tests down under.

My Wedding Day, August 11, 1979 – in Lansdowne for a change!
On the left is Peter Dunne, my father-in-law, then my mother, Cassie,
myself and Anne, Anne's mother, Mary, and my father, Willie.

Willie John and myself at the
reception – Donal Lenihan,
myself and Willie John, were a
continuous link in the second row
from 1962-1990, except that
Willie John, of all people, was
dropped for the Welsh match in
'64.

Phil Orr, myself and Harry
Steele at the reception.
Harry was a back-row-
forward who ended up on
the second row. He was
probably as good a man
as ever played in the
second row for Ireland,
'pound for pound'. Philip
Orr and myself played for
Ireland together 40 times.
He got 49 consecutive
Caps, was dropped for
two games and returned
to get another nine Caps.

1980: my first and only try for Ireland! I was more surprised than the crowd.

Ireland v France, one of the rare occasions I won the lineout for Ireland!
(© Getty Images)

passed the security. If we were ever stopped we just uttered one word 'vomit'. It always did the trick.

On one occasion in the Spring of '69 a couple of us 'bucketted' our way into a drinks reception before a very important wedding. The talk was of yachts, property deals and holidays abroad, a rare thing in those pre-Ryanair days. It was the first time any of us had tasted champagne even though I think I'd surreptitiously polished of a stolen bottle of Babycham in the milking parlour one Christmas when I was about 17. We grew bold and stayed for the meal. The bride's people thought we were invited by the groom and vice versa. I almost blew our cover when I asked the mother-of-the-bride if the bride would prefer Waterford Crystal or a few quid as a present.

'One does not give money as a wedding present,' she replied.

Her husband came over to us a few minutes later.

'I know you two are crashing this. I saw you come in with the buckets.'

'Ah no', I replied. 'that wasn't us at all.'

The father of the bride got a fit of laughing: 'Enjoy it lads. Best trick I ever saw.'

And he spent most of the rest of the night telling us of the high jinks he got up to himself when he was our age.

And of course there were girlfriends. But we will not go into any of that. The girls I walked out with would never have had anything to do with me if I plastered the details of our relationship all over this book. Suffice to say, I remained friends with every girl I ever went out with.

But football was as important, and sometimes more important than anything else.

At the time Kerry was going through one of the worst periods in its footballing history – we had lost the last three All-Irelands we played, two to Galway and one to Down,

and the selectors began scouring the county for new talent.
Keohane made sure I got a trial in the early summer of 1969.
It was played in Fitzgerald Stadium, Killarney, and I literally
ran into Mick O'Dwyer, one of the greatest players in the
game, who won four All-Irelands in his illustrious career.
Later, as a coach, he managed Kerry to eight All-Ireland titles.
Early on in the contest I hit him a shoulder and got it just
right: he went down hard and I fell on top of him. O'Dwyer
was fit to kill me, and as we left the pitch at the end of the
game he turned to me and said, 'You'll never make it.' Then
he walked off and just left me there.

O'Dwyer was referring not just to our joust on the pitch
that day but also to the weekend before, when a few of us
from Currow had gone to Waterville, where Mick lived, and
drank far too much.

I knew what Mick meant, even though he said it in anger.
If you wanted to play for Kerry it was not enough to be able
to dish out the hard stuff, you had to be able to play football
as well. And there wasn't much room for drinking and
carousing, not if you wanted to achieve something in sport.
O'Dwyer took his sport seriously. I have visited Mick's
hospitable hotel in Waterville many times since and we often
laugh about that day. All the same his words stuck in my
head – many times during my rugby career I found myself
looking back to that day in Fitzgerald Stadium.

I was picked at full-back for the Kerry Junior team and
we made it through to the All-Ireland final in Croke Park
that year. It was a supremely joyous moment for me. I
thought back to the small boy who had gasped for breath
when he first caught sight of the famous stadium all those
years ago. It was another dream fulfilled.

But when we were beaten it was a terrible disappointment.
Our opponents, Wicklow, were simply the better team, but
we were eaten alive back home. Kerry was not supposed to

lose an All-Ireland final, least of all to one of the weaker football counties like Wicklow.

Heaven is winning an All-Ireland, and you never forget losing one. More than 30 years later I was interviewed on Radio Kerry by the much loved sports' broadcaster, Weeshie Fogarty, who had played that day against Wicklow. We spoke about rugby and Triple Crowns but at the end of a long interview Weeshie dropped his head as if remembering a great disaster and said, 'Moss, Wicklow '69. We lost it on the sideline.' In other words, our selectors made mistakes. All those years later, it was still remembered.

I couldn't bear to answer so I made a joke of it. 'We lost out on the sideline all right, Weeshie. They should have taken the two of us off.' This wasn't true. I actually played reasonably well and Weeshie didn't put a foot wrong. The broadcaster didn't respond to my hop ball. It was too soon for closure. After all, it was only 35 years since we'd lost that junior final.

* * *

At the start of my fourth year, in 1969, my brother Brian joined me in UCC. I used to hitch to Kerry quite often and my mother didn't want the two of us on the road in all weathers, so she decided to buy us a car, a Fiat 600. The car became famous among our friends as it was known to carry eight in its time.

We never had much luck with that car. I took a wrong turn off Moore's Island one Patrick's Day and finished up in the middle of the parade among the floats and the marching bands. The marshals asked us to leave and told us we were, 'a bunch of useless sponging student langers we're financing with our taxes and a disgrace to the country in front of American tourists. And shag off back to Kerry.' In the end

Brian and myself sold the old Fiat to raise money for food and drink, but we had to sell it outside of Cork, as no garage in the city would touch it.

It was my final year and when I got back that September I knew I had to start thinking about studying hard for the June exams. I wasn't really thinking about a career at that stage; I didn't know what I wanted to do. All I knew for sure was that there was a lot of football to be played before my finals came around.

I was still training hard – the boys on our squad were tough men when it came to socialising yet football usually came first. It showed on the pitch. We won the double that year, 1969: the Cork County Championship and the Sigerson Cup, the two major club and university competitions in one year. I was full-back beside Jim Coghlan, a close pal to this day, and we never played better than we did that season. I often joked in later years that Coghlan was my domestique but the truth was that he was seven steps ahead of everyone else and invariably knew when I was going to be skinned by some lively full-forward with mustard up his arse. That was the great thing when I turned to rugby. All the lads I marked were my own size.

We walked away with the Sigerson, beating University College Galway in the final by 5-12 to 0-3. The perfect game.

We beat Billy Morgan and Nemo Rangers in the Cork County Championship semi-final by a point and went on to win the final by a point against St Nicks, the football wing of Glen Rovers. Brendan Lynch, who won an All-Ireland for Kerry that year, won the match for us with a free, three minutes from time.

I was proud of our victories. We were heroes in the college and back home in Kerry, where the idea of Kerrymen winning the Cork County Championship went down very well indeed.

Aside from football, the best thing about university was the friends I made there. We all mixed and gradually I got to know the rugby crowd who trained next to us on the Mardyke and began to socialise with them. The Western Star, run by Nuala and Starry Crowley, was their pub – Starry toured with the Irish team to Argentina in 1952. It was a home away from home for all of us, a place where you would never be stuck for a loan if you needed it. We GAA lads, by and large, socialised at Nora and Bill Ludgate's bar. Bill, a tall, well-spoken man, loved students so much he couldn't wait for the summer holidays to end. Nora, like Nuala, was a lovely woman and was always advising us to meet nice girls, study hard and go easy on the drink. We ignored her advice, except as to meeting the nice girls. Much as they doted on us, the Ludgates were never going to get rich from our student drinking. A pint cost 2s 1d, or about 12.5 cent in today's money, so we didn't spend much when we went out.

There was no hostility between the Gaelic and rugby clubs but we weren't as close as we should have been, thanks to the divisive GAA ban. The GAA simply banned its players from playing rugby or soccer and from attending matches as a spectator. We couldn't play rugby and they couldn't play football or hurling. There was even a ban on attending rugby dances. The ban was enforced by vigilantes who roamed the countryside, looking for transgressors. Sometimes they hid behind ditches and more times they skulked behind girthy trees outside country dance halls. The origin of the ban was political. It went back to the time of the Troubles but the diehard anti-everything-British brigade made sure it was still implemented. And, at the time, many of our lads thought the rugby lads might have been looking down on us. The rugby lads were for the most part graduates of the private schools where Gaelic football was a foreign game, another less publicised form of discrimination.

The barriers between us were finally broken down at a novelty match, organised mainly by the student doctors. Con Murphy, a medical student who seemed to know everyone in college, was up to his eyes in it. And there were other undergraduates like Billy O'Mahony and Pat Parfrey, as well as Dr Dave Kiely, Professor Eddie Fahy and a good few others too numerous to mention. Con had to be very careful. His father, Weeshie Murphy, was one of the greatest players Cork ever produced, but as well as that Weeshie was Chairman of the Cork County GAA Board, and had warned Con not to disgrace him by playing soccer and rugby in college. Nowadays these things hardly matter – Con is a top practitioner in sports medicine and has been team doctor to the Cork football and hurling teams for many years – but back then they mattered a great deal.

I had a close call myself just a few days before the match. I was a big Cork Hibs fan and went to as many soccer games as I could manage. The Sunday before we played our rugby challenge, I tried to get in the schoolboys' turnstiles at a match and got stuck. Three or four men had to lift the turnstiles off me. For many anxious minutes I was literally stuck to the ground, terrified a vigilante would spot me. The slagging was unmerciful.

'Go easy lads he's expecting triplets. Piglet triplets.'

'What class are you in now?'

'Where's your mammy and daddy little boy?' references to the fact that I was stuck in the under-14 turnstile.

I don't think I ever went as red in my life. And all for the sake of the price of a pint.

Billy Morgan was taking an even bigger chance playing in the match. He was the top keeper in the county and had a high profile nationally. If he was caught, it was curtains for him. But Billy was always his own man, and if he thought that what he was doing was right and the rules were wrong, then he ignored the rules.

The novelty rugby game was a dangerous experiment. It was the first time since University College Cork was founded that such an event took place. Simply put, the friendship of a bunch of young lads overcame years of prejudice. When we travelled over to the Western Star in convoy and laid down a challenge to the rugby club we made history. In the end the match was organised between the two pubs on the back rugby pitch in the Mardyke. Murphy's Brewery put up a barrel of stout and each of the pubs did likewise. The UCC first fifteen rugby team was barred from taking part, as were most of the better players from the second fifteen, though they might have slipped in one or two good ones from the seconds onto the final team. We took on the pick of the rugby club's third army, comprising specially selected units from the pick of the College rugby units known as the Bulldogs, Beavers and Badgers. None of these boys could be accused of training but most of them had played at school and knew what they were at.

We Gaelic players took to the field with only a rudimentary knowledge of the game. I passed the ball once by punching it GAA style with my fist and I fielded another ball high over my head, GAA style again. I got clattered in the ribs for my ignorance. On one occasion I passed the ball straight from the lineout to Billy Morgan, who was playing out-half, and he was floored for his troubles. Even though we were great friends, Morgan wouldn't spare you if he felt aggrieved, and he had a lot to say to me.

'Mossy that oval-shaped yoke is a ball and you are supposed to pass it and not shovel it out like cowshite from some Kerry dunghill.'

I spent half the match offside and disgraced myself by calling the referee some choice names, which was fine in football but not in rugby, where you just shut up and accepted the decision. For all the mix-ups, I enjoyed every minute of the game, and we won 6-3. It was, we decided, a classic encounter, with Billy Morgan kicking the winning drop goal from 25 yards out – a distance that stretched nearer to the halfway line as the porter sank in.

The first half of the post-match socialising was held in Starry's and the second half in Ludgate's. The proprietors had attended the game and exchanged good wishes for the first time, even though their pubs were not much more than a mile apart.

My main recollection is of the celebrations on the night of the game. I enjoyed the match immensely but I didn't see myself as changing over to rugby as long as the ban was in existence. I still had football ambitions. I was now playing at a standard I thought I would never reach and I didn't want to sacrifice all the status and hard work.

My second game of rugby was in the Nunan Cup. The Nunan games were played on a 'pitch' in the heart of the campus called 'the quarry', a pit that had probably been quarried for stone in previous generations. On one side, students crowded together to watch the match; on the other there were rocks and a wall shutting out College Road.

The rules were hardly out of the RFU manual. It was a lot closer to cad than rugby. If you got a ball close to the line at the bottom of a ruck you could, if you were lucky, crawl through the ruck. I often heard of the crowd invading the pitch but in the quarry games the crowd was sometimes invaded by the players.

After a series of battles with only sporadic outbreaks of rugby we finally found ourselves in the Nunan Cup final, the 'Sciences' versus the 'Engineers'. We felt the pitch was a bit too fast and decided to flood the quarry the night before, drenching it with a garden hose. It poured rain immediately after we finished and the match next day was played in a swamp. The touch judges, who were the only two senior players allowed on the pitch, invariably gave the throw to their own team. They were not allowed to touch the ball, but they were allowed to fight.

I did a bit of fighting myself. I invaded the crowd and threw a few digs but swiftly moved back to the relative safety of the pitch before I was killed. The ground was so mucky that anyone not togged out could not venture onto it, which was just as well: I would have been punched into the middle of next week if the engineers caught me. Rough and ready as it was, in my six years at UCC I never saw a dirty blow landed in a quarry game. Then one Christmas not long after I left the college, bulldozers moved in and the quarry was filled. It is now the site of the Boole Library, and the Nunan Cup, sadly, is no more.

But rugby was growing on me. My fellow students were encouraging me to take the game more seriously. I was still committed to the GAA but I began to attend more rugby games and I was beginning to gain a better understanding of the how the game should be played. And Johnny Senior's words kept coming back into my head.

I did well enough in my final exams but the thought of facing into the real world of working and making a living got me down. I had grown too used to the good life.

That summer the hard work in the farm went some way to getting me ready.

As my father said, 'Moss my dear man (I always felt a life lesson coming on when he called me my dear man), I expect you to fulfil a certain function in relation to the running of this farm – work it's called and it's a condition you will need to look into on a permanent basis very shortly. If you stay in college any longer you will finish up in the same class as your own children.'

Four

Doctor Keane

September came around and it was back to Cork again. I'd decided over the summer that a Masters would be the next step for me. I thought it would keep me out of trouble while I enjoyed another few years of the good life. One of the advantages of the MSc course was that I was being paid for giving tutorials and for lab work.

I got myself settled into a tiny bedsit on Magazine Road. It was designed for one person, preferably a scrum-half or a waif. But there were three of us squeezed into 'the cupboard' as we called it. We were all over six feet five and as bulky as one of my father's well-fed bullocks. The idea was that we would prefer to make publicans rich rather than landlords.

I'd been made captain of the UCC Gaelic football team in December 1969. My year as captain was in the middle leg of what became known as the glory years, an era kick-started by our trainer and coach Denis Philpott, a Cork City St Finbarr's man with a passion both for football and the university. His determination to beat University College Dublin (UCD) – our main rivals at the time – was palpable. Another major influence on college football in those years was Denis Leahy, an army man from Collins Barracks who put us through our paces.

I'd known it was going to be difficult to maintain the

spirit that had won the Sigerson and Cork Championship double the year before, but we'd all been well up for it and the big thing was that we were all great pals. Rows had been settled quickly and we'd trained in the Mardyke for months, right through until we headed off to play in the Sigerson Cup weekend in March 1970. We'd beaten UCD by three clear goals, then got the better of Queens University Belfast by five points in a hard-fought final. Ray Cummins, the Cork star, hit two goals. Kerry All-Ireland medal winner Dan Kavanagh not only took the roof off the net, but almost did away with the foundation as well. It had been a terrific victory, and I was a proud man when I lifted the Sigerson Cup over my head that day. It was two-in-a-row for UCC and as I started training again that September I was hoping that maybe we might make it three-in-a-row that year.

After the win we'd spent a week in raucous celebration back in Cork and then I'd gone home for a weekend to tell my father all that had happened – on the football field at any rate. Dad had a young collie he purchased from Wicklow to keep Rover Keane company. He called the collie Fenton, of all things, and the dog, loyal as he was, was always the first to greet me when I arrived home every month. Fenton became a friend and a mentor of sorts. I got it into my head for some reason that my career would last as long as he stayed alive. It was just superstition on my part, but so it proved: fourteen years later Fenton was dead and so was my rugby career. At this point, though, he helped give me my entrance into the game. I played my first official rugby match under the name 'Moss Fenton'.

It was a way of avoiding the ban when I was asked to play for UCC's second team in December 1970 at the Mardyke. 'Fenton is promising and will soon make the University College Cork first team,' the *Evening Echo* reported, 'if the rough edges are knocked off him.' If I'd been caught playing rugby by the vigilantes I would of course have lost by GAA status, but by now I was getting hooked on the game.

At the other end of the sports grounds, the university's GAA teams were to play a challenge against the Nemo Rangers club, but as things turned out it was the night after The Cowpunchers Ball, a notorious piss-up organised by my faculty, and only five of the footballers turned up. I was excused from playing, as it was only a friendly game. The GAA club were more than sympathetic when it came to helping me out so I could balance the rugby with the football. Left without an opposition, the entire Nemo team and their officials moved down to watch the rugby. I was afraid I might be reported and would get a year's suspension. Most of the Nemo boys could be trusted to be tactful, but it only took one to ruin my GAA career. There was such a man at the match but thankfully his hands were tied: if he had made a report, the Nemo club itself would have been grounded for a year just for watching me, Moss Fenton, togging out for UCC junior rugby team.

I loved every minute of every rugby match I played and began to realise for the first time that I might just make it at the sport. The game suited me. I was now just one of the gang in the rugby club and the more I got to know the rugby boys the more I liked them. If they had been a shower of snobby city boys, with accents and too many manners, I would have given the game up straight away and quite possibly would never have played again.

I played my first legal rugby game with UCC's junior team in Musgrave Park on Easter Sunday 1971. On that same day, the GAA lifted its ban on Gaelic players playing other sports. I had to admire the humour of the *Echo* reporter covering the game who wrote that 'Fenton was dropped for Moss Keane, the well-known GAA player.'

We were inspired that day by a dynamic pack leader, prop

forward Rusty McDermott, who we nicknamed 'The Drover' because of his great ability to lead a pack from behind.

The GAA's decision had been a long time coming, and met stiff resistance all along the way. Even at a local level, when the GAA in Currow voted on the issue in the run-up to the decision at the GAA's National Congress, my father, my brothers, yours truly and our club captain Derry Mangan had been the only ones who voted in favour of abolishing the ban. There were many diehards who refused to accept change, though I must say that when I was picked to play for Ireland a few years later, everyone – GAA players and officials included – backed me 100 per cent. By then even the most fervent advocates of the ban realised that the rule was an anachronism.

The university rugby club felt I had potential, especially Dr Dave Kiely, who had great faith in me; he was also UCC's selector on the Munster team. Another doctor, Billy O'Mahony, who had first introduced me to the game in that famous novelty match, had no doubt that I would make the grade. O'Mahony had a good deal of experience of playing with converted GAA players, and firmly believed that Gaelic football complemented rugby. 'The GAA recruits,' he maintained, 'are more natural ball handlers. Some so-called rugby experts are treadmill men, and only kick a ball when they've accidentally missed someone's arse. Second rows must push in the scrums and the lineout is your main area where you jump to compete for the ball. Your job is to win the ball and get it safely out to your back line. Under no circumstances attempt to do anything sophisticated with the shagging thing. It's as simple as that.'

Whatever about that, I had new skills to learn too. Scrummaging killed me. After five or six scrums I was knackered. It took about three months of hard coaching before I was comfortable in the scrum. After a year, though,

I could scrummage all day long.

I was sailing under two flags now. I played with the Gaelic football team and we were still keen contenders in club competitions.

We won the Sigerson again in 1972 after a poor year in 1971 when we lost both the Sigerson and the County finals. Brendan Lynch scored a last-minute goal in the semi-final against UCD in '72. He took a free from 14 yards out in the dying seconds of the match, and sent the ball flying past ten UCD players defending the goal-line. There was one small space in the top right-hand corner and such was the power of the shot the ball was in the back of the net before anyone could get a hand to it. It was one of the most amazing goals I have ever seen.

We won through to the final of the All-Ireland clubs championship also, which gave me another chance to play in Croke Park, this time against Bellaghy of Derry. We were beaten once again, this time by a point. We couldn't begrudge Bellaghy their victory – as sectarian violence worsened in Northern Ireland, these players risked their own safety just to go training, and in any case they deserved to beat us. Still, it was to be my last chance of winning an All-Ireland medal.

I played senior and junior rugby for the 1971–72 rugby season as well, usually on the same weekends on which I played GAA. The seniors had a poor year but the juniors made it to the Munster Junior Cup final. We were beaten by Highfield in Musgrave Park. Playing matches brought me on more than any training sessions and I felt I was making a solid if not spectacular contribution. I was giving away far fewer penalties and was beginning to understand the subtleties of the game but I still had a lot to learn. The day of the Munster Junior rugby Cup Final I had already togged out for the GAA All-Ireland clubs' semi-final against Claremorris of Mayo. I was playing a lot, on both pitches, and loving it. While all this was going on I was also in the process of trying to complete a thesis for my Masters Degree in Microbiology.

That summer I was picked on a large Munster panel for weekend training in Limerick. This was a big step forward and it helped my confidence enormously. It meant I must be doing something right and I was progressing in the right direction. It was mainly endurance work under the Munster coach Noel Murphy, and the level of strength and fitness it demanded was an eye-opener for me.

A few weeks later in September I did an interview with the Department of Agriculture on a Monday afternoon in Government Buildings, O'Connell Street, Dublin. It was the day after we played Muskerry in the Cork Senior football semi-final in Bandon. I got the job. Better again, my first posting was in Cork, in the dairy science laboratory, and I was still eligible to play with UCC. My worries were over. Things had worked out fine.

My parents showed up for the graduation ceremony in the autumn and it meant a lot more to them than it did to me. They were delighted and a little bit overawed by the pomp and formality of the ceremony. The graduates and the professors were all dressed up in their coloured gowns and mortarboards with the austere oil paintings of past college presidents looking down on all of us in the old grandeur of the *Aula Maxima*. My mother and father sat there without saying a word. I have to say I was moved at how thrilled they were when I came back down with my scroll. It brought home how hard they had worked for me and how lucky I was to get the opportunity of the university education they could never have aspired to. They were delighted for me and very, very proud.

I had managed to keep my place in the Munster squad all through that autumn and I did well enough at the squad training sessions to win a place for Munster's game against Ulster in Thomond Park just a few days after the graduation. I was the first player who came straight from Gaelic football into representative rugby after the ban and the move attracted a good deal of attention. There were newspaper articles and I was even mentioned on television after the 6 o'clock news. My parents got a great thrill out of that too. For the most part the people back home were hoping I would go the whole way and win a cap, but there were others who resented the fact I was playing 'a foreign game'. It was as if I was after spitting on the flag. But I was delighted and there was no way I was going to let myself get walked on by small-minded bigots. I was certainly nervous. The fast track to representative rugby was all very well, as was the publicity, but newspaper praise never won anything for anyone. I wondered was it all a bit too soon for me.

I was due to mark Willie John McBride, a legend who would get a place on any World XV and probably as captain as well. As things turned out he wasn't going at full tilt that day. He just did as much as he needed to. I sensed if I got stuck into him I would only rouse him up so I left well alone and concentrated on the ball. Willie John had seen and done so much, I got the impression he was saving his energy for bigger events.

I mustn't have done too badly on him because a few weeks later, in November, I was included in an enlarged Irish squad for a weekend training session in the Belfield grounds of University College Dublin under national coach Syd Millar. This was my first senior Irish squad session. Now I was in contention for a cap. My old friend Dr Billy O'Mahony coached me in short-cuts, cutting corners, short-changing push-ups, tying my bootlaces – whatever I needed to know he was on hand to tell me. I was absolutely exhausted when he was finished with me.

I was training with the Irish team but it was all happening a bit too fast. I felt like an impostor. I didn't even have a proper grasp of the feckin rules and here I was letting on to be a rugby player. It was like at Mass when you're not sure whether to stand up or sit down at different parts of the service. You just mimic those around you. I copied Willie John. The thought of playing for Ireland was there somewhere in the background but I suppressed it. I was half expecting someone to tap me on the shoulder and say, 'who let you in here?' All I wanted to do was not to show myself up at the squad sessions.

I was picked to play for Munster against Leinster at Lansdowne Road. We won but we cared little for the victory. The day before the match we'd all gone to see a film in the Adelphi cinema in Dublin when all of a sudden there was the sound of explosions – bombs going off in Sackville Place. The cinema was evacuated. I found myself outside, standing on the street in my socks – I had slipped my shoes off inside and forgotten them in my haste to get out of the building. It was a day of mayhem and murder in Dublin. No cause was worth it. Our small cause was diminished by the event. To this day the identity of the bombers is hotly disputed. Suffice to say whoever it was carried out a callous and cowardly act.

Even with all the rugby I was still togging out at full-back with UCC's Gaelic team but by now I was giving rugby priority. And there was another change; I had to hold down a full time job too. There were times when I would have greatly benefited from the power of bilocation. But I was young and strong. I thrived on all the activity. And I was by now a past master at balancing my schedule. The rugby and GAA clubs co-operated and did their best to oblige.

The focus all through, from a Munster point of view, was the clash due between Munster and the All Blacks on January 16, 1973. There was history here, even though I knew little about it. I was told soon enough by Noel Murphy our coach, a former Irish international and a Lion:

> Moss you are no longer an experiment you are a Munster man picked to play against the All Blacks. The All Blacks beat us 6-3 in 1953 and in 1963. Munster could have won both games. I played in '63. Best game I ever played in. We had a last minute penalty. It was just barely wide. Moss this is very big. Bigger than all of us.

Noel Murphy, who coached as he played with passion and fire, made life very simple for me:

> Just go out and cause mayhem. Disrupt their lineout. Stop them getting quick ball. Stand up for yourself and your team. Kerrymen have more All-Irelands than anyone else – you're afraid of no one. Kerry are the All Blacks of Ireland. That's why we picked you.

I was well aware I was representing Kerry. I was also representing the honour of the GAA, as I saw it. It was my first big game, but, in a way, I was still under the impression that I shouldn't be there. The GAA club turned out to a man. My dad couldn't make it down but he told me he'd bought a new transistor radio and he would have it in the cab of the tractor with him. I suppose he didn't realise how big a game it was. Remember the Keanes were new to rugby.

I was never as nervous.

The build-up in the dressing room before the match against the All Blacks was like no other I had experienced. This was special. Noel Murphy was emotional, almost in tears when he spoke of near misses in the past. Our captain,

Tom Kiernan, the renowned full-back and for many years the most capped Irish player of all, said the last few words before we ran out. He pointed to his temple and said: 'We must use this. It's there for us. Brains and courage are an unbeatable combination: Munster; Munster; Munster.'

I was shaking as we ran on to the field but I was fired up. You just had to be.

One of the GAA boys, I think it was my flatmate O'Meara, shouted out, 'Come on the Kingdom.' The crowd was right down on top of us. I recognised faces. Friends for the most part and guess who? – the fecking vigilante from the Cork County Board.

I knew very little about the All Blacks – I got a shock when I saw them perform the *Haka*. It was the first time I had ever even heard of the famous Maori war dance, never mind seen it performed before my eyes. I was mightily impressed, but not frightened. If anything it got me even more fired up

It was brutally tough from the kick-off. I was a new boy and I was tested straight away with a fair shoulder charge that winded me but I was soon back at full belt, ready to respond in kind. And when these formalities were disposed of we settled down to play a seriously hard game of rugby. It didn't take me long to get a tutorial on the New Zealanders. They played fair if you did, but if you didn't, watch out – they'd kick the shit out of you.

Murphy had emphasised: 'If you miss a tackle, you're finished. The All Blacks are ruthless when it comes to punishing mistakes. Missed tackles cost tries.'

If it moved we tackled it.

We got on top in the forwards' battle. Just. Midway through the second half I got myself into a bit of a scrap with Andy Haden, the Blacks second row. I stopped him from jumping for the ball in the lineout. He didn't like it very much and fists flew. Haden would never use the boot in a stand up fight – he was old school. Our hooker, the late great Jerry Leahy, came in to separate us, and got a few accidental wallops for his trouble. One was from me. Munster never left a teammate isolated. Neither did the All Blacks. But there was no badness there, no stamping or eye gouging.

I was well able for the pace and intensity. I even enjoyed it. There were no formalities with these lads. It was great. You just gave it everything and so did the All Blacks. The game was tight. There would be no tries. We went three points up. Kiernan kicked a fine penalty.

My second row partner was John Madigan from Charleville and he was as strong if not stronger than any of the All Blacks. Behind the scrum we had Barry McGann, who kept the All Blacks on the back foot, the traditional Munster tactic for playing the New Zealanders. It stood to us: we were three points up as injury time ticked into the fifth minute.

Then there was a penalty for the All Blacks. The crowd, as is the custom in Munster, went completely silent as the kicker took aim. I said a little *Hail Mary* as we stood absolutely still while the ball sailed by, but for once my prayers weren't answered. Trevor Morris levelled it from far out. The final whistle blew. Chance gone.

Munster had come within seconds of pulling off a huge shock. Up to then no Irish side had beaten the All Blacks. As a team we were bitterly disappointed. We could have been further ahead before that last-minute penalty kick.

The game was by far the toughest I had played in any sport up to that. I'd had doubts going into it, but afterwards I knew that if I improved a little bit more I would wear an Irish jersey some day.

A few months later the Irish selectors decided to take a look at me. In April '73 word came through that they were looking at a number of options for the second-row berth alongside Willie John McBride and that I was one of them. I was asked to play as a guest for Shannon against Galway Corinthians on the back pitch at Thomond Park. The fixture gave me eight or nine days to get cracking with my fitness. And I did – no drink, early to bed, long runs and sit-ups and push-ups. There was no such thing as going to a gym – it was almost considered unmanly.

The day before the game I decided to go into the Western Star to have a mineral, meet the lads for an hour, then head back to the flat. But when I arrived the Aintree Grand National was about to start and I had a small investment on a horse by the name of Red Rum. It was possibly the greatest Grand National of all time. We watched top weight Crisp go out in front and jump the fences as if they were sods of turf. We witnessed the great Red Rum keeping at it, staying in the race. We cheered to the echo when he beat the gallant Crisp on the line. And at that moment my chances of filling Ireland's second-row spot next to McBride went from even money to 20-to-one. I was in funds for fun. So was everyone else in Starry's who had backed Red Rum. I decided to have a pint, maybe two at the most, but when I tried to leave someone produced another one. I extended my deadline. In the end I left at closing time and stopped at Jackie Lennox's chipper on the way home.

I headed for my trial in Limerick the next morning with a fairly muzzy head. I didn't play too badly, just not nearly good enough for the task ahead. The great servant to Irish rugby, Dr Mick Molloy, was recalled to fill the position on the Irish team. It was just as well. I certainly needed the extra year; I was still a novice at the game. Mick was the better player and deserved to get in ahead of me.

In the meantime, I still wore the skull and crossbones of UCC's Gaelic football team. We made it through to the semi-

final of the Cork County Championship that year. It was
the game that brought my Cork GAA career to an abrupt
end – I was sent off.

Jim O'Sullivan, the prince of GAA reporters, wrote a
report on the match in *The Cork Examiner*:

> A highly questionable decision by the referee to
> send college full-back Moss Keane to the line
> fired the students with a driving force which
> brought them back into the game and won it
> for them three minutes from the end. The
> incident which led to the rugby star going off
> occurred in the 49th minute when he was
> clearing a ball out near the right sideline, and
> was taken down by a trip. He got up, and after
> running back shoved the St Michael's player to
> the ground. It was surprising that after ordering
> Keane off he took no action against the offending
> player.

To his eternal credit, Neilly O'Keeffe, the man I was supposed
to have struck, said that I had not hit him. The deliberations
of the officials were held in camera. By any standards I was
innocent but I was found guilty all the same and suspended
for two months. I felt I was very badly treated. I loved GAA
all my life and all I had ever wanted was to win an All-Ireland
for Kerry. I was very disillusioned after the hearing and I felt
the Board had a lot to answer for.

As recently as April 2005, the Cork County Board
opposed a motion at the annual GAA conference to allow
rugby and soccer to be played at Croke Park. The motion
was a goodwill gesture to Ireland's rugby and soccer teams,
who were about to find themselves without a ground to play
in while Lansdowne Road was being redeveloped. Cork was

one of only two counties in the Republic of Ireland to vote against the motion. More than that, the Board effectively denied GAA clubs in Cork, most of whom supported the motion to open-up Croke Park, the right to express their views on the issue – they barred clubs from voting on procedural grounds.

What is it with some people? Rugby is an All-Ireland sport. I respect people who argue that the GAA is in competition with rugby and soccer for the allegiance of young players, and should not offer their facilities to other sports for that reason. That's a sound argument. But I greatly resent being told I am not Irish enough to play in Croke Park. Those people who push this point of view should take a long, hard look at their definition of what it is to be an Irishman.

Irish coach Syd Millar took me for a drive after an inter-provincial match against Ulster once. Syd didn't say a word until we ended up in the Shankill Road, the loyalist heartland of Northern Ireland. Even the sidewalk was painted in the red, white and blue of the Union Jack. Syd knew I had no comprehension of what it was to be an Ulster Protestant Unionist, hence the tour. But despite the gulf of under-standing that separated us, as men we hit it off almost immediately – brothers in green shirts. Forget about anthems, flags and emblems, it's the wearing of the green that counts. The green jersey, that is. You should see the pride the Ulster lads display, on and off the pitch, when it comes to the wearing of the green. Irish rugby owes so much to them, to people like Syd Millar who put aside religious and political differences for the good of the game. On the rugby field, we were all one.

The GAA did in fact vote to open Croke Park to other sports by a large majority in 2005. I was proud of Sean Kelly, President of the GAA, who won the battle that day. The

Kilcummin man was a credit to Kerry. But back in 1973 Sean Kelly had yet to be heard of and I was off the team. When UCC won the Cork County Championship, I played no part in the final due to my suspension.

They couldn't stop me celebrating, though, and I celebrated with gusto. When two of our team, Brendan Lynch and Con Murphy, interns in the North Infirmary, had to report for work on the night of the match, I felt so sorry for them that I rounded up the lads. We appeared in the hospital late that night with two bottles of whiskey and a few crates of beer. Unknown to the two interns I slipped on a white coat, hung a stethoscope around my neck, and went around to the wards offering a drop of whiskey to the sick and infirm. I got them all singing – a woman from Beara even got up and danced.

The following Sunday after Mass my mother was accosted by a neighbour from Currow. 'Is your Moss going for a doctor now?' she asked. My poor mother didn't get a chance to reply. 'I saw him in the North Infirmary last Sunday night,' the neighbour continued. 'They're all mad about him in there. He has such a lovely bedside manner'.

Five

Picked for Ireland

My football career for UCC was over. I missed the camaraderie more than anything else. Rugby was now my number one sport. I was being touted as a future international and I knew I would never make the Kerry senior team so the choice was easy in that sense. But I could never turn my back completely on football. I loved the game far too much for that.

It was now time for other changes as well. I had my Masters and I'd got good experience in my first job but I was growing out of it. I needed more money to survive. Lads who'd started out with me were settling down and having families.

After seven memorable years I decided it was time to leave Cork and the student life for good. In fairness, I'd had a good run at it, six years in college and seven years in Cork. I'd nearly have stayed another seven if I thought I would get away with it, but I had to face up to reality and take on a job with a good salary. The lab job was fine and I enjoyed the work and the company but I needed a career. At my going-away party I summed up the consequences of my departure: 'It's good for Cork and myself.'

I was moving to Dublin to work for the Department of Agriculture in the dairy hygiene area. When I told one of the lads back home about my new job he said, 'Dairy hygiene Moss – is it how you wipe cows' arses?' The job involved implementing EU regulations so I told him I was in charge of putting nappies on cows. Dublin meant that I would have to play my rugby with a city club so I joined Lansdowne FC in September 1973. I'd had a few other offers but Lansdowne was the only real choice for me. Apart from the pressure my friend Frankie Forrest put me under, I was already half in love with the place. Lansdowne Road is the oldest international rugby ground in the world. And it was seen as a Munster club, the home of former Munster and Ireland players like Paddy Berkery, Barry McGann, Gordon Wood, Mick English and Pat Whelan. I had played for UCC against Lansdowne and came away with the impression that it was a very democratic club with no airs or graces, where every member was treated the same, whether they were a Lion or the left outside with the third team. It was always Lansdowne for me, and so started a love affair that has continued to this day.

Even though I had been told by one or two prospective clubs that I would be better off to stay down south if I wanted to keep my place on the Munster team, in fact I played for Munster later that year. That game against Argentina was undoubtedly one of the dirtiest games I ever experienced. The Argentinians were up to all their tricks – eye gouging, booting, grabbing private and non-private parts. At 15-15 we got a penalty, well out of range of goal. Phil O'Callaghan, who had been on tour in Argentina a few years earlier, issued the instructions to our out-half, Barry McGann.

'Put it up in the air, Barry.'

'No better man,' McGann replied, and his high, hanging kick gave us just enough time to get to the front. We ignored the ball; each of our eight forwards picked an Argentine forward to clatter, and at the end of the move there were eight Argentinians stretched on the grass.

Final whistle.

Another draw.

I was beginning to understand what it was to play for Munster. You never gave in. It was as simple and as complicated as that. And you left nothing go. This was done not just to seek revenge but to send out a signal to future opponents. It was also to lay down a marker for future Munster teams.

Half of Munster moved to Dublin in the seventies, mainly for economic reasons, and took over a good bit of the city, so I was among friends from the start. I was crashing on the floor of a flat belonging to two lads from UCC, ex-St Brendan's boys, Jim Coghlan and Denis Coffey. There wasn't enough room to swing a kitten never mind a cat. One evening, with nothing much to do, I decided to wander down to the club for a look around. When I reached Lansdowne Road I got a real thrill as I gazed out on the field on that lovely autumn evening. The grass was green – there wasn't a scar on it – and soon I would be playing on the hallowed ground every fortnight. I made my way to the back of the stands where the Lansdowne thirds were training.

'Tough going,' I said to a small man standing beside me. To my eyes the training looked savage.

'Ah, he's going easy on them,' the man replied. 'A few years back,' he said, 'the training was really hard. There was a weekly run out to Templeogue, a round trip of about twelve miles. It was discontinued when the boys began taking the bus back, jogging in the gates of Lansdowne Road as fresh as an impostor in an Olympic marathon.'

After we'd introduced ourselves the small man told me I better get myself used to the concept of hard training. 'Moss,' he said, 'you have a good bit of conditioning on you after being out to grass for the summer.'

Thus began a friendship that lasted nearly 30 years. The small man was Con Murphy, kitman at Lansdowne, the smallest man ever to play for his country. He was only five-foot-six and nine-and-a-half stone weight when he won caps at full-back, and the only man capped before and after the Second World War. He also played soccer with Bohemians and was a junior soccer international. He loved rugby and Lansdowne, and never missed a training session at the club. He stood on the sideline in all weathers, no hat or cap on his head, too wrapped up in the training session to care about the rain.

I needed to get myself somewhere to live in the vicinity of Lansdowne. I found a flat on Garville Avenue in Rathgar and moved in with two friends of mine, Jerry and Frank. The lads told me they were short one to help with the rent.

The flat was almost opposite the residence of the Taoiseach Jack Lynch and his wife Maureen. Mrs Lynch was devoted to her cat, a big cranky-looking thing whose photograph was framed in the Garda cabin in front of the Lynch's house. The cat got an occasional kick in the arse if he happened to stray from the precincts of the Lynch household – I was never much of a cat lover – but, that apart, we liked our neighbours. Mind you, it was hard to know what they thought of us: Jack was later to tell me that after we were evicted the price of property in Garville Avenue went through the roof.

Our flat developed into a kind of 'rambling flat', where all manner of people came and went at all times of the day and night. We discovered a footprint on the ceiling once and none of us could ever figure out how it got there. There were times when people crashed on the floor and left next morning without any of us having a clue who they were. The door was never locked, as there was nothing worth stealing. We had no television, no radio or stereo, nothing to tempt even the poorest thief. I was hardly ever there between work and training.

My first month's training was torture. We trained on the back pitch of Lansdowne Road, in the shadow of the East Stand. Tuesdays were a killer, when we sweated out the weekend, starting with an eight-lap warm-up. It was only when the evenings began to shorten that I was afforded some relief. The floodlights had a limited range, so I would dodge behind one of the huge concrete pillars in the East Stand and sit out a couple of laps. I kept a bottle of Lucozade hidden behind my private pillar for my tea break. Sometimes there were other dodgers, every man to his own pillar.

One night I was propping up the stand when Con approached me. He handed me my bottle of Lucozade without a word. I drained it in one slug. 'You're going to have to train on your own,' Con said. 'There's a lot more of you to get fit than these other lads. If you're going to eat and drink for two, you're going to have to train for two as well.'

I was of the firm opinion back then that there was no point in burning myself out in the early autumn when the real action only got going after Christmas – there was no Heineken Cup then, and only an occasional autumn international. I think my ducking and diving was one of the reasons I survived so long. Con and I got talking and he agreed with my approach. He was rarely wrong.

Con was what club rugby was all about. Even in the simple things, like having your kit together, as bagman he made sure I always had my gear in order. More than that, he could discuss rugby all day and all night. Con was a natural storyteller. He gave an especially vivid account of hearing shots as a small boy playing in his back garden in Kilmainham. The shots were the most significant of many in Irish history; they were the volleys that executed the leaders of the 1916 Rising. But there was a moment he hated to talk about, a dropped ball in a Triple Crown decider from 30 years earlier. He used to look up and hold his hands out as if he was playing Wales once again and the ball was dropping out of the sky and he'd say, 'I let the Triple Crown through my fingers.' My heart went out to him.

When I did go on to win a Triple Crown, it was as much for Con as for myself, and when I told him so, it brought tears to his eyes.

Con was being hard on himself. On a wet day the old-style ball was heavy and slippery and impossible to catch. Con also had great days in the green shirt, like the time in Lansdowne Road when two French second rows carried the small man 50 yards while he refused to let go of the ball, or the day in 1947 when he captained Ireland to a 22-0 win over England at Lansdowne Road. Amazingly, he was dropped for the next game and was never picked again. He was 35 and I suppose his time might have been up.

Con knew me better than I knew myself. He never gave me too much praise or too much criticism. He explained the game intelligently, jumping to his feet in his enthusiasm to put his point across. This coaching was vital for me. I was like a man who starts school at 21 – I had never played the game at secondary school and needed an intensive course in what I had to do to become an Irish international. If UCC had been my cradle, Lansdowne was my finishing school, with Con as the headmaster.

Under Con's supervision I trained on my own as well as with the team, when coach Tony Twomey took charge. Tony had no favourites: he tortured each of us equally. I owe him a great debt. The hard work paid off by Christmas when we won the Leinster Senior League in a game against our co-tenants at Lansdowne Road, Wanderers. We had four current and future internationals on the team. Vinnie Becker and Mickey Quinn starred in the backs, while Con Feighery was my second row partner. He was an extremely sound performer and even though we were in competition for an Irish spot, he still shared all the insights of his experience. Lansdowne was that kind of club.

A few days after the League win, I played for the Rest of Ireland in a game against the Combined Universities. The match was a trial, played to select the teams for the final trial for the Irish team, which was to be held on the first Saturday in January. I lined out against Leo Galvin, an adversary who, like many others, became a lifelong friend. Galvin had international experience already, and played well for Ireland against Argentina as second row partner to Willie John McBride. Willie John was likely to be selected anyway, so the choice of player to partner him was probably between Galvin, Kevin Mays who had played in the previous season's internationals and possibly, with a bit of luck, myself.

The pre-trial was one of my better games – I even managed to score a try – and after the match I was told I was on the Probables for the trial itself. The Probables were the first team, playing against the Possibles. I was in pole position.

I didn't celebrate just yet as the main aim still lay ahead. I took it easy at our work Christmas party and missed the elongated lead into Christmas around Dublin. The season of goodwill in my adopted city seemed to start around the beginning of December and finish up around the end of the rugby season. It was more like 90 days of Christmas, and it was very easy to get sucked in. Work was definitely not taken as seriously back then and it was unheard of for someone to be seen in an office after seven in the evening. There were probably about 20 sports cars in the entire city and you would still look up to admire a Merc or a BMW. It was more easygoing than it is now and a lot more fun, even though money was scarce. There were no computers or mobile phones so it was much more difficult to ascertain your every movement or your net worth to your employers. We were just happy to have a job and, unlike thousands of our contemporaries who'd had to emigrate, we could go home for the Christmas.

Christmas, for me, that year was training every day in muck up to my ankles. The field I trained in looked as if it had been grazed by a herd of bullocks from the amount of running I did there. My old friend Michael O'Shea from over the road, helped out, as did my brothers Brian and Matt, and between them they pushed me hard. It was a regime we continued every Christmas for many years afterwards. My father wanted me to run on the road but it was too dangerous in the wintry darkness. Anyway I didn't want the locals to think I was turning into a Yank, as it was only Americans who ran on the road back in those days.

The funny thing was I didn't lose any weight over Christmas; in fact, I put on nearly half a stone. A few months in flatland living on take-away was replaced by a holiday at home in Currow living off my father and mother's excellent food, most of which came from our own farm. Home bacon with our own cabbage; homemade brown bread with eggs gathered from our flock of Rhode Island Reds. The turkey was even one of our own; I'd killed her myself.

I hardly visited the pubs in the village over the holidays. In fact, I didn't visit them at all. I knew that the trick was not to go to the pub in the first place, where there was the danger of being drawn into the craic. I like a drink, always have, but I could give it up when-ever I had to.

It was only a few weeks later that I was carrying a rattling crate of Guinness up the narrow stairs, hardly able to see my way in the twilight of the 45-watt bulb much favoured by Dublin landlords back in January 1974.

I had a bit of good news and I wanted to share it with my flatmates. I clattered into the flat. Clothes and newspapers were booted to touch. Shoes and books were shoved aside. We were poor housekeepers at the best of times.

'Wake up, ye lazy whores,' I shouted, at the top of my voice, ripping the blankets off my friends.

They were still rousing themselves when I opened the first bottle and handed it to Frank. The warm Guinness fizzled out of the neck and onto the bedclothes and the floor.

'Ah, Moss, what's going on? Were you on the piss or what?' asked a half-awake Jerry.

'What is it, Moss? Did you lose your virginity?' Frank enquired, taking a sup from the bottle. 'At least you're back to yourself. We thought you were turning into a monk.'

Over the past few weeks I had carried on training like never before, and cut my consumption of liquor to a fraction, just a few quiet pints. I had learned my lesson the hard way. It was binge training.

But there'd been temptation. A few days before the Ireland team trial my friend Dr Paddy Crowley was getting married in Cork. I had to go; Paddy was a great friend from college days. And once again Cork was a temptation I couldn't resist. All my old college GAA pals were there and my new rugby friends togged out beside them. The wedding itself was wonderful. To put it mildly, the discipline of the previous three weeks had gone out the window. I'd woken up in the house of another pal, Dr Con Murphy, directly across the road from the Western Star. 'Jaysus, Moss,' I'd said to myself, 'you shagging gom.' All the horsing around the haggard back home at Christmas and I'd cut loose a few days before the trial.

On the way back to Dublin that Thursday morning, Frankie Forrest had given me a bollocking about my carry-on the previous evening. I'd tried to tell him that my intense training regime of the last few weeks would stand to me, and anyway, Frankie, I'd countered, 'weren't you on the piss too?' Frankie had replied, with some justification, that he wasn't playing in a final trial for the Irish team on Saturday.

I thought I had blown my chance again, and when I'd played only a fair game in the trial I cursed myself for going on the rip at the wedding feast in Cork.

My flatmates had seen the state I was in when I came back from Cork, so they didn't bring up the trial as we sat there drinking the Guinness.

There was silence. I put my hands over my face and took on the pained, doleful expression of an undertaker on a day when he has no funeral. They were diappointed for me and didn't know what to say. I let out a sigh, followed by a longer sigh and then I let out a roar.

'You know what it is, lads,' I told them, 'I've been picked to play for Ireland.'

They jumped out of their beds and danced a jig and we did a bit of scrummaging practice on the floor. The crowd in the flat underneath thought there was a herd of bullocks upstairs, but when they realised they weren't going to get any sleep they took their beating and came and joined us.

We celebrated till late that night. I knew there was an Irish training session next morning and everyone had to be on the bus outside the Shelbourne Hotel at 10 am. I'm afraid I let the occasion go to my head, but it's not every day you get picked to represent your country.

I woke up at 9 am. My alarm hadn't gone off, mainly due to the fact I hadn't set it the night before, and my car was still in Ballsbridge, about five miles away. It was Sunday morning. No one went anywhere on Sunday morning, except to go to Mass. Taxi drivers took the morning off and buses were scarce as hen's teeth and even if I did get a taxi I didn't know where the training session was to be held. And every public payphone I passed had coins stuck in the slots; I couldn't even call in late.

I set off at a run for the Shelbourne, thinking that the bus would have long departed, along with my first cap. I was cursing myself. It was 10.25 am when I finally showed up. The bus was there – coach Syd Millar had delayed it, although I learned that if another five minutes had elapsed it was gone, and so was I – out of the Irish team.

I got on the bus and sat beside the hooker, Dr Ken Kennedy, who was on his own in the front seat. I wasn't there long when the bus was informed of the stink of stale porter off my breath – there had been no time to brush my teeth. No one took much notice other than to have a good laugh about it, and as it turned out the training session wasn't too arduous. The three-mile race to the bus had been much tougher.

Family and friends were delighted for me but I kept out of the limelight as much as possible. I was afraid things might not go according to plan in Paris and I reasoned if I was out and about showing off what a great man I was the fall would be even more painful, it being a well-known fact a fall hurts more when you come down from high up.

Once you get picked for your first cap, the press will want to find out about you but I continued to keep a low profile. I wasn't even in the phone directory and didn't clock in too often at the number I gave the Irish Rugby Football Union. And of course it was the days before the mobile phone, when a man could go missing and stay missing.

The legendary Sean Diffley, then of the *Irish Press* and later of the *Irish Independent*, found me. His mother lived a few doors down from the flat in Garville Avenue. He made contact and arranged a rendezvous upstairs in Murphy's Pub, Rathgar. I liked Diffley. There was something of the gentleman about him, and he had a great sense of humour. The interview lasted a long while, and we enjoyed a drink as we spoke. The following morning, I was at my desk in the

Department when the phone rang. It was Sean. He couldn't remember a word I had told him. I strongly suggested that our next meeting be held in a café.

Diffley wrote a lovely piece, which I still have. I was nervous of meeting the press, but he treated me with great respect.

The preparation for my first cap wasn't ideal. There was still something of the student in me and I was living a carefree lifestyle like most of the lads I hung around with. Rugby internationals lived ordinary lives back then, except for a few weeks every year when we were in the spotlight. And we all had jobs – rugby was a game we played for fun. We had the same holidays as everyone else. There was no pay and the IRFU weren't exactly throwing expenses at us. Fun is why the game was invented and that is why William Webb Ellis ran off with the ball at Rugby school. This was something I never lost sight of, and was one of the reasons I survived so long.

In the early days I did a lot of binge training, only doing serious stuff coming up to a big event. Like the man fixing the roof the day before the storm. But from my first cap on, and for the next 11 seasons of my international career, I trained as hard as anyone. I would never have survived otherwise. I never missed a Five Nations match in those eleven seasons, playing 44 games in a row. Neither was I ever dropped.

But that was all in the future and I had to try to persuade myself I was good enough to play for my country in Paris. The days went slowly. I scoured the papers to see if someone said something good about me. For the most part they gave me an easy ride and it bolstered my confidence. It was traditional to keep the Saturday before your first cap free from club duties and Lansdowne captain Dermot Power duly obliged. It was real now. The free Saturday gave me time to think. Time to worry, too. I trained that week as usual with Lansdowne as the international squad only came together the Thursday before the game. I noticed the Lansdowne lads were careful about coming into any physical contact with me at training.

We all shared the same dressing rooms, from the First to the 3rd E's, the eighth team. One lad from Waterford, Tom Keane, a good friend and son of legendary hurler John, sat beside me after training and said, 'Moss I'm worried sick. I have been subbed up to the Third B's. I hope I don't let the lads down.' And he went on for a good while in the same vein.

I just nodded my head at the end and told him I knew exactly where he was coming from.

Six

International Championship

My first cap was in the Parc des Princes, Paris against the French on January 19, 1974. You couldn't get a tougher opener. The days leading up to it were hectic, with telegrams, letters and calls of congratulations.

I took two days out of my annual leave to cover the Thursday and Friday before the game. I was nearly broke. My paycheck ran out when I had to hire a dress suit and buy a pair of black shoes and socks for the after-match dinner. The boys in the flat decided to hand me over their few quid and stay in that weekend. We managed one last meal in the Pronto Grill in Ranelagh where you'd get more liver than lamb chops or sausages. There was no shortage of chips or bread, but the butter needed to be spread very thin to cover the entire acreage of the sliced bread. There was tea but there was a small charge for the extra boiling water and the waitress generously waived this in honour of the fact it was my first cap for Ireland and we were good customers.

The Irish squad assembled in the Shelbourne Hotel for lunch on the Thursday before the game and then went training for a few hours in Belvedere RFC grounds in Anglesea Road. I was the first man on the bus. It was a peculiar feeling to train in front of a few hundred onlookers and to be asked to sign autographs for the kids afterwards. It was a great thrill; I was wondering if any of the youngsters would come up and ask me. They always seemed to pick me out, too, probably because I was so big. 'Look, Dad,' one young lad said to his father, 'a small giant!'

On the bus to Dublin airport the butterflies started to flutter, not because of the game, but because of the bloody flight to Paris. I had a savage fear of flying. Any other mode of transport would have been fine. Sean Lynch, the St Mary's College prop and an experienced traveller, had the same problem, and when the two of us were put together it was a disaster. The panic multiplied logarithmically.

Lynch told me of a flight he took on the Lions Tour of New Zealand in 1971, when the pilot put the plane on automatic, came out of the cabin, and began serving teas and coffees. The plane was an old Fokker Friendship and this was a one-man show. Lynch got frantic and wanted a parachute.

Lynch and myself cracked each other up. Willie Duggan hadn't arrived on the scene yet, but when he did he panicked the lot of us even more. In any event, we made it to Paris. With his feet on the ground, Lynch was a great ally. He was rated the best scrummager in the world in 1971 when he played with the Lions in New Zealand. The Kiwi scrum was demolished on that tour. It was worth anything to have a man of his standing looking after me. I knew he would be with me all the way on and off the pitch, whatever about in the air.

I roomed with the late, great Terry Moore, the Highfield and Munster Number eight. It's a small world – his brother-in-law was Starry Crowley, patron of the Western Star. You couldn't meet a nicer roommate, calm and easygoing – the ideal partner for a rookie.

A good night's sleep was followed by a crisp dry Parisian day on Friday. We had a light run out and then came the traditional trip to the Irish embassy. Lynch hauled me aside at the reception. Maybe it was the bond we had established through our mutual fear of flying, but he adopted me for the weekend.

'Moss, you just can't be seen drinking beer at the function,' he told me, 'even if it is only one or two. If they see you you might never pull the Irish jersey over your head again.'

There were soft drinks, of course, and there was Tio Pepe, served in tiny glasses held between finger and thumb. I had hard, shovel-size hands and the delicate crystal nearly snapped in my fingers. I sank a few glasses of the stuff and there was a nice little buzz off it. The Tio Pepe was tasty. It reminded me of the sherry trifle my mother used to make for us as a treat on Sunday.

When the food was served I stuffed myself on the first two courses and polished off what was left on the boys' plates as well, thinking there wouldn't be much more coming. There were four more courses. I couldn't even touch the last one. If the French are as well fed as this, I thought, they'll hardly be able to walk around the field.

Friday night's sleep was not as good as the previous one. I dropped off quickly but the phone rang at about four o'clock in the morning, and that was the end of my sleep for the night. It rang again, some French fecker acting the bollix. I got up out of bed to see if I could spot anyone in the phone-box across the road but luckily for the hoaxer he wasn't in it. Terry made sure the phone would ring no more anyway. He pulled it clean out of the wall.

Rugby players always look out the window the minute they wake up. The sky over St Lazare was blue; the day was to be fine and dry. I lay on my back at about seven o'clock with my palms under my head, looking down at my long toes dangling out over the end of the bed. The cot was far too short. Where would those toes bring me today? Would I be able to hold my own? Would I disgrace myself, make some terrible mistake near our line? Terry was still sound asleep. I coughed a few times and tossed around the bed in the hope I might wake him up but it was no use. Terry would have been good to talk to; the calmness just oozed out of him.

I knew my family at home were even more nervous. My mother never let the rosary beads out of her hands. Canon Matt, my uncle, offered up Masses. The whole of Currow and beyond were holding their breath. I said a few prayers myself and that helped a little.

Breakfast-time couldn't come quickly enough, and when it was over a few of us went walkabout for an hour or so, trying to focus on the match that afternoon. There was an early lunch but I didn't bother with it as I had eaten enough at breakfast, and by now the butterflies were beginning their metamorphosis.

The lack of sleep was worrying me, but there were stimulants on offer. One of the backroom boys prepared a strange concoction to soften the lunch. It was basically eggnog, enhanced with some form of alcohol, and everybody who wanted it received a glass. There was a bit of a kick off it. It was a big thing back then, a swig of whiskey or a drop of poteen before a game. It was the same in Gaelic football. It never did anything for me, and in any case the practice was eventually discontinued, probably for the best.

Shortly after lunch the squad assembled in a big room in the hotel for the team talk. We were on our own now with our captain, Willie John McBride. This talk consisted of a half-hour of complete silence, when you concentrated on your individual responsibilities in the match that lay ahead. I thought the 30 minutes would never end. It brought me back to the retreats in St Brendan's, when the whole school had to observe the rule of silence for a weekend. It was the

longest half-hour I ever spent in my life, I who was up half
the night and had already spent the morning thinking about
my responsibilities. All I wanted to do was get on the bloody
field. Then all of a sudden Willie John exploded into the
most fiery speech you could ever hear. It left me bursting
with passion and pride.

Fifteen minutes later we were on the bus heading to the
Parc des Princes, escorted through the city traffic by
gendarmes, travelling at high speed. I wished they hadn't. I
hate fast cars. They put the fear of God into me.

Irish supporters had been assembling since Friday
morning and on our morning walk I met several people from
home. We met wagonloads of French supporters too. They
didn't know me, but they recognised the likes of Willie John,
Fergus Slattery, Ray McLoughlin and others and gave them
a fair bit of a barracking when they came off the bus. It
didn't seem to bother them unduly. Slatts said it was just
part and parcel of rugby weekends and helped to get him up
for the battle that lay ahead. It was all in good spirits, in any
event. Most of the French supporters had travelled up from
the south of France, and this was a weekend in Paris for
them just as it was for the Irish.

As the pre-match atmosphere built, my nerves all but
disappeared. This was what I had wanted all my life, a big
day in a big stadium. And if it wasn't to be Croke Park, Parc
des Princes wasn't a bad second choice.

As we made our way into the stadium, there were a
hundred offerings of 'Best of luck, Moss.' I was approached
by a few lads I knew from the world of Gaelic football. Before
a big Gaelic game they would tell me cheerfully, 'Kane, you
big useless bollix, you better play well today.' The locals had
a habit of changing Keane to Kane, depending on the
occasion. Today, though, I was Moss. And they were
euphoric, totally positive when it came to cheering on the

Irish rugby team. I could sense their passion, and once you feel it you know you simply have to raise your game in response. If you can't react to that kind of support, you might as well not be there at all.

The French stadium was newly built. I had played on the back pitch the year before when Lansdowne met Racing Club de Paris, and I had looked up at the stands that day and wondered if I'd ever play in the real thing. Now my dream was a reality.

It was a game we should have won.

We ended up losing 9-6 after a tough battle. It was a game we could have won, should have won. Stewart McKinney scored a perfectly legitimate try that was disallowed by Scottish referee Alan Hosie. I have no idea why that try was disallowed; and judging by their expressions, neither did the French. And of course one of them cut me up with his jagged boot, but I came back on after a quick makeover. We hardly left the French 22 in the last few minutes, but we just couldn't convert the territory into scores.

The post-match dinner was full of speeches and good humour. I got on well with the French, save for the stamper, who kept well out of my way.

We did a tour of Paris that night. Willie John McBride has a story in his book about my pulling a ring of sausages out of a bistro and half ways into the next parish. If I did I can't remember it and I would say there might be some confusion on his part but I do recall some lunatic going for Willie John for no particular reason other than he was Willie John. He had a knife, but I took care of him – with a good old-fashioned puck in the gob.

After all Willie John covered my back during the game. The reception was top class. I had a great night, satisfied that I had played my best. I even ate a feed of escargots. But of course the lads didn't tell me what I was eating until I polished off a couple of plates. Mick Quinn told me they were Normandy prawns.

I woke up the next morning suffering from those escargots, but generally pleased with myself. My teammates told me I did fine and seemed to accept me as one of the lads. I couldn't have hoped for more.

There was a feeling at breakfast, and in the days that followed, that we could do very well in 1974. Ray McLoughlin said as much to me in the corridor of Lansdowne Road before we went out to play Wales in our second game that season and my second cap. Ray was a superb motivator. Sometimes in the course of a game he would whisper, 'Come on the Kingdom,' and this would get me going. He was tough as nails with the strength of two men, but he was smart too, and probably had the best tactical brain I ever came across in rugby. Ray felt there was no reason why we shouldn't win the Triple Crown.

'Moss,' he continued, in a deadly serious voice, 'here I am without any tangible success after playing for my country for nearly 12 years. McBride is the most famous rugby player in the world, but he's never won anything for Ireland. And you can come in and win a Five Nations in your first season, hardly knowing the difference between knocking-on and a knocking shop. Moss, you'll play for Ireland for many a year. Trust me. You have what it takes. Believe in yourself. But we need you to go from a beginner to a seasoned pro in one game.' He paused to let his words sink in. 'You have it, Moss.'

He paused and repeated again: 'Moss, trust me.'

'I trust you, Ray. I'll die out there if I have to. I promise you that.'

Then, as we were about to run onto the pitch, Ray turned to me and said, 'Moss, it's my last chance to win anything in a green jersey.'

Ray's words did it for me. I was ready for Wales.

My family turned out in strength. There was no question then of flying to Paris for the first cap. People didn't go anywhere much back then unless it involved emigration. My aunt, Sister Iznard, defied her superior's instructions not to attend my first home cap. She simply ignored them, and was duly disciplined on her return to the convent. 'I would have gone,' she said, 'even if they threatened me with excommunication.'

We stepped out on the pitch and the welcoming roar of the Lansdowne crowd. Nothing prepares you for it. It's as if you're a score up before a ball is kicked. If you were to ask me now, all these years later, what it is I miss the most, it's those first moments when you cross into the field of play at Lansdowne Road, with Ireland's supporters in full voice.

We knew we were better than Wales but we missed chance after easy chance. It was my first encounter with Geoff Wheel, who was to be the fulcrum of the great Welsh team of my time. He made his debut facing Willie John McBride that day. Geoff had some sort of involuntary twitch in his shoulder, and Willie John, thinking that the shoulder movement was a prelude to an invasion of his territorial waters, clattered him. Geoff told me afterwards he would have been highly insulted if he hadn't been hit by Willie John; I think he regarded it as some kind of rugby rite of passage. Geoff was a rookie and it was the tradition to soften up rookies, though with this Welshman you might as well try to soften up a rock.

I think I had a good game but at the final whistle we had to settle for a draw. It was a major disappointment. At any rate, at the end of the match McBride came up to me and said, 'That wasn't too bad, big Moss.' I must have grown since the French game.

Ray was the last man in the dressing room. He just sat there, almost motionless. 'Come on, Ray, let's get out of here or it'll be closing time,' I said, summoning up my courage. That got him up and out of it. Even though his eyes told of the pain in his heart, he still managed to say, 'Well done, Moss. You did all that was asked of you.'

That was enough for me.

The Welsh game was a terrible disappointment. We should have beaten France in Paris, when we were denied by that disallowed try, but against Wales it was our own fault: we just didn't put them away. Ray's face told it all: I remember thinking I would love to win something with him, for him.

For the moment, though, we put the downs behind us and looked forward to the next match. That was the great thing about the Five Nations, or the Six Nations as it is now, every game was a championship in itself. And we were a very happy squad of players. We were different ages and personalities but we just seemed to click together, even if we didn't always know how. Every time I spoke to Stewart MacKinney he would reply, 'Pardon, Maurice?' even though I thought he must understand what I was saying half the time at least. When he spoke to me in his rich and incomprehensible northern brogue, I would just nod my head and say 'That's right, Stew,' irrespective of what he was saying. One day we finally made a communications breakthrough. I was in the shower after an Irish squad session and Stewart was washing himself in the berth beside me.

'Maurice, you were obviously down home in Kerry at the weekend,' he remarked.

'I was indeed, Stew. How did you figure that one out?'

'Because there's a blade of grass stuck between the two cheeks of your arse,' he answered airily, continuing with his own ablutions.

After Wales, next up were the English at Twickenham. We were the underdogs in most people's eyes, but our captain had a different view and soon put us in the picture. He went ballistic in the dressing room. He blamed England for everything from Eve's seduction of Adam to the disappearance of the dodo, and had us champing at the bit, ready to take them on. I was astonished. I was under the impression that because Willie John was an Ulster Protestant he would in some way tone down his pre-match address to the troops. But that was the thing about playing with the northern boys: we transcended politics. It didn't take too long for me to reconcile my Republican heritage with the diverse political and religious backgrounds of my teammates. There was no border in the Irish dressing room; we were united to play for Ireland. I felt a surge of pride as I ran onto the pitch at Twickenham, ready to take on the English.

Willie John's speech worked. I went into that game with a shoulder ligament injury and was hoping it would loosen out as the game went on. We raced out of sight of England, leading 26-9 with the opposition dead and buried. Or so it might seem. One thing I learned about playing England that day, and later, was that they never gave up. But neither did I and I should have. My shoulder was very sore. It got to the stage where I couldn't even lift my right hand over my head. I was contesting the line out with one hand. I was afraid if I came off I would never get a place again. I didn't even tell Willie John I was hurt. I got it into my head I would be looked upon as fragile or that I would be seen as a quitter. The pain was almost unbearable but I played through it.

The English kept chipping away and cut us back to a slender five-point lead in the last few minutes. I could feel the huge Irish crowd at the game willing us to hold on. They would revel in a win and I put myself about a fair bit that day. We held the line in the end. For Ireland it was three wins in a row against England, and we were the first of the home nations to beat them twice in a row at Twickenham.

Mike Gibson was the man of the match. He always played

well in Twickenham. He had destroyed England on the occasion of his first game there ten years previously. Here he played as if he had watched the game beforehand. He was just so far ahead of everyone else in terms of quickness of thought and anticipation. He simply glided past the English as if they weren't there. Sometimes when I had the opportunity to look up out of the bottom of a ruck, I'd notice him drift into a space where there was no sign of activity; next moment the ball would find him there.

Fellow Lansdowne man Mick Quinn had his best game ever for Ireland that day. Nothing seemed to bother him. Mick's calm seeped through the team. He was only in his second season at the top level but he played as if he had been there forever. When England scored a try and we were all walking slowly back behind our own line for the conversion, he says to me, 'Ah, cheer up, Mossy. At least you went back on the right side this time.'

Mick was referring to an incident the season before when we'd played University College Cork at the Mardyke, and out of force of habit I had walked behind the UCC line after a Lansdowne try. Problem was, I was playing for Lansdowne.

The graph was curving upward all the time. My first cap had been a loss; the Welsh game was a draw and now a win against England. The first international win at that. I had a terrible fear I would never appear on a winning Irish team and might end up as a question in a pub quiz: 'Name the only Irish player to win 20 caps and none of them on a winning team? Answer: Moss Keane.'

The dressing room was full of yahooing and singing, backslapping and general goodwill towards all. The best place in the world is an international dressing room after a big win. You can't wait to get out to celebrate with family and friends, but at the same time you want to stay there forever.

Once the game was over we got on extremely well with the English. They preferred to socialise with us more than with anyone else. It was another stereotype I was glad to knock down; the 'auld enemies' were for the most part sound men, good for a laugh and a few beers too.

I didn't overdo glorying in the win that night. There's an old Kerry saying, 'Walk easy when your jug is full.' In Kerry, they never let you lose the run of yourself. On the morning of our next game, against Scotland, my father was on his way by train to Dublin in the company of a few rugby men from home, when someone asked him if he had a good ticket. He had the best seat in the stadium, about the length of a three-prong pike from where the President of Ireland sat.

'It's wasted on me,' he said apologetically, 'I don't know too much about the rules of rugby.'

'Don't worry, your son knows even less', quipped the smart-arse sitting opposite him.

My father's first cap went well all the same when we pipped Scotland 9-6 in our last game of the season at Lansdowne Road. We did just about enough to win. Some of the older players were simply dead tired, but we stuck together and toughed it out. The win was great, but we were left with a sense of what might have been. We knew we should have won the Grand Slam. It had been years of near misses, glorious defeats and hard luck stories since our last Five Nations success. As far as we were concerned, we'd blown it.

Mathematically, of course, we still had a chance of winning the championship – we led the table by one point from Wales and France. When the last games were played, we needed Wales to lose to England and Scotland to beat France. Trouble was, Wales and France were the dominant rugby nations – England hadn't beaten Wales for years and Scotland were given no chance against the French.

At this stage I felt bad about the season. It wasn't so much for myself, because I was delighted simply to have held my place, but for the old hands like Ken Kennedy, who was the most capped European hooker, and of course for McLoughlin, Lynch, McBride and Gibson – Dad's army as they were known.

Next up was Scotland against France – it would decide the Championship.

I couldn't bear hanging around Dublin so I hit for Currow. It was a fine, dry, bright spring day and I brought Fenton for a walk up to the field above the top field. That was a great Kerry one – the field above the top field. Castle Island lay in the distance and the sun shone on the Brown Flesk down below. Our good land was nearly all below our farmhouse. Up where I was it was wild and windy, full of rushes and bogholes. I walked and walked in the heavy going until I sensed the match was over. I meant to eat a good supper then and watch television at home with my mother and father. There was no point in going down to the village for a few pints because everyone would be trying to console me.

Or nearly everyone. There was one man who never stopped knocking the Irish team and the game of rugby. Rugby, he said, was no better than tearing and rooting like oul' pigs looking for food. And I was well suited to that, he continued, what with my size and everything. And it was as well I had the bit of rugby to play as I would never have made it at Gaelic football because I was so big and awkward. And the rugby couldn't be that hard to play either because if a very middling footballer like me could make a go of it, what wouldn't the likes of the truly great Kerry footballers do if they took it up? And it was just as well they didn't as it would be a total waste of their talent. The man was older than my father and when he started I just had to shut up and take it. Respect your elders was the etiquette I grew up with. The rest of the parish, though, caught every ball with me and tackled every opponent, and prayed and lit candles in the parish church and sent cakes and puddings to the house as gifts when I came home.

I was trudging back along old, muddy tracks, with my head down waiting to hear the worst. I took my time. The longer I stayed on the hill the longer we would be in the lead in the Five Nations. Fenton took on my mood and slunk along beside me. Then I noticed my father coming up the hill as fast as he could manage.

'Moss, ye won the International Championship. Come on, your supper is ready. Pancakes.'

Seven

Tough Times

That first season changed my life a fair bit. During the summer I was recognised in the street, was asked for autographs by kids and I was even sent over drinks by complete strangers. I found it easier to talk to women as well. It was a question of guerrilla warfare. You took your chances as the occasion arose.

But I still had to get up for work every morning and I continued to live in Garville Avenue in the rambling flat when you could expect callers at any hour of the day or night. Then back home at weekend after four hours' hard driving. A big bag of dirty clothes for my mother and two days of feeding and rest. Life continued pretty much the same as before as far as Kerry was concerned. They were glad I'd done well and congratulated me, but it wasn't the All-Ireland I'd won, was it? On Sunday night back to Dublin. Five hours. It was always an hour longer going back up with the traffic on a Sunday night. It often seemed to me that those of us not forced to emigrate all lived in Dublin. There were very few jobs back home. I could have had the farm but I made my choice and I had no regrets. The farm meant milking cows, morning and evening. It took over every facet of your life and meant there was little, if any time, for socialising.

One day around this time a strange thing happened to me in Grafton Street in Dublin. I was meeting up with a friend who was running late so I was waiting around. I happened to glance in at a model in the window of a clothes shop – a tailor's model that is – because I was thinking it might be about time to buy a new suit. I was trying to see the price when I got a tip on the shoulder. When I turned around a bald man, as bald as the model and nearly as big as myself, handed me an egg. It had just been boiled. I juggled the hot egg around, like a full-back who has trouble fielding a high ball, before I knocked it onto the pavement. I looked around, but the tall bald man was nowhere to be seen. To this day it bothers me. Who was he? What was he up to? And why me?

The rugby season that year and those that followed promised much, but, like the curate's egg, the performances were only good in parts. Edmund Van Esbeck summed it up well in his book *Irish Rugby 1874-1999* when he described the years between 1975 and 1978 as 'poor performances followed by great and unexpected victories'.

We beat England in Lansdowne Road at the start of '75, a victory that raised everyone's expectations. I marked Chris Ralston in that game. I was jumping all over him so much in the lineout that in the end he flared up and threw a punch at me. I ducked and Ralston's fist connected with his teammate, flanker Peter Dixon instead and laid him out. Worse again, from an English point of view, Peter had been having a stormer. From my point of view it was a classic case of killing two birds with one stone. I was smiling broadly while Peter was tended to by the doctor, the physio and the Red Cross, and when I caught Chris's eye I made a gesture with my fingers – not a V sign, but a kind of a childish strumming of my lips. Chris was like a dog on a leash after that, dying to get at me, though he couldn't and he didn't. I never enjoyed anything as much in my life. Chris saw the funny side that night – much later that night. It took a while for him to loosen out but we got on famously after that.

After the England win we were hot favourites to win the Five Nations, until Scotland beat us 20-13 in Murrayfield. Bubble burst.

Then we had a big win over the French, 25-6. I was lucky to be left on the field that day. I spotted the player who did me in Paris the year before, or so I thought. I let fly and he was soon pumping blood from above his eye. But it was the wrong man, a case of mistaken identity. The referee didn't make eye contact. I'm gone, that's it I said to myself. But he gave me a chance. The man who nearly took my eye out in Paris escaped again. If I'd hit anyone else in that game I would have been sent off for sure and I would have been regarded as a loose cannon by the selectors.

After the big win against France expectations took another swing upwards. Next Wales hammered us 32-4 in the Arms Park. A black day, the less said the better. None of us did too well, myself included. Willie Duggan was the exception as usual.

The highlight of that up and down season was beating England for the fourth year in a row. The strange thing was that England were favourites every single time, except for that '75 win. But even though we had beaten the favourites, I sensed we just weren't the same team that had won the championship in '74.

We had a good few of the 1974 Lions in our side, but they were worn out, as is often the case following a Lions' tour. And at the end of the season Willie John McBride, Ray McLoughlin, Sean Lynch and Ken Kennedy packed it in. I think it was the Welsh game that did for them. That was the day, I think, they realised their best days were over. This left a huge vacuum, which even a strong rugby-playing nation would have had difficulty coming to terms with. These men had been through it all for a decade and more. They were the kind of men who only came along every 30 or 40 years. They were leaders. Tough boys who never flinched when it came to the rough stuff. And of course they were all Lions. They grew old together and left together, and it proved very difficult to fill the void they left behind. It was no one's fault. It was just a fact of life that Irish rugby was not able to muster the same playing numbers as Gaelic games and soccer. Everyone loves rugby, everyone supports the national team, but not many play the bloody game.

Syd Millar also packed it in as the Irish head buck cat. In '74 Syd had coached Ireland to our first international championship in donkey's years, and he was the man who won with the Lions in South Africa in 1974, their most successful tour of all time. He was technically gifted and as shrewd as a small farmer, always making the most of his resources, and he worked harder than anyone for the game. And most important of all, he had great time for me.

When Roly Meates stepped in as coach we had, by any standards, a couple of torrid years, winning just one game out of ten. They were very difficult times, and the longer we went on losing, the worse it got. Roly Meates was a fine coach. I can safely say he enjoyed the support of all the players, but even though we had new stars like Willie Duggan who were making a big impression, we had simply lost too many big guns, and all in one go.

Roly was open, honest and he knew his rugby. He was an excellent forwards' coach and there was nothing he didn't know about scrummaging. He started off on the right foot when he picked Tom Grace as his captain. Mike Gibson had captained the team for a couple of games but the great man just didn't like the job. Gibson was a perfectionist when it came to rugby, and he knew the captaincy involved a lot more than giving a talk in the dressing room. He wanted the time and space to concentrate fully on his own game and he was man enough to admit it. Tom Grace, the leading try scorer on the Lions South African tour in '74, was the best man for the captaincy. He was an all-round athlete. I remember taking him on in the 16 lbs shot one day in Trinity College. He lofted the weight the best part of 48 feet, leaving this muscle-bound bollix in the lurch. Grace was smart too. On leaving UCD, he looked around and saw that Lansdowne already had the two best wingers of that era – Alan 'Dixie' Duggan and Vinnie Becker – and he promptly joined St Mary's College. There he became one of a long list of Irish captains to come from that great club in Templeville Road, a club very close to my heart too.

One day during this time I was the victim of a send-up. The mimic was good. He could do a nice imitation of English journalist John Reason. And one day he kept me on the phone for nearly an hour pretending to be Reason who wasn't exactly my biggest fan anyway. The joker said he was doing an exposé on cheating in rugby and accused me 'of pushing in the lineouts and jumping in the scrums,' which was of course near enough the truth. I never discovered the identity of the hoaxer. I have my suspicions. I often wonder if he had anything to do with the curious incident of the egg on Grafton Street.

I might have had a bit of a laugh at the whole carry on if we were still winning, but we were not.

These were tough times for Irish rugby, even though we suffered only two 'humiliations' – getting a real hammering from Wales, 34-9, in Lansdowne Road in '76, and going down to France, 26-3, in Paris the same year. There was an incident or two in Paris once again. The French were attacking about 10 metres from our line and lost the subsequent ruck. I picked up to feed scrum-half John Robbie and found there was no sign of him – he was tied up in another skirmish. I saw Barry McGann standing about 20 yards away but decided there wasn't much point in trying to reach him from where I stood. Instead I tried to go around the side of the ruck and was confronted by the French wing forward Jean Claude Skrela. I sold him what I thought was a perfect Gaelic football-style dummy, but he didn't buy it, so I chucked the ball hurriedly to Mike Gibson who was close by. He really didn't want to know about it – the pass was about ankle high – and the huge French prop Gerard Cholley was on top of him in a flash. Gibson was pulverised in the tackle.

My excuse afterwards was that if Skrela had known anything about Gaelic football he would have bought the dummy, and if Mike Gibson was as good as he was supposed to be, he would have held the pass. I was forgiven. Sometimes you just have to be brazen.

It was a miserable season. The best we got out of it were lovely white togs. Up until then, players were given togs and socks at the beginning of the season. We were allowed swap one jersey – if we swapped a second we had to pay for it ourselves. And we had to keep our kit clean. I was friendly with the girl in the flat downstairs and just before the match against Wales she popped my togs into the washing machine along with a pair of black knickers (the girl's, not mine) which ran in the wash. I lined out against Wales in togs of indeterminate hue, and it drew much comment from press and spectators alike. A man playing for his country in dirty togs! Enter the Irish Rugby Football Union, heroes of the game. We had new togs and socks for every game after the Welsh match. I suppose we should be grateful they didn't charge us for them.

We weren't playing well and Scotland beat us 15-6 at Lansdowne Road. Gordon Brown was the star that day. My only consolation that season was beating England once again and breakfast with Harry Steele.

The night before the match at Twickenham I asked Harry to order breakfast-in-bed. This was a serious treat for those of us living in flatland.

'Ah, Moss, you do it,' he'd complained.

'No, Harry, I'm the senior man, and anyway they wouldn't have a clue what I'm saying, especially over the phone when they wouldn't be able to read my lips.' I think I might have called him a lazy Ulster something or other, but it wasn't laziness that was stopping Harry from sticking in our order. He was fairly sure they wouldn't be able to understand him either.

'Harry, do you want to be parading down to the dining room in the morning and have some fool telling you how to play rugby and talking about "phases" and "binding" and rubbish like that? Well, do you?' That outburst did the trick. Harry had conceded and phoned down our order.

The following morning the breakfast arrived on silver platters. We lifted the lids, ready to tuck in, and discovered four plates of kippers in front of us. It transpired that Harry had ordered the newspapers along with two full breakfasts. In his strong Northern brogue 'newspapers' are pronounced 'newspippers'. 'Pippers' became 'kippers' in the hands of room service.

I ate the four plates, plus the fry. I finished the kippers too quickly and began to feel unwell on the bus to the game. Normally you couldn't sicken me; I had the constitution of a goat, if not the agility. This time, though, I deposited the whole lot mid-way between the 25 and the halfway line at Twickenham. That was the one place Barry McGann never landed the ball all through the match.

McGann, our canny out half, controlled that game. Without doing much running, he just placed the balls so they were hanging over the pockets and we cued them in. He scored a seriously intelligent drop goal of his own as well. McGann always knew what to do. That was his greatest asset, and he had the smartest boot in world rugby; that day he kicked as if his feet were blessed by the Pope. He was a player who never panicked, and that coolness made him the ideal man to close out a tight game.

Brendan Foley played alongside me. It was the start of a great partnership and an enduring friendship. Foley was a mighty second row, and, like his son Anthony, he gave it a lash every time he pulled on the green shirt of Ireland or the blood red of Munster. Foley was afraid of no man, not even Willie Duggan. His kids take after him – his daughter Rosie has captained the Irish ladies rugby team.

For some reason Foley was dropped a couple of times while I was left on the team. At that point the team was doing so badly, anyone could lose their place. 'Moss,' Foley pleaded, 'you better play well today or I'll be dropped again.'

I played well enough, but our saviour was Tom Grace, who scored a great try in Twickenham. We hung on to our slim lead and came away with a 13-12 victory, which meant we had avoided being whitewashed in the Championship. It was our fifth consecutive win over England, a record I suspect will never be broken. We had the hex on England in those years.

If things were bad in internationals, they didn't get much better at club level. Lansdowne were the hottest of favourites to win the Leinster Senior Cup, and we put our money down confidently with the bookies. We all invested a few quid – the pool was meant to provide us with enough cash for socialising if we were lucky enough to win the cup. It was a kind of an insurance policy. But it was more than just the money; back then the Leinster Senior Cup was the most important domestic trophy open to Lansdowne FC. We got to the semi-final against Trinity College (Dublin University). I was marking a skinny 19-year-old second row from Tralee by the name of Donal Spring. It was the cup, so I didn't spare him. Nothing dirty, just tough. But I couldn't quieten him, especially in the lineouts. He was playing out of his skin and knew how to use his elbows to protect himself.

The score was 4-3 for us with a few minutes to go. Trinity kicked ahead and I chased back. Their winger, Brian Doyle, raced up in pursuit of the kick, outside the touchline and off the field of play. Mindful of our collective investment, I ran across the 22 and slammed into him. Spectators fell over from the fall-out and there was an outbreak of scuffles.

I had reasoned that if I took the winger out off the field of play it would have been outside the referee's jurisdiction. It was a bad call and the referee awarded a penalty.

Conor Agnew kicked the penalty from the touchline – 6-4 for Trinity. Final whistle.

Game lost. Money lost. Dirty looks. Moss wants to disappear up his own arse.

It was the biggest shock in Lansdowne for years. I got a bollocking after the game from our Kiwi coach, John Barry. 'Of all the men to do it,' he said. 'With your experience!' I tried to argue my case but it was unsustainable. I was a seasoned international by then. I had let my club down. I felt terrible.

Maybe it was fate – nothing I did that season turned out right. Later on in the year I was giving a hand behind the bar in the old Lansdowne clubhouse with Eddie Byrne, a stalwart of the club. We locked up and hit across the back pitches in Eddie's car. My jennet, as I called my car, was tied up on the other side of Lansdowne Road. We drove through the old stadium and out the gates into the back pitch at the rear of the Old East stand. Outside the 22 on the back pitch we dazzled a few rabbits. They stood stock still, caught in the glare of the headlights.

'I never ate a rabbit,' I said to Eddie.

Hint taken. One of Eddie's pastimes was to go off hunting in the mountains. He took his rifle out of the boot and took aim at the rabbits. I even fired a shot myself, and, fortunately for the rabbits, I missed.

Lansdowne Road may be a vibrant international rugby ground on match days, but this was nine o'clock on a dark night. We were in the middle of one of Dublin's most exclusive suburbs, just a mile from the British embassy. The troubles in Northern Ireland were at their height. We were only just out of the grounds when we saw the flashing lights. Another police car followed and a squad of heavily armed soldiers raced by seconds after. And next day there was a story in the papers that the police were investigating a possible paramilitary shooting incident, in the vicinity of the British Embassy.

* * *

In the days before the Irish tour in New Zealand that summer we were seen as no more than an appetiser for the All Blacks before they took on the Australians. Bob Messenger, rugby correspondent with the *Irish Press*, forecast that we wouldn't win a single game. He was a Kiwi, and his brother Ron was President of the New Zealand Rugby Union, so his view gave us an indication of how the All Blacks saw us.

I arranged my holidays to coincide with the tour, as I pondered flying for 24 hours. I was nearly tempted to ask them to send me by ship, anything bar flying. The IRFU made it clear if I had a problem with planes there were plenty more to take my place.

We arrived safely to be met by just a few Irish fans and the New Zealand tour organisers. I was beyond myself with excitement. Taking on the All Blacks in their own backyard. Off work for six weeks with dinner served up every day, £10 a week spending money, with the best of company, in the home of rugby.

It was the first time I had toured with Ireland and I loved every minute of it. I played in every game, bar one.

The 1976 tour was managed by the late Kevin Quilligan of Garryowen, with Tom Grace as captain and Roly as our coach. Fergus Slattery, who had decided not to travel, was a huge loss, but Ireland always has an abundance of talented back row forwards, so we would hold our ground there. All in all, we were a happy bunch, and it showed on the pitch.

Our first game was against South Canterbury and we confounded the critics by winning 19-4. We made it two out of two when we beat North Auckland. Then the legendary provincial side, Auckland, beat us in Eden Park after a crazy refereeing call that saw us lose 13-10. We were robbed. I'm not sure what exactly transpired – I was too far behind the play – but I took our lads word on it.

We stayed in Palmerston North for the fourth game against Manawatu. It was a tactical call by the management team. Palmerston North was a dry town on Sundays and the cunning tour manager reckoned that if there weren't any pubs, we wouldn't get any drink. He was wrong.

Three of us went to evening Mass in Palmerston North and we were just about to leave the church when the altar boy told us the priest wanted to see us.

He led us to the presbytery, where Fr Gallagher from Donegal greeted us and welcomed us to a treasure house of delight. Before our eyes stood a full-size pool table and a couple of crates of lager. Fr Gallagher and yours truly beat Willie Duggan and Pat Whelan in the best of about 15 frames, and while we played we drank what cans were in the house. Fr Gallagher was the best of company.

Months later my mother showed me an article Fr
Gallagher wrote in the *St Martin de Porres* magazine. He
recalled the great sense of warmth he felt when he saw three
thoroughly exhausted Irish players make a huge effort to go
to Mass, despite the fact that they had had a very hard game
the day before. 'They were,' he wrote, 'a credit to their
upbringing and their faith.' My mother was delighted. The
mention of me in a holy magazine meant more to her than
all the write-ups in the national newspapers. It gave her
bragging rights, which she would never exercise, among her
peers. But she was sceptical enough when it came to the
pastor's interpretation of our motives. Mother knew me better
than anyone.

We beat Manawatu after another battle, and after that
we experienced a savage onslaught from Canterbury. There
was nothing dirty, just hard ferocious rucking where you
were kicked out of the way if you wandered offside.
Canterbury were the perfect rugby machine, the benchmark
of what a good club could be. They would have beaten the
pick of the Five Nations.

We came back to defeat Southland in Invercargill in the
southernmost tip of New Zealand, a coastal town famous
for its oyster beds. All through the match Phil O'Callaghan
kept winding up his opposing loosehead prop by calling him
'oyster belly'. Unusually for a New Zealander he had a good
bit of a gut on him. It drove the Kiwi shellfish lover absolutely
crazy. But Phil was unbeatable as a scrummager in his day
and never have I seen a New Zealand front row so tormented.
Pat Whelan was incredible as well, tougher than any of the
Kiwi hookers I played against in my time, and Phil Orr kept
the scrum upright at all times.

We went into the test game with a record of four wins
out of six, which was better than anyone expected from a
team of rookies. We'd now had the benefit of having played

together for five weeks, and it showed.

The New Zealand press were trying to write us up. They said 'we were brave' which usually means they think you have little ability and will be hammered out of sight. In fairness to them they were never abusive and in private proved to be very good company but we fed them a fair share of misinformation, like we hoped to hold the All Blacks to 50 or 60 points – off the record of course. They did the *Haka* for us and as usual it was ferocious and noble at the same time. And there was the usual hard hitting in the early stages, but again there was no foul play unless you went looking for it.

I remember thinking during that game against the All Blacks that we had the pack to beat them. Our front row of Phil O'Callaghan, Phil Orr and Pat Whelan were in the ascendancy – quite literally: the All Black front row was lifted up and out of it. The pack was well able for the tough stuff too, but in the end we missed three easy penalties and lost 11-3. It was a game we should have won. What we lacked was self-belief. It was only after the match that we realised we were every bit as good as them up front.

On the way home, we stopped off in Fiji and beat the locals 8-0. I was worn out but was rested for that match. Rugby in New Zealand takes more out of you than anywhere else in the world.

We enjoyed Fiji. The people appreciated our visit and responded with a level of generosity I have never experienced anywhere else. The Fijians were not wealthy, but they shared whatever they had with you. I was invited into one house, no more than a shack with a tin roof, and my Fijian host offered me a drink. There was one can of Coke in the fridge. I had the impression it was bought specially for the occasion. The little boy of the family couldn't take his eyes off it.

'I'm fine,' I replied, 'give it to the young fella.'

The man wouldn't hear of it. In the end, his son and myself shared the can between us.

I gave the Fijian my official Irish top as a parting gift. Well, I gave him Mike Gibson's Irish top – I had given my own to a girl from Wellington. It fitted her. I also donated an Irish tie. In fact, Shay Deering's tie. I had lost mine under the bed in some hotel.

And when I handed over my small gifts, you would think I had given the boy and his dad a million pounds. Whatever their material circumstances, they were very happy, that father and son, and I often think about them.

Later that same day I decided it was time I learned how to swim. The sun was lovely. I was roasting. And if I could learn how to play rugby at 23, surely I could learn how to swim now that I was 27. I jumped into what I thought was the shallow end of the pool for a paddle, thinking that if I could get up my courage I might even let the water go above my belly-button.

Three of the lads were relaxing by the pool when I jumped in. They saw me go down and thought I was messing. I could hear Whelan laughing and he said something about Archimedes.

I went down again.

The lads were in stitches laughing. I was choking, unable to keep myself up.

I would have died; it was a matter of seconds. I could feel my eyeballs popping. My hands and legs were kicking and threshing. The more I tried to stay afloat the more I sank. When I thought I was breathing my last, Shay Deering jumped in and pulled me out. I thanked him by walloping him in fright and kicking him in a sore place. As soon as I got my breath back I looked around for Whelan. He couldn't be found. In fact, he stayed out of my way for the next couple of hours.

The amazing thing was that Deering had his arm in a sling when he jumped in the pool – he had a dislocated shoulder and torn ligaments since the game against Auckland. Deering saved me, but we couldn't save him. He died a young man. He was without doubt not only a marvellous, gutsy, honest rugby player, but also one of the finest men I ever met.

The day after returning from New Zealand, I lined out at full-forward for the Civil Service GAA club in the Dublin County Championship. I had continued playing Gaelic football all through my early years at Lansdowne – it was a great change from the rugby, and of course I never lost my love for the game. I would play with Civil Service on Sundays after having played a rugby match the day before.

There were a number of reasons why I joined Civil Service, but the main one was Tom Woulfe. Tom, a classmate of my Uncle Matt's in St Brendan's, was a North Kerry man who was instrumental in getting rid of the ban on GAA players playing foreign games. I felt I had to play for his club. Danny Lynch, the GAA's present PRO and the best possible company, was another flatland emigrant who persuaded me to join the Service team.

I lined out at full-forward in the game against St Vincent's because I said I'd let someone else look after Jimmy Keaveney. Keaveney was so good he could play for Kerry. There was no use in trying to horse him out of it, he was a hefty boy and had bottle to burn. In any event, the natural progression in Gaelic football was to move from the backs to the forwards, and then onto the scrap heap. As a result I ended up being marked by Gay O'Driscoll, one of the toughest men on the Dublin team. Thankfully it was a friendly encounter – I hadn't the energy for anything more. Although on landing after fielding one high ball, I got a sneaky elbow, which shot across my chest. I pretended I didn't even feel it, though the wind was knocked out of me. Afterwards I said to Gay, it's a good job you're small or you might have done damage.

The Dubs I played against were every bit as tough as the men I met on the international paddocks. It was tough football, especially if you were a Kerryman, and even more so when you were an Irish rugby international. To them I was just another big Kerryman, while I loved playing against some of the best Gaelic footballers in the history of the game. The next best to Kerry, that is.

During the '70s the Dublin-Kerry rivalry was as intense as any in the world of sport. The whole year was defined by the result of the Dublin-Kerry clash. It was city versus country. If we won it was a good year. If we didn't it was a bad one.

Many of that great Dublin team had a wonderful affinity with Kerry. Their captain Tony Hanahoe married a Kerry woman; Robbie Kelleher built a palace in Ventry and win or lose they would all turn up for the Listowel Races.

Dublin beat Kerry in the 1976 All-Ireland Final and in the great semi-final of '77, but Kerry came back to take the title the following year – the first of a magnificent four-in-a-row. When I saw just how good the Kerry boys were, I knew I had done the right thing to pick rugby. I would never have made it at that level but their class, their fitness, their loyalty to the green and gold, and their success inspired me.

Gaelic football, at least for me, had always been a great help in playing rugby. It helped with the catching and handling side of rugby. Most footballers are natural ball-handlers. It also helped with speed off the mark, co-ordination and anticipation. But rugby destroyed whatever bit of Gaelic football was in me. Rugby ruins you for football. It's down to the different shapes, the oval and the round. Not that I had much chance to kick the ball where I was stuck. The games are similar in that there's a good deal of physical contact, catching, kicking and running, but rugby, in the second row especially, is geared towards strength and grinding. It has changed a fair bit since my time with more emphasis placed nowadays on ball skills and athleticism. Football needs more explosive speed and manoeuvrability and as my training was all geared towards stamina and strength, I began to slow up. Not that I was ever a sprinter to begin with.

I missed the GAA from the minute I retired in 1977, but I could no longer cope with playing the two sports. The GAA was good to me. I won a few bits and pieces, played with some of the greatest names in the game and, most importantly, I made many friends and no enemies. I suppose I didn't do too badly for a man who was too big for the game, and never made a school team.

But now my sole focus was on rugby.

EIGHT

The Lions

1977 was a year of downs and downs. Up to then I was
always healthy, thank God, and had suffered no serious illness
since my days in St Brendan's. I was beginning to believe in
the illusion of my own invincibility. I hardly ever had a cold;
I could eat a raw dog and it wouldn't give me so much as a
burp and as for hangovers – what hangovers? I was never
tired and had no bother following a hard day at work with a
tough training session.

My work was demanding, but I was well able for it. From
time to time I would be sent to check out the far-flung regions
of the Department's jurisdiction. I once spoke to a dairy
farmer from Wicklow for two hours without understanding
a word he said. He wrote a letter to the Department
complimenting me. He said, I was the best inspector he ever
met and the first man he ever met who really understood
'what it was like to get up in the middle of the night in deep
snow in the Wicklow Mountains to pull a calf from a narrow
gauged cow.'

On another one of these trips I met a woman who,
curiously enough, lived in a greenhouse. (Too warm in
summer and too cold in winter, well by night anyway.) She
praised me for being the only inspector she ever encountered
who was able to resist saying 'people in glasshouses shouldn't

throw stones' when she complained about the smell coming from a neighbouring farmer's silage pit.

Most of the people I met were hard-working and just trying to survive in tough times. I knew from working on the home place that these people weren't in farming to make vast riches. They had a connection to the land for historical and family reasons. Money was scarce and the Department's budgets were tight enough. I always tried to help out but I had to keep it in mind it wasn't my money I was spending. I used the rules to help people, if I could, but I never broke them. I learned a valuable lesson when I was about ten. My mother sent me down to a neighbour's place with a half crown. I was instructed to cross the neighbour's new-born baby's palm with silver. I did just that. I flashed the half-crown across the baby's palm like you would a swipe card today. But I swiped the money as well. My mother found the half-crown in my trouser pocket. She was never a woman for physical punishment but she was well capable of exacting full retribution. I was kept under house arrest for two weeks and when I was left out it was only to do hard work around the farm.

We could have done with my mother's farmyard psychology in the rugby season that cursed year of 1977 – we failed to win a single game. The nearest we got to a win was against Scotland. They beat us 21-18 in Edinburgh in the second last game of a terrible season. They should have beaten us by more – they scored three tries but failed to convert any of them. The game ended badly for me, too. There was a bit of messing going on in the front row. The standard procedure in the second row manual for sorting out such matters was to throw a dig, which I did. The result was a penalty against us. Scotland put it over from way out to win the game.

'Not a word lads,' I warned the boys in the dressing room

after the match. 'Omerta.' I put my finger to my mouth.

But someone cracked and I was hauled outside during the official dinner and given the greatest roasting I ever received in my life. Wins were scarce back then; we could not afford to hand penalties to the opposition.

I went back to the dinner in a sulk with my teammates, Scotland, the ref and the coaches, but most of all with myself. Strangely enough, my second row partner Charlie Murtagh, who played well on the day, was dropped for not putting himself about enough but I wasn't.

The pressure I felt, compounded by the defeat, became too much to handle, and when we got back to Dublin Tom Grace and myself headed straight to Sean Lynch's pub in Aungier Street. It wasn't Tio Pepe we were on either. Sean did his best to console us, but it was no good. We decided to head for Davy Byrne's in the middle of town, just for one.

A common touring signal when you were in trouble with a fan and needed assistance, or just wanted to tell someone who was boring you to feck off, was to tug your ear. We were only in Davy Byrne's ten minutes when I noticed that Tom was pulling at his earlobe, and I guessed it wasn't an itch. He was trying to get rid of some punter who was annoying him and he needed help. I moved in to sort the problem out, brushing awkwardly against the punter. He went backwards and tripped over a stool. The barman rushed out from behind the counter. The punter lay on the floor as if he was a soccer player looking for a soft free.

'Jesus, Moss,' Tom said, 'we're done for.'

The barman looked furious.

Tom Grace, Captain of Ireland, chartered accountant, thrown out of a packed Dublin pub – it would be the talk of the town within hours.

The barman stood over the man lying on the ground and roared: 'You're barred!' He escorted the punter to the door and then went back behind the counter and poured us two pints.

The frustration we felt at our performances was agonising. There were times when some players didn't play well or might have come up a bit short but I can honestly say we gave it everything we had. People were sympathetic for the most part, but some, especially after a few drinks, could be abusive. I usually just walked away. What else was I to do? There was one occasion when I poured a pint of Guinness over a critic's head. I greatly regretted this action afterwards. I should have drunk it myself.

In those far-off days of amateurism, a lot of things were done by trial and error, in a hit and miss manner. We were operating with archaic structures. Back in the 1950s Paddy O' Donoghue, the great Bective Rangers player, had to go to work on a Saturday morning before lining out for Ireland in the afternoon. Further back, in the 1930s, my wife Anne's uncle, Pat Lawler, a farmer from Dunlavin, would go to the Saturday-morning mart before taking his place in the Irish team for the game in the afternoon.

Much of the abuse fell on our coach, Roly Meates. The whole squad all got on well together even in those dark days and I can't ever remember dissension against Roly. There were no secret player's meetings or any organised politicking. Roly was a good coach and a decent man. He was fair and knew his rugby. He is still involved as scrum coach to Leinster and is as good as you'll get in that capacity anywhere in the world.

Roly Meates, in fact, was far ahead of his time in many aspects of our preparation and training. He would bring a number of us to his house in Clonskeagh to show us videos of previous games, while his wife Heather laid on some food, which I very much appreciated as I still lived in a flat. Of course, we nearly always ended up watching the video for enjoyment rather than analysis, but that was our fault: poor Roly eventually gave up on us. He resigned as coach at the end of the 1977 season when we were whitewashed. His departure was sad but the team had only won a single international in his time as coach. Roly bit the bullet, but in reality we the players must take most of the blame.

Irish rugby just wasn't ready for Roly, either at player or official level. The IRFU was honest and adhered to an amateur ethos, but the other countries had gone too far ahead. We played by the rules. No money was handed over except for expenses, and they were miserly. It was symptomatic that Roly had to resort to calling unscheduled extracurricular sessions to improve the fitness levels of the players living around Dublin.

I have some sympathy with the IRFU's approach. Rugby is, after all, a game. The men who ran the game were almost all amateurs themselves and gave willingly of their time on a voluntary basis. In their view it was a pastime, fun for players and fans, but our opponents saw it differently. Scotland were nearly as useless as we were. The French team were never overburdened by strenuous jobs. England were under-achievers, but they had a huge player base. There were strong rumours that the Welsh boys were getting a few pounds on the side. It was called boot money, as the notes sometimes showed up miraculously in a man's boots. There was none ever showed up in mine.

The season wasn't long over when I found myself in a doctor's surgery in London. The doctor looked me up and down and I suppose he must have been saying to himself, how is this fella going to last three-and-a-half months, playing rugby for the Lions in New Zealand? My shin was gashed and was red raw.

Geoff Wheel, the Welsh lock, had been ruled out of the tour the week before the team were due to depart. Albert

Agar, the Lions' secretary, had announced that Geoff had 'a slight heart condition, which makes it race under stress'. I thought that was the case for nearly everybody, so I'm not sure what the big deal was, especially as the doctors announced in the same communiqué that Geoff 'could play tomorrow if necessary'. Doctors differ and rugby players stay at home. At any rate I had been offered Geoff's place on the team – the fourth Irish player to join the tour.

I was pleased to have been picked for the Lions even though I was also disappointed not to have made the original party. And I felt sorry for Geoff, though at the end of that rainy New Zealand winter I was firmly of the opinion that Geoff had been the lucky one.

From an Irish perspective, the tour could not have come at a worse time. We'd just been whitewashed in the Five Nations Championship and this was reflected in the small number of Irish players originally selected in the 30-man Lions squad. The only Irish players picked at the outset were Willie Duggan, Phil Orr and Mike Gibson. I became the fourth when Mr Agar announced that I was to be Geoff's replacement, but as yet I didn't know this, because I was incommunicado down in Dunmore East in County Waterford, in the sunny south-east of Ireland.

I was on a tough tour of my own, with a gang of lads I knew from Dublin flatland. From time to time we would head off for a weekend to play Gaelic football against teams we knew we could beat. I went off on the trip to Dunmore East on the very same Saturday I was selected for the Lions. I spent that afternoon playing a friendly football match in Dunmore East, talking with my opponent about the quality of the porter and the women of the locality. While all this was going on, the Lions' management were scouring the country looking for a man answering my description.

That night we went to Harry's Bar, a pub sited just below

road level, and patrons had to negotiate a steep flight of steps to gain admittance. Being the awkward man I sometimes am, I slipped and gashed my shin on my way down. I took no notice of the injury. Harry supplied a bandage and I anaesthetised myself with a few pints, oblivious of the fact that I had been chosen to tour New Zealand. Amazingly, no one else had heard the news either.

I went back to Dublin and to bed early on Sunday night, having missed all the sports' bulletins and the Sunday papers. I swallowed a couple of headache tablets to kill the pain in the leg and thought I'd take Monday off work as my leg was very sore. Someone knocked at the front door and threw stones up at the window but I didn't answer. I was sure it was one of the lads looking for someone to go on the tear. I put my head under the blankets and dozed off.

The leg was a small bit better the following morning so I decided to go to work after all. The phone rang in the office as I arrived in. It was Ronnie Dawson, head of the Lions in Ireland.

'You need to be at Twickenham next week for a medical and a few days' training,' he began.

'Why?' I asked.

Dawson broke up laughing on the other end of the phone.

'You've been selected for the Lions!' he said.

I had just three days to get my things in order if I was to go. I had a few misgivings. It would mean taking months off work without pay. Luckily consumer credit wasn't dished out as easily in those days so the monthly monsters of credit card bills and standing orders had yet to gobble our pay cheques. I knew there would be a small tour allowance, but losing out on a quarter of a year's pay was a big sacrifice. My fitness levels were very poor. Lansdowne had made an early exit from the cup that year and I hadn't done any training of any description for a month. I had a wounded leg and knew

I had a job on hand to pass the medical.

And what stuck out as a big, obvious warning was that the likes of J P R Williams, Gerald Davies and Gareth Edwards had not deemed the tour attractive enough to bother with it. These stars had been to New Zealand before and they seemed in no hurry back. They were smart men, and perhaps I wasn't; I agreed to go. The Minister for Agriculture granted me special leave to help me on my way. I had no time to get down to Kerry to stock up on fresh clothes washed by my mother. Back in those happy days in Ireland our mothers did everything for us. I had no idea how to go about washing my clothes and at the time I had no steady girlfriend who might have done it for me. I was about 30 years of age before I could even peel a potato without taking half the potato away with the skin.

I arrived at Dublin Airport with a modest bag, big enough to hold two underpants, four pairs of socks with holes in five, a jumper with no elbows, a pair of jeans, a pants for good wear and three bottles of Lucozade, just in case they didn't sell it in New Zealand. In my kitbag were rock-hard boots (two), unrelated socks (three), togs with a tear up the side of the thigh (one) and jockstrap (one).

I met William Patrick Duggan of Kilkenny by arrangement at the airport bar. We were by now confirmed in our fear of flying so we needed a couple of drinks to calm us before we got on the plane. Willie had two huge suitcases and a massive kitbag.

Willie asked me if my bag was hand luggage.

When I told him it was all I had he said, 'Where the feck do you think you're going with the small bag? Do you realise,' he continued, without waiting for an answer, 'that we are going to New Zealand for three-and-a-half months and not to London for a weekend? What are you going to do for gear?'

I pointed down at his suitcases.

We were based in Richmond and trained in Twickenham. It was all very pleasant; good food, a few pints every night without doing the dog on it. History was made when I organised the first ever game of Gaelic football to be played in Twickenham. A combined Ireland, Scotland and England side beat Wales by 2-12 to 1-11. Wales actually scored more than that, but I was also the referee. I took no nonsense from anyone and fiddled the score into the bargain.

Meeting up with men who were hard opponents in the recent past felt strange, to say the least, and very different to amalgamating the four provinces when we all played for Ireland. I wondered how I would get on with English second row forward Nigel Horton, who had floored me as I trotted blithely across the pitch in Lansdowne Road when England beat us 4-0 just a few months earlier. As it transpired we both played second row in the first match of the tour against Wairarapa Bush in Masterton, and got on fine.

After a few days' preparation in London we set off for New Zealand. The flight was a killer for anyone, but for a man with long legs and a phobia about flying it was ten times worse. And some hours into the 30-hour journey, Duggan was beginning to sound as if he might complain all the way to Auckland.

He finally dozed off, leaving me awake. Late in the night the captain announced we were over the North Pole. I was really excited – the North Pole!

'Wake up, Willie. Wake up.'

'Moss, this better be good.'

'Willie, we're over the North Pole.'

Duggan looked out the window, then gave me that raised eyebrow. 'Well, if we are I can't see any fecking reindeers,' he said, and went back to sleep.

When we finally arrived in Auckland, after a stop at Los

Angeles where there was a total cock-up with the visas, it took all of two-and-a-half minutes to realise we were in the rugby hotbed of the world. There was a huge crowd to greet us, all clamouring for autographs. Everyone from the customs officials to small children had questions about scrummaging and tactical ploys I didn't even know about myself. One little old lady walked slowly towards me. She beckoned to me to bend my head so she could whisper something in my ear.

'Keane,' she said, 'Frank Oliver is going to kick the shit out of ya.'

Welcome to New Zealand.

I was the first to bed. My head-clock was in a mess. My room-mate on that first night in Wellington was Peter Wheeler, the English hooker. I woke him up to the sound of a beer bottle being opened at 6.30 am New Zealand time. Peter was a little taken aback so I told him that it was 6.30 pm at home now, when I would be dropping into the local after work for a pint, and I didn't want to upset the system too much. That was as far as my acclimatisation routine got. Later that morning, coach John Dawes told me that if there was any more of that kind of carry-on I would be on the next plane home.

We went training on the very first day. I had been told to keep myself fit by the Irish Lions selector, Syd Millar, but I never thought I'd get called up and I was way below par. I was miles behind the rest on the training ground and my shagging leg was killing me. I still managed to get through the full session, though.

We played golf and some pitch and putt to pass the time. I was only a hacker back then and not the sweet-striking 18 handicapper I am today. Mike Gibson, on the other hand, was almost good enough to turn pro. He used to wince when he'd see me hitting the ball. Bobby Windsor remarked that if the New Zealanders ever wanted to put in a few bunkers, all they had to do was follow behind me with a lorry-load of sand.

I struck up a friendship with the tour manager, the amiable Scot, George Burrell. We had some great chats as the tour progressed, though I honestly believe he only barely understood my brogue. Coach John Dawes, who had captained the Lions on their last tour of New Zealand, was pleasant and fair to deal with. He'd laid it on the line after he found out I was drinking beer on my first morning in New Zealand, and I respected him for it. We got on well most of the time.

The Lions tour of 1977, which ran from May to mid-August, was the last of the long tours, involving a total of 26 matches, including one in Fiji on the way home. It was a murderous schedule for amateur players. The players, in fact, were an afterthought – it was all a money-making exercise for the New Zealand Rugby Football Union. We received a daily allowance of about three euro. Only 30 players had been picked to travel and by the time we were halfway through the tour we were decimated by injuries. We had to traipse down to the nearest hospital for treatment from local physios. 'Doc' Murdoch, a Kiwi from Auckland and the NZRU liaison officer gave a great rub if you were stuck, and he did more for us than anyone on that tour.

To my surprise I was picked to play against Wairarapa Bush in Masterton in the first match of the tour. The plan, Dawes and Burrell explained, was to get me fit by playing matches. It was the best training of the lot.

I got a shock when we went out on the pitch: the scoreboard listed us as 'British Lions'. In other games it was worse: 'British Isles'. I didn't even bother discussing it, there was no point, but I felt I was playing for a team that never officially existed. We should have been listed as the British and Irish Lions.

My old friend Nigel Horton togged out in the second row with me. Early on in the game he was hit from behind with a punch he didn't see coming and suffered a very bad eye injury. Willie Duggan replaced him and Derek Quinnell from Wales moved to lock.

Before the tour began, we were told that, if the going got tough, we should get stuck in as a group. We totally adhered to this advice. Willie John once famously said that it was important to get your retaliation in first, and the previous Lions outing, to South Africa, had been more like a war campaign than a rugby tour. On a codeword of '99' the whole pack attacked as a unit. It was a matter of self-preservation in times when referees did not give as much protection as they do now and few if any incidents were captured on camera.

I wasn't sure what to do when Horton was taken off but I didn't have long to wait before I found out – Duggan had a right go from the moment he came on, and I wasn't leaving him on his own. In fact, Duggan took on the whole of New Zealand during that tour. He was fearless. To tell the truth, even though I never told him, I was in awe of him and very proud to be his friend. He was without doubt the toughest man I ever played with.

The Masterton game set the tone for the whole tour. It was played in atrocious weather. The rain came down cold, like spears of icy water. The three months of the tour, in fact, proved to be one of the wettest winters ever experienced in that part of the world. If they ever make a movie about Noah's Ark, New Zealand will provide the ideal location.

I looked up at the cold mountains and I thought of Killarney and how warm it would be there right then, coming up to June. I'll never forget the cold – sometimes I think it hasn't left my bones to this day. We won the game in the finish, after a mudbath on the pitch, and I had a good game despite my lack of fitness and my gashed shin. I was, I suppose, well used to muck and shit anyway. I even made a try.

When we got back to the dressing rooms after the game we discovered the showers were broken. Water came out all right but it was freezing cold and as brown as Guinness. The Kiwis made some lame excuse about a broken pipe. Remarkably, the same thing had happened on the previous Lions tour. We were shivering, half-naked in the dressing room until George Burrell organised blankets from the nearby hotel. My abiding memory is of watching Willie Duggan leave the dressing room, a woolly blanket draped over him, and walking barefooted through the crowds, holding his shoes in one hand and a cigarette in the other. He looked like a Roman senator who has fought a hard but victorious campaign and doesn't want to give the vanquished the pleasure of seeing how much he suffered to beat them.

'Soft kind of a day, William,' I said consolingly. Duggan didn't reply. He was cross with me. I had thrown a punch at Turley, the Masterton flanker, missed, and hit Willie instead. He was still a bit sore.

I didn't play in the second game, but I did well against Poverty Bay East Coast in the third match. I was marking an 18-year-old lock by the name of Cameron. He was a good player, but he was very light and very green. I could have done him serious harm if I was bad enough.

Willie and the great Ian Kirkpatrick spent the afternoon belting each other at the back of the lineout. There was one great scrap; Willie and Ian stood toe to toe and just went at it. They tested each other out and neither was found wanting. After we won the match, they were inseparable in the clubhouse.

I was beginning to understand what it was all about. You had to earn respect in New Zealand, where there was no such thing as an easy game. I was beginning to get fit, my leg was fine, and I was enjoying the physical confrontations. I found I was as strong as any of my opponents. Even so, I was not picked for the Taranaki game – the probable test team against the All Blacks, was picked for that one. Horton and the late Gordon Brown were chosen to play second row and succeeded in controlling the lineouts. The scrum was a big success too, so I was left warming the bench. Taranaki had a good record against touring sides and beating them was a feather in our cap.

We had a small celebration back in the hotel, and when a fire alarm went off I was blamed. George Burrell was very annoyed and christened me 'Rent-a-Storm'. It was a storm in a teacup; more importantly I was back again for the King Country Wanganui game, which we won, and next up was Manawatu Horowhenua, the sixth match of the trip and my fourth. It was a dirty, mean-spirited game.

Willie was booted in the head twice and the referee did nothing about it. Unlike the scrap with Ian Kirkpatrick, this was bad work, and Willie had to be carried off and stitched. When Terry Cobner, the captain on the day, also went off injured, Bobby Windsor led by example. It was a pitched battle on another miserable afternoon. Willie came back on, bound up like a mummy with all the bandages. Brynmor Williams scored a great try to win the game for us.

That night New Zealand television showed the kicking Willie had been given. The cameras caught two players deliberately kicking and stamping on him while he was unable to defend himself. The Kiwis were horrified. Curiously, the only person who didn't seem to be all that put out about the whole thing was Willie himself. The man from Kilkenny, the home of hurling, wouldn't let on he was upset. And Brian O'Driscoll thought he was the first Irishman to be given a synchronised New Zealand clean-out at the ruck. This kind of carry on has being going on for years in New Zealand. I'm not saying Brian or Willie were deliberately targeted in a premeditated way but it was obvious all through that trip that our tour captain Phil Bennett was selected for extra rough treatment. A tackle might be a fraction late and the toll mounted up to such an extent that Bennett was only operating at a fraction of his best form. That said we dished out a fair bit ourselves. But we did not put the boot in deliberately nor was their any conspiracy to target players among ourselves in the dressing room before the game.

Unlike the Lions of 2005 we didn't complain too much either. It wasn't considered manly. In fact Willie didn't complain at all. He just wouldn't have it said that they succeeded in putting him out, even in a small way. All the same Brian O'Driscoll was put out of the tour and the tackle was dangerous. No mistake about that – New Zealand were on the back foot. They were genuinely embarrassed by the actions of their captain. I applaud O'Driscoll and Gareth Thomas of Wales for having the courage to speak out but the subsequent condemnations and spin were carried on for far too long.

For the most part I found the New Zealanders to be a sporting nation, intense yes but far too good at the game and far too much in love with rugby football to resort to organised and premeditated dirty play. But there were times when they stepped over the mark and there were times in 1977 and 2005 when the New Zealand Rugby Football Union put victory and image before fair play and the best interests of the game.

Around the time Willie's hair was parted by the Kiwi kicking in the momentous Manawatu game, the Tour Court was convened for the first and only time on tour. I was appointed judge, largely due to the fact that I had more offences against me than anyone. I was a recidivist underpants and socks thief. There was a whole range of other felonies on which I will plead insanity. The business of the court would have been delayed for weeks had I been put on trial. Bobby Windsor was the clerk of court.

'All rise for his worship the right honourable Mister Justice Maurice Ignatius Keane.'

I wore a fireman's hat in place of a wig. There were malicious rumours about that I had hosed our captain with a fire hydrant. Tony Neary was the prosecutor and Elgan Rees appeared for the defence. The whole tour party was present at the proceedings. While I cannot go into details due to judge/client confidentiality, I was a hanging judge. Among my rulings, was getting one player, who shall remain nameless, to go down on all fours and chew a bone for acting the dog. All fines handed down went into a communal drinks' fund, over which I had full control.

Next up was one of the toughest games of the tour, Otago, so the drinks money was put away untouched in a safe place (my arse pocket) for the night of the game.

I was the third choice second row by the time we arrived in Otago. Brown and Horton were before me, but Horton broke his thumb and I came on after 35 minutes.

I had cross words for Nigel as I ran on as a sub. 'Never hit a man with your thumb sticking out like you were hitching a lift,' was all I could say to him by way of comfort. I didn't know the thumb injury would put him out of the tour. It was my fifth game in seven and I needed a break, but it wasn't all that bad a tally for a man whose only pre-tour training was a game of Gaelic football in Dunmore East.

After the match, the English policeman, once my sworn enemy, was on his way home. I knew I was in with a big chance of a test place once Nigel Horton left, but I had huge sympathy for him all the same. He put himself about on the tour like no one else, except perhaps Willie. He could have stayed on in New Zealand, if he wanted to, but Horton was such a competitor he would have been miserable hanging around while we played. That day in Carisbrook, one of the great rugby grounds of the world, we showed real resolve to beat Otago, 12–7, who had beaten three out of the last four Lions teams they played.

Billy Beaumont was summoned to join the Lions' and his legend began on that tour. Willie Duggan welcomed him with the earnest advice, 'If I was you, I would shag off back home.' From my point of view, I knew Billy would push me all the way for a test place, but I was playing the best rugby of my career and I was in pole position, having done well in every game. I was glad to see Billy on a personal level, because we always got on well together, but I was worried about the competition that lay ahead.

I needn't have bothered; my tour came to a halt in the next match. I was carried off with concussion in the game against New Zealand Universities in Christchurch on the Tuesday before the first test. I was dazed. I thought I was in Vancouver with Lansdowne, which I had been three years previously when I was also concussed from a kick in the head. Willie came down from the stands and stayed with me in the dressing room. A doctor finally appeared and warned Willie I should under no circumstances be allowed to play rugby again for at least two weeks.

We sat on our own until the rest of the lads came in after the game, which we lost. It was the first defeat of the tour and a bad blow to our morale. Fair play to the Universities, it was a great win for a young team.

All that night in Christchurch my head was in a real spin. I went to bed and have no further recollection of anything that went on. I tried to train the following day but I felt so groggy after scrummaging practice I left the pitch and vomited. When I was selected to play in the first Test the following Saturday, I pleaded with George and John not to pick me. I knew I was in no fit state to play. Willie also passed on the medical advice to George.

Fran Cotton, one of the stars of the Lions' Tour to South Africa in '74 had been very annoyed when he didn't make the team, and here was I not wanting to play. That's the big problem on a Lions' tour, keeping the players who don't make the Test side happy. You can have all the camaraderie in the world but you have 30 internationals, the pick of the English, Irish, Welsh and Scottish teams all vying for a Test place. It was bound to cause tensions and it did.

The selectors picked five of the Welsh tourists and three Irish tourists in the pack for the first Test. I knew I was in a mess going into the match. I was still wobbly on my feet and vomiting up all my food. I had a constant headache and my long-range vision was still blurred. I persuaded myself I could manage. In the event, I have only a very hazy memory of the game. I know we were well beaten in the lineout; we only won two in the second half and lost about 75 per cent overall. I barely knew where I was, though I must credit my immediate opponent Frank Oliver, at number two in the lineouts, who was very, very good on the day. I should simply never have played. It was a mad decision. In the end we were beaten 16-12. Nowadays a player would be obliged to take a compulsory three-week layoff, and even then there would be all sorts of scans and tests in case there might be any lingering damage.

I was in a terrible state after the game and went straight to bed. Monday morning training was a nightmare. As we were jogging around the pitch I suddenly saw two Billy Beaumonts and two Willie Duggans, and thought that that must be impossible because each of these men was unique. The problem was solved in my mind when I saw two sets of goalposts where I knew there was only one. I changed course immediately and headed for the two dressing rooms, and clattered into the wall that held the door I saw in my head. The funny thing is that I remember all this part.

George Burrell appeared some time later to ask me to go back out. I can't remember what I said to him but I'm sure it was choice. I went back to the hotel in the tour bus and went to bed at lunchtime, and didn't wake up until Tuesday morning. Someone was telling me that the bus was leaving in 20 minutes for training. I said, 'They don't need me to drive the shagging thing, do they?' and went back to sleep, rising only for lunch and tea. I eventually woke up on Wednesday morning feeling fine. My late grandmother used to say that it was no harm being your own doctor from time to time. That, as far as I know, was the end of the concussion. Others say it still lasts to this day.

It's an ill wind that doesn't blow somebody good. Billy Beaumont blossomed as the tour progressed and deservedly played in the last three tests, while I was restricted to a few mid-week matches for the Dirt Trackers, the team that played against the so-called weaker New Zealand sides. If you ask me, there was no such thing as a weak team in New Zealand, and they were all eager to beat the Lions.

One of the nightmares on the tour was flying. I would nearly prefer to spend three-and-a-half months in the monastery on Lough Derg than go through that again. We criss-crossed the skies above New Zealand. We were flying from Hamilton in Waikato to Wellington when our plane appeared to be losing altitude, not unlike myself in the lineouts. I was sitting beside Ian McGeechan. 'Don't tell me,' he said, 'we're going to have this all over again.'

'Ian,' I asked, as the plane dropped at alarming speed, 'what the fuck are you talking about?'

'The Lions had a close call in South Africa in '74,' he told me, 'when birds were sucked into the engine and the plane began to dive. We had to make an emergency landing – we were lucky to survive.' This situation appeared to Ian to be something similar but he was quite calm about it.

I said an *Act of Contrition*, just the short form: 'Bless me, Father, for I have sinned.' Gripped by terror, I felt I would not have time for the unabridged version. The plane seemed to be dropping out of the sky. Then just when we all thought we were done for, the pilot straightened her up and we were on our way. Panic averted, for the moment. We found out afterwards that the pilot had decided to make a figure of eight to impress his friends down below.

For the following trip, from Wellington to Auckland, a few of us decided to take the train. We left at 8 pm on Sunday evening and didn't arrive until 9 am on Monday morning, just in time for training. The equivalent flying time was about 90 minutes. I doubt if any of us had any sleep either; the bar was open all night and Willie Duggan and Bobby Windsor, the Welsh hooker, were great men to shorten a journey. Bobby told about a thousand jokes and never repeated one. We fell off the train, went training and spent the rest of the day in bed.

The All Blacks beat the Lions in the second Test without me and the Lions won the third Test without me. It was to be our only win in the Test series. My last chance to get back in the side was to play a blinder against the New Zealand Maoris. All four Irish tourists played in that game. We came back from the dead to win 22-19, but it was a hard-won victory. Willie Duggan had to depart the scene once again after a Maori tried to break his jaw. Willie had put his body on the line all through the tour, with the inevitable result that he hardly ever trained – nine time out of ten he was off to the local physio in whatever region we happened to be in for repairs. There were a few other chronics as well, but none were hurt as often as Willie. He just didn't know the meaning of the word danger. Phil Orr had a stormer in the Maoris match, and George and John certainly erred in not picking him for the Test. He was to show the rugby world just how good he really was in subsequent seasons. Mike Gibson also had a great game, but he too was largely ignored on the tour. Gibson was suffering from back trouble throughout the trip and was constantly on the physio's bench, but even so he should have been picked for the last two tests. When Ireland toured Australia two years later, Gibson was the star in two Test wins. Mike had brought his wife on the tour and I think the management held that against him. I often covered for Mike when he went off to see her – she stayed away from the team hotel – but wives and sweethearts were simply not to be encouraged in those days.

When I wasn't picked for the third Test, I decided to have a holiday for the rest of the trip. I was worn out by then anyway. I lost the run of things, though, and socialised far too much over the next four weeks. It was probably one of the wildest time of my life. I was always grounded by visits home to Currow; they steadied me and I returned to a type of sensible reality with my core values topped up. The trip was too long and I began to get frustrated with the fact I was only involved in a peripheral role. One night I let off a fire alarm and a hotel had to be evacuated. It wasn't a premeditated thing. I was walking down the hallway with Phil Bennett at 4 am and I just reached out and let it off. I was severely spoken to by George. All I could do was apologise. George seemed to understand my frustrations, and I think he knew I felt terrible. He accepted the apology and a promise it would not happen again. I was lucky to have met such a sympathetic manager. I heard stories of players who got themselves into bother on tours who weren't picked at international level long after the tour was over.

I got on far too well with the New Zealand rugby public.

I think they respected the fact that I wasn't found wanting in the rough games. I loved the people, their sense of humour and their absolute allegiance to the All Blacks. Off the pitch, people were hospitable to a fault. I found it hard to buy a beer; in fact, after a visit to a brewery we loaded 30 cases of beer onto the team bus, one for each player, each case labelled 'Lion Beer'. The whole population was into rugby and knew more about us than our neighbours back home, which I found very flattering.

I was unlucky to visit the country in the worst weather in living memory. There wasn't much anyone could do about that, but as the weeks passed the unremitting rain depressed everyone. It was a huge factor in undermining morale. And the camaraderie on the tour, with a few notable exceptions, was fairly superficial. Phil Bennett, the captain, did all he could to keep us together, but it was an uphill task.

When the New Zealand tour finally ended we headed to Fiji for four or five days. The New Zealand Rugby Football Union gave us no chance to holiday or rest up once the last Test was over. It was pack your bags the day after the final game – we were not wanted anymore now that our crowd-pulling tour was over. We were very bitter over that. We had raised a lot of money at the turnstiles, yet some of us were nearly broke. The Lions set-up was truly amateur.

It was mid-August, Fiji's dry season, and it was very hot. No one gave a damn about rugby, least of all the Fijians. John Dawes told me that I was a sub for the centre position and when I heard that I didn't even bother togging out. I just put on a tracksuit and a straw hat I had found somewhere. When Gordon Brown was injured Dawes told me to strip off and I simply refused. I'd had enough of it.

When I got back to Dublin I felt terrible. I felt drained and I spent most of the time sleeping. I had no energy. Even my appetite was gone. After a visit home I decided to see the doctor. I was lucky I hadn't left it go any further; I was diagnosed with some sort of jaundice or hepatitis. There was a fair bit of it about in New Zealand that winter. I was ordered off the booze immediately. My doctor and mentor, John Craig, told me the normal prognosis for an illness like this could keep me out of rugby for a minimum of six months. There was also a question of taking more time off work and I was uncertain of how I would cope when I went back to the Department. John Craig told me my liver function tests were somewhere outside the normal – in other words, they were in bits – and I had to stick to a strict diet. It brought me to my senses. If my rugby career wasn't over, it was certainly on hold. The doctors felt there was no way I would be ready for the following season.

The tour had taught me some hard lessons about looking after myself. Yet I have never blamed George or John for picking me to play in that first Test. They were different times: rugby men just got on with it and I was never a great man to say no. I have only myself to blame.

I met George again in Paris in 1985. He was over with the Scotland side playing France. He invited me to visit him in Galashiels the next time I was in Scotland.

'George,' I said, 'I might just arrive at your door some day soon.'

But it was 16 years later before I made the journey. It took us a few days to get to Galashiels, a rugby-mad town in the border country. My wife Anne was dying to meet George – I was never done talking about him – and I had a bottle of whiskey in my hand as we called to his house. A lady answered the door and told us George had died just a few days before. I was very upset. George was a thoroughly decent man, with a good sense of humour and a great heart.

There was another reunion that did come to pass. Some of the Lions of yesteryear were assembled in the Celtic Manor

Hotel in Wales in May 2005 as part of the send off for the 2005 Lions.

I was interviewed by Chris Rea before hundreds of people and he reminded me of the time I'd told Nigel Starmer Smith of the BBC that the highlight of that '77 tour was when I heard Kerry beat Cork in the Munster Final.

'And what was the next best moment?' asked Chris Rea.

I steadied myself. I was sick and tired of old Lions going on about how they could never understand a word I said. I took a deep breath. 'Slowly Moss,' I said to myself. 'Aisey up,' as if I was talking to Gubby, the crazy pony.

And then I replied in my clearest and slowest voice:

'Ah Chris, it had to be when I saw the clothesline of Ireland. Sorry I meant to say the coastline of Ireland.'

They all heard me and the laughter went on for a good while.

NINE

Munster and the All Blacks 1978

I suffered badly from the illness I picked up in New Zealand. I was constantly tired. I had to take even more time off work. And that was on top of the leave I was granted to go on tour. The Department of Agriculture treated me very fairly.

Even when I went back to work I was exhausted after just a few hours. There was no drink so the evenings were long. I had no interest in socialising anyway. I just didn't have the energy for it. A good few of my friends were beginning to settle down and get married, but I had no interest in taking such a drastic decision. And anyway I hadn't met the right woman, or more importantly she hadn't met me. I had an idea I would take up the marital tactics of the old Kerry bachelors, who only ever began to think about settling down when they passed the two-score mark. And even then, the courtship could last another ten or twelve years. I was well settled in to bachelor life.

I had a fairly good job, so money was never a problem even if I didn't have enough to scatter about foolishly. And there was the freedom I had always coveted since my days in St Brendan's and long before that. But I was now a veteran in flatland terms. My neighbours were younger and there was less company of my own age in the immediate neighbourhood. There were fewer callers to the rambling flat. And many who visited brought small babies or auctioneer's leaflets for houses they were planning to buy. There were more who called wondering if I might go for a pint but I was off the stuff. And I stayed off it without any great difficulty.

The hepatitis I'd contracted during that Lions tour was looking certain to put me out of the '78 season when Noel Murphy was appointed Irish coach. I'd always had a good relationship with him and I knew I would be in the frame in spite of the Lion's Tour. All I had to do was get myself right and not just from a rugby point of view. I took over the top floor of a two-storey house in Kingswood Heights near Tallaght, well away from the city centre. I'd decided that it was time to move away from flatland and the lifestyle that went with it. I spent a few months there out of harm's way, passing the time by writing; I filled four full pads of foolscap paper. I just jotted down stories I'd heard when I was growing up and all sorts of things that came into my head. The writing was a way of figuring out where I was in my life and where I was going. I knew it was time to take stock. There would have to be changes. I just could not continue with the madness of the last few weeks in New Zealand. There was no rugby, even though I did go down to Lansdowne every week just to stay in touch.

My beloved Aunt Jo had an inclination towards alternative medicine as a back-up to the normal treatments, and told me of a herbal practitioner in Dunboyne by the name of Sean Boylan. When I went to see him, I knew immediately that he was genuine. Years later he became famous as manager of the Meath Gaelic football team as well as for his skills as a herbalist. Sean sent me home with a herbal liquid which would help cure my liver. Thanks to him and John Craig, I began to feel a little better. But I was till suffering from endless exhaustion. I was even tired after walking up the stairs.

But I had another doctor as well – my mother. When I had to take even more time off work I just couldn't hack it. It was time to head home for Currow. I sensed I just needed to be looked after for a few weeks. I helped out a little around the farm. Nothing much, just a few small jobs. Feeding calves and the like. My mother fed me with our own meat and fresh vegetables and made sure I got plenty of rest. My colour was coming back and I felt a little bit stronger every day. The day I faced into the fourth spud was a milestone.

Back in the city I started to go for walks. Nothing too much, just a couple of miles. By mid-November I was back in harness, working in the Department, beginning to train with Lansdowne and playing with the Probables in the Final Trial for the Irish team just after Christmas. It was a huge turnaround. I knew then the full meaning of the old saying 'health is wealth'. I enjoyed my club rugby more than ever even though I didn't play for Munster in the Interpros, but I was selected for all four internationals in 1978.

When Kingswood Heights was sold I moved to the top floor of a house off the Navan Road, well away from flatland yet again. I was taking more care of myself now, though during the move across the city all my writing disappeared. But the thought process that went into it stayed with me. The reflection and getting it down on paper changed me profoundly. I was a stronger man on every level and I began to play good rugby.

The international season started off with our first win in nearly a year-and-a-half. The win over Scotland at Lansdowne Road brought a sense of relief more than the joy of victory. We were a much-improved team; Noel Murphy had worked hard with us and brought new blood into the side. When Tony Ward came on for his first cap, he was so classy at out half that he just lit up the game. You could hear the buzz from the crowd whenever he had the ball in hand. Donal Spring from Tralee made it an all-Kerry second row. Donal was light but mobile and he had absolutely no fear. I was very proud to have a Kerryman with me in the second row – Donal Lenihan would team up with me there a few years later, but he was only half a Kerryman. Spring was with Trinity at the time and went on to join Lansdowne, where we had many good years together. Dr John O'Driscoll played at wing forward for his first cap and also did well.

Despite our good start, we went on to lose our next three games. France beat us in Paris, where the pitch was like an ice rink. We were sliding all over the turf, especially in the scrums, and the ground was so hard I could hardly walk the next day. Still we dominated them in the scrum. We were very unlucky to be beaten by a point, a sore point in more ways than one. My good friend Jean Pierre Rives got his fingertips to a Wardy drop goal attempt. I would eventually finish my career without a win in Paris.

We gave Wales a good game of it and could have won when Mike Gibson raced for the line, only to be halted by J P R William's stiff elbow. It should have been a penalty try and a sending off. The crowd booed the referee and J P R for the rest of the game. It was a professional foul in an amateur match, but though I didn't like it I thought it a shame that J P R was booed. He was the most physical back I ever played against, and no angel, but I had done a lot worse. In my experience referees often favour successful team. We eventually lost 20–16 and Wales went on to win the Grand Slam.

The results were not going our way but we were playing good rugby, so naturally we lost to England – when we played badly we beat them. The bare results read like another mediocre performance, but the opposite was the case. We could have won all four matches; they were that close. We played with boot, bite and brains, but it was just not to be. One consolation was that Tony Ward was voted European Player of the Year, and deservedly so.

I played for Lansdowne in the Belvedere Sevens towards the end of April. I was a strange choice for a Sevens tournament, but ours is not to reason why, though I think there might have been an epidemic of injuries in the club. I went home to the Navan Road after the game, but I was too restless to stay there and went back again to Belvedere.

It must have been fate because I travelled back half way across the city for no particular reason other than there was nothing on television. I spotted a lass in the clubhouse bar. She was pleasing to the eye and from my discreet observations she seemed to be a good humoured sort of a girl, so I made it my business to talk to her. We've been talking ever since, most of the time anyway. After about two weeks I felt I had known Anne Dunne all my life.

The first date could have ended in disaster. I arranged to meet Anne in Lansdowne the following Saturday night. The place was packed and Anne couldn't find me. I was actually waiting for her outside the old clubhouse. Anne was on her way home when she spotted a car with several empty Major cigarette boxes up on the dashboard. She had no idea what kind of car I drove, but she strongly suspected from the dishevelled state of the banger, and the evidence of the fags, that it could well be mine. Anne went back again and found me. Later that night Anne confessed she would never have looked at me again if she thought I had stood her up.

We started to go out. A good bit. And I made sure I nailed down our exact meeting points from then on. I said to myself very early on, 'Moss if you keep going with this woman there is a high probability you will lose your bachelor status.'

That summer I bought a house in Knocklyon, a three bedroomed semi-detached. I was sick of living in flats and halves of houses. I was now nearly 30 years of age and felt it was time to put down roots. I was delighted with the house. It was a big move for me but I'd had a serious chat with myself after the debacle in New Zealand and knew it was time to move on.

Anne said to me one day, during the summer, 'Moss you're putting on a bit of weight isn't it about time you got back training?' My boots were so hard I had to throw them away. We only used the one pair back then so I trained in runners until I got new ones. The training made me realise how unfit I was – I was a stone overweight and I had hardly taken a walk that summer, much less run. I was drained, too, after the international season and the hepatitis. I decided to stick to my old beliefs. There was no point in being the fittest man on the pitch in August when the serious stuff began in October. And that October the All Blacks were coming. I had unfinished business with them. I felt I was a bit naive back in '73 with Munster and with the Lions the summer before but now was an opportunity to get even.

According to my mother, a Kerry mystic used to say that 'a man who isn't his own doctor by the age of 40 is a fool'. It's the same with a rugby player or any other sportsman at around the age of 30. You have to know your own body and how much it takes to get fit. There's no point in leaving all your best work on the gallops when it's the racecourse that really counts.

I was fit enough to train seriously by about the middle of September, time enough to be ready for Munster versus the All Blacks in Thomond Park on October 31, 1978. I worked back to it gradually, going for a run with Donal Spring most days at lunchtime. He was good company, a law student with a penchant for telling yarns, most of which I believed until I got to know him better. He even talked me into going to the gym in Trinity College, but I couldn't handle it – too claustrophobic. Instead I did my few sit-ups – 300 – and a couple of hundred press-ups to get the shoulders into trim.

Tommy Kiernan was the Munster coach. He was meticulous but not in an annoying way – there's nothing worse than a coach who concentrates on small things that don't really matter. Tommy organised squad training in Fermoy, County Cork. We were a very scattered group (and not just geographically): six of the team were Limerick based – Moloney, Dennison, McLoughlin, Whelan, Foley and Tucker; four lived in Dublin – Keane, Ward, Canniffe and Spring; four came from Cork – Bowen, Finn, Barrett and Cantillon – and then there was Les White who hailed from somewhere in England; at that time nobody knew exactly where.

There were no floodlights in Fermoy so the selectors had to turn on the headlights of their cars instead. I'm sure Kiernan did this deliberately, though he will never admit it. The thought of preparing to take on the greatest rugby team in the world by training under 'floodlights from Cortinas and Ford Escorts' gave us a real lift. It made for a lot of fun, too. Brendan Foley would pass remarks like, 'Tommy, can you switch to dims? Mossy is having a gawk' or 'turn on the indicators, Mossy is about to turn,' which had us laughing as we worked out. We worked hard, too; the regime was tough. Nothing scientific, just hard running, but Kiernan had an eye for players and could tell at a glance if you were carrying a knock or had a touch of flu or, worst of all, if you had been out drinking the night before. There was one area of the pitch where the lights did not reach, which provided us with an escape from his all-seeing eye.

One night I headed for the dark of this black hole, totally knackered, and met full back Larry Moloney lying down on the grass.

'Are you all right, Larry?' I asked.

'No, Moss,' he said, 'I'm going to die.'

Kiernan must have known we were there but he knew when to allow a bit of slack. He also knew how to push us. He had something of the gift of his fellow Corkman, the great racehorse trainer Vincent O' Brien, and knew instinctively how to train rugby players. Then he brought us to London for a preparatory race – we played Middlesex and they thrashed us soundly. It was no surprise; most of the team had been out on the piss the night before. Ill-disciplined as that might sound, Kiernan had his reasons for allowing it.

One was that the All Blacks spies would report that we were useless. Middlesex had an All Blacks coach and he would be bound to pass on the word that we were no-hopers. Secondly, there was the group dynamics of a bunch of young lads hitting London and having a good time, breaking down the barriers between them. The yarns that follow keep you going through the hard slog of training. And, thirdly, Tommy could assess exactly where we were in terms of fitness at that stage of the season.

We went on to play London Irish, two days later, a club side, and barely scraped a draw, and had a final trial sometime in October. Afterwards Pat Whelan, Captain of the Probables, was called out of the dressing room. He was back five minutes later, and beckoned me over.

'There's been a coup,' he said, pronouncing the 'p' at the end. Donal Canniffe, our scrum-half, and yet another Lansdowne clubmate, had been appointed captain. He went on to play a hugely important role, both in the build-up and in the match itself.

Pat accepted the decision without complaint. He was a team player and just got on with it. And the captaincy wasn't as big a deal then as it is now.

The All Blacks were in Britain at that stage. They hammered the London Counties. Middlesex was one of the London counties, so by that measure the All Blacks would eat us without salt.

We went into a squad session a few days before the game. Kiernan told us we would win. Olan Kelleher, the sub scrum-half and the most photographed non-playing member of the squad was certain we would win. The rest of us just wanted to perform to our optimum and take it from there. We made no provisos of any kind.

Instead, the day before the game we went for a boat trip on the Shannon and threw Kiernan into the cold water. We all ended up soaked to the skin in the end. Wardy always makes out that we gelled that afternoon and he was right; it was the making of us. I believe really successful teams must have the upmost respect for each other, and we all got on very well. There isn't a single player on that squad I ever want to avoid.

Kiernan organised a man by the name of Vincent O'Connor to look after physiotherapy on the morning of the game. He pulled every one of our toes and fingers and the cracking and clicking of bones nearly drove me to distraction, but I felt free and loose afterwards.

There was no need for a big speech. We all knew who we were playing and what was expected of us.

The All Blacks lined up and performed the Haka with the usual menace and threat. I whispered to Foley, 'Will we ask them to dance?' He just smiled.

Thomond Park was packed to the rafters, with 12,000 plus inside. Years later many multiples of that number claimed to have been there. The atmosphere and support of the crowd was incredible from the off. Maybe they sensed history was about to be made, though I was concentrating so hard I barely heard them. *The Fields of Athenry* hadn't yet been written so there was no unifying song on the terraces. If someone sang *The Banks of My Own Lovely Lee* the Limerick lads would have been offended and if *The Rose of Tralee* was sung that wouldn't satisfy the Cork people, and so on. Maybe that's why the new breed of Munster supporters chose *The Fields of Athenry* as their signature tune – Athenry is safely situated in Connacht.

The Blacks took control early on. Then Christy Cantillon, a gutsy, open-side wing forward with a real turn of foot, backed up Jimmy Bowen's brilliant first-half break and we scored near the posts. Wardy was in his element. He was a confident player and he just looked a class apart. Seamus Dennison hit Stu Wilson with the hardest tackle I have ever seen and this lifted the whole team. I think that rather than the try was the moment we knew we could win the game.

For my part I spent the day trying to disrupt Frank Oliver, who had cleaned me out in the First Test with the Lions the year before. Andy Haden was another lineout expert and I shouldered him Gaelic football style every chance I got. I struck no blow during the game. The only incident was when Les White was hit and it was all my fault. I'd instructed Les to stand on Haden's toe when he was jumping for the ball; we called that a toe-job. But the All Blacks gave us plenty to do in the lineouts and after a while Les had enough of it. 'That's me finished with the toes, Moss,' he said. 'You'll just have to jump higher.'

Brendan Foley consigned me to playing behind my very good friend Ginger McLoughlin. 'But why?' I asked. 'Aren't ye both Shannon men. It's only natural that ye play on the same side.'

'No, you're better than me,' he answered. 'Keane, I hate to say it, but you're the best scrummager I've ever seen, and Ginger has very high standards. He's a kind of a scrummaging perfectionist.' I thought he was going to cry if I didn't agree.

My head swelled to the size of a watermelon to hear a Limerick man praising me; it was like winning an Oscar. I should, of course, have known better – Foley knew from experience that his clubmate's diet was causing him to produce too much gas. I discovered that in the scrum, and learned quickly to scrummage low – methane is lighter than air, a fact I knew from the bit of science I picked up at UCC. Moreover, if you scrummage low enough you will avoid being crushed between the prop and the hooker's hips. My new technique helped me to avoid the cauliflower ears most second rows pick up from constant friction in the scrum. I have Ginger and Foley to thank for this development and my beautiful ears.

But I still picked up a dose of the dreaded herpes. The All Blacks prop, Gary Knight, played with a bandage around his head. He picked up the virus a few weeks before and, in the days before very much was known about herpes, passed it on to Ginger and me. My head was so low to avoid the farts that I was in constant friction with other players' heads, and herpes spreads with contact. In November of every year I get a major flare-up on the top of my head. It is a constant reminder of a memorable day.

We had the better of the All Blacks in the scrum, where Ginger proved he was as good as anyone in the world. That day was the making of his international career. And outside the scrum it was our tackling allied to their poor use of the ball that won us the match.

It was a famous victory, 12-0, perhaps too famous: I get embarrassed when people talk of how we humiliated the All Blacks at Thomond Park. We didn't. We beat them, that was all. They were the best rugby team in the world and went on to achieve the Grand Slam in the course of that tour. I believe it's the only time the All Blacks were held to a scoreless defeat.

It was reported that towards the end of the game a bit or

argy bargy broke out and I said to Andy Haden, 'You've lost the match. Do you want to lose the fight as well?' Maybe I did, but it doesn't sound like me, and I have no recollection of saying it. There was no chatting with the All Blacks. If you wanted to do one of them you did it at your peril. And they were very sporting on the day. In fact, I thought we were lucky more penalties weren't given against us. Believe it or not, there were no penalty kicks at goal that day.

Still, we were the better team and it was a proud moment to have beaten such opponents and prouder again that we kept them from scoring. The win helped in no small way to erase the embarrassment I'd felt after my Lions' Test performance.

Munster had a good overall record against the All Blacks. In my three Munster matches against them we drew one, won one and lost one. The aggregate score in the three games was 19–17 to Munster, so the win in Limerick was no fluke.

The fans' enjoyment and subsequent elevation of the win to a quasi-religious experience was as much a compliment to the might of the All Blacks as to anyone else involved. In May 2005, at the launch of a vivid and truthful account of our victory, in the book *Stand Up and Fight* by Limerickman Alan English, Tommy Kiernan said: 'We had a good day. We won a famous victory against opponents we will always respect. Let us move on and allow later generations make their own history.' It was the right way to sum it up.

I didn't go to the official dinner on the night of the match. Instead I had a few quiet pints with my old pal Billy Morgan and my new pal Anne. I was happy with my life and most of all with Anne, and I knew it was only a matter of time before I was going to ask her to marry me. There was the usual inspection by both sets of parents. By Christmas we knew this was it, and said as much. There wasn't much point in hanging about and we were engaged by St Patrick's Day the following year.

That night, though, Anne drove us home early. I would be facing the All Blacks again the following Saturday, playing for Ireland and the last thing I wanted was to face a wounded All Blacks, suffering from a hammering, and me suffering from getting hammered after a big celebration in rugby mad Limerick.

As it turned out the New Zealanders beat us with a last-minute try by hooker Andy Dalton in Lansdowne Road. They deserved to win – we were unable to reach the heights of the Tuesday before. In fact, the All Blacks won all their other matches on that '78 tour. Five of the successful Munster team played – Larry Maloney, Tony Ward, Pat Whelan, Donal Spring and myself.

Their visit to Ireland had significance beyond the games we played against them. Donal Canniffe's father, Dan, died suddenly in Cork during the match in Thomond Park. The All Blacks' manager, Jack Gleeson, was diagnosed with liver cancer on his return home and was dead within a few months. When I look back on those days now, I think of two fine men from different hemispheres and the roles they played in the drama enacted that day in Thomond Park.

Many years later I found myself in the second row of the Dunamaise Theatre in Portlaoise. Earlier that evening Anne had ordered me to dress up, saying she was taking me on a surprise outing, and I knew better than to refuse. She landed me into John Breen's play, *Alone it Stands*, a dramatic recreation of the events of October 31, 1978.

Niamh McGrath, who played me, made a clumsy entrance and opened with the immortal line: 'I'm taking the ball and your fingers, you ugly sheep-shagging bastard.'

Poetic licence.

She was a petite girl of about five-feet-feck-all bulked out with shoulder pads, and went about the stage tackling and mauling everyone in sight. She was brilliant. By the end of the play I actually believed she was me. I went backstage afterwards with Seamus Dennison to meet the cast, and Seamus and I had a few drinks for old time's sake. It was a great night.

The play toured all over the world and was very well received in Australia! There was a West End run and every now and then it pops up in a theatre in Dublin. The wonderful thing about our famous win is that the television coverage amounts to only ten minutes from one pre-digital camera, which leaves loads of room for myth and legend. There is no evidence to contradict us.

The Munster team of '78 was invited to a special charity production of *Alone it Stands* in the Belltable Theatre in Limerick. The high-energy show has lots of simulated rugby action. Brendan Foley sat beside me and he leaned over at one point and whispered:

'Hey, Keane, that small girl playing you, Karen Scully…
'

'What about her?'
'She jumps higher than you ever did.'

TEN

Winning Down Under

After the All Blacks win I was on a high. The win instilled a confidence in us. The feel good factor spilled over into the Five Nations. Ginger was picked for his first cap against France on January 20, 1979. Mike Gibson of Lansdowne, Gibbo, was also awarded a cap as was Colm Tucker, another hero of the Munster All Blacks' game. Fellow Kerryman and Lansdowne player, Dick Spring came in for his first cap, continuing a find tradition of brothers playing for Ireland.

We played well and drew 9 all. Wardy's tactical kicking was brilliant and we went on to have a good season. We beat England, but, even though we were playing well, we lost narrowly to Wales in Cardiff after scoring a record 21 points. We then had a draw with Scotland in a game we should have won easily.

Wardy was the star that season and at the end of it he was voted European Player of the Year. He was now the superstar of Irish and world rugby. Tony Ward was a smashing guy, shy even and he never let the fame go to his head.

The concluding stages of the Leinster Cup were played after the Five Nations. Dick Spring was captain of Lansdowne that year. Dick was a young barrister and spent a few years in New York working as a waiter and in construction to pay off student loans. He brought leadership and organisation to Lansdowne on his return.

I was in line for the captaincy, what with being well-established on the Irish team by then and having toured with the Lions. Dick approached me and asked if I was interested. Being a Kerryman, I said 'maybe'. I asked him if he was interested and, being a Kerryman himself, he went so far as to offer, 'maybe I might'. 'Maybe', as I understood Dick, meant 'yes', so I told him my 'maybe' was a 'no', but I was happy with his answer. Building on such subtle interplay, Dick Spring would later go on to negotiate less delicate matters as a politician, like the IRA ceasefire in the North of Ireland and the terms of the Good Friday agreement. He wasn't a bad negotiator even then. He was the youngest ever leader of the Labour Party and the youngest ever Tánaiste (deputy Prime Minister) and remains a great friend to this day.

I had no problem with Dick taking over; it was the best call for Lansdowne. We hadn't won a cup for seven years and it was beginning to get everyone down. It was one of the worst losing sequences the club had experienced in its 100-year history. We came up against Blackrock in the semi-final of the Leinster Senior Cup. We were decimated by injuries in the pack to such an extent that one journalist called us Snow White and the Seven Dwarfs, with me in the lead role, towering above everyone else. The game finished in a draw. We finally won home by a nose in extra time in the replay. My good friend Willie Duggan and myself never came to blows at any stage of the two games, but we didn't spare each other. You'd never think we even spoke to one another if you saw the way we leathered into each other on the pitch. The second game was decided by a superb Dick Spring try. It was beyond doubt one of the most crucial of Lansdowne tries and involved a back movement so intricate that it could only be figured out if you were a seagull viewing from above.

We met Terenure in the final. Throughout the first half, I was getting cleaned out in the lineout by a fella called Gerry Mullaly. He was 6ft 9in and I was finding it impossible to beat him in the air. Dick came up to me and demanded, 'Who's the Irish international here? Is it you or Mullaly?'

Shortly afterwards, Dick came back for another go and asked me if Mullaly spoke Australian. Ireland were due to go to Australia in a few weeks time. I'd had enough of his enquiries and told the future Tánaiste to fuck off and mind his own business. Dick left me alone after that, but he knew he had me going – I went on to win every ball that came near me in the second half. Lansdowne won by 20 points. We'd won the Leinster Senior Cup. The first of three-in-a-row. It was a fine side containing household names like Spring, Becker, Quinn, Canniffe, Gibson, Moroney and domestiques like Kearney, Nyhan, D'Arcy, Nuzum, Kavanagh, Boylan, Conroy and MacWhite.

That season seemed to go on forever but when things go well you never feel battle weary. Next up was the Irish summer tour to Oz.

Anne came to the airport and kissed me goodbye. Willie Duggan was astounded by this public display of affection and returned with a Mills and Boon entitled *Love Long Distance*, which he presented to me in public. I made an effort to read it on the usual tortuous plane journey but I gave up after about six lines and passed it on to a cattle jobber's wife from Offaly. I missed Anne on the tour and it was hard enough to get through on the phone in those days, but I was kept busy and didn't have time to get too lonely.

I was one of only three players to tog out in all eight games on that Irish tour to Australia in 1979. Mike Gibson and Fergus Slattery were the other two.

I was honoured to be included in such illustrious company and mentioned this to our coach, Noel Murphy. 'Moss,' he said, 'it was the only way we had of keeping you out of trouble.' Murphy also knew that games were the best way of keeping me fit and because of my size I was well able for the punishment.

In 1978 Wales had been eaten up by the Aussies in both Tests after they had won the Grand Slam. The Australians hammered the All Blacks in the Bledisloe Cup just a few weeks before we turned up. The Irish team was definitely not the favourite when we arrived.

During that first week in Perth all the squad were billeted out in pairs for an evening meal in private houses, a novel idea that was a big success. I was paired with Ulster centre David Irwin, a touring rookie at the time. He was a great roommate and, unlike Willie Duggan, he was tolerant of the odd fit of snoring and anxious to be home before dawn. We were a bit apprehensive about staying in private houses but our hosts, Flora and Gordon Simpson, turned out to be lovely people. It was a real home away from home and we were fed like gamecocks. I was delighted, because I had had enough of hotels on the New Zealand tour to last me a lifetime.

Gordon was a massive man who originally hailed from County Armagh. His uncle was Henry O'Hara O'Neill, who played international rugby for Ireland in the 1930s. By a curious coincidence, he had attended University College Cork, where he took the same degree as me. That's where comparisons ended – he went on to head the Ministry of Agriculture in Northern Ireland. Some time after our visit, Gordon in his wisdom purchased a young trotting horse – the sport is extremely popular throughout Australia – and named it 'Moss Keane'. It was a peculiar honour, and I told Gordon that I hoped the horse would run faster than I did.

'Never mind, Moss, he's only a trotter,' Gordon reassured me.

The horse turned out to be reasonably successful. Sadly, Gordon passed away a few years ago, but we had happy memories of a wonderful night in his company and I maintained contact for many years afterwards.

On the pitch the tour was a huge success. We won seven of the eight games, including the two tests, which created a little bit of history: our Irish team was the first team from the northern hemisphere to win two Tests down under. But we could hardly have had a worse start when Ned Byrne was badly hurt in an accident. Ned was an All-Ireland Senior Hurling medal winner with Kilkenny, but packed in his successful hurling career to give his full attention to rugby. We went to the races a couple of days before our first game and on his way home that night Ned was knocked down by a hit-and-run driver and very badly injured. He spent the next five weeks in hospital in Australia. The driver, a young lad from out of town, was showing off to a girl, and to her credit, she reported the crime to the police. The driver was sent to jail but that could not fix Ned's injuries. He never regained his old form. It was a cruel blow to a great man and a great sportsman.

There was more off the field controversy surrounding Tony Ward, who arrived in Australia as our number one out half. He was the new pin-up boy of Irish rugby and the centre of attention from the moment the tour started. Everyone wanted a piece of him, especially the press and Australian women. Wardy was unfailingly polite to both, even though they hardly gave him a minute's peace. He was in a serious relationship back home and didn't socialise very much, not even to take a drink with us. When it came to relations with the press, he was before his time. He was no publicity fiend, just a very polite young man, sometimes too polite for his own good. He posed in a swimming togs for an UK tabloid, not for any financial gain but just because they asked him to. Most of all, Tony simply loved sport – he played soccer almost as brilliantly as he played rugby.

Ollie Campbell travelled as our number two out half. He had been capped at a very young age in 1976 against Australia and was subsequently overtaken by the brilliance of Wardy. By 1979 Ollie had matured into a serious rugby footballer. He was smart and classy, a brilliant tackler and a superb kicker.

Some argued Ollie Campbell played himself onto the first Test team with an impeccable display against Queensland when he scored all of our 18 points but Wardie scored 19 in the next game to create a new Irish record. It was a tough call, and the selectors called it in Ollie's favour. The decision could have been handled better, especially in light of the publicity that surrounded it. Wardy only found out he was dropped when Pa Whelan told him on the bus on the way to training. It was a tough blow. There was huge controversy back home over the decision, with publicity almost reaching the levels of the Roy Keane Saipan saga.

In fact, the two of them played in the second last match against Sydney, the only game we lost, though that was not their fault. There were some tired legs in the park that day and Sydney came from behind to win by three points. The selectors didn't deem that experiment to be a success.

I was deeply privileged to play with both players, winning a Triple Crown with one and beating the All Blacks for the first time ever with the other. I would have either of them in my world team and maybe both. I often thought Ollie would have made a fine full-back. You could make a case for either player – the difference between them was so fine, it split the country down the middle. What was nice was that Ollie and Wardy remained friends in the teeth of one of the most heated public debates ever seen in Irish sport.

There was great camaraderie on that trip – at the very least, those who were disappointed hid it well – and there was heart and spirit in the team. In the first test in Brisbane, with Australia having the better game and leading 12-9, our full back Rodney O'Donnell was taken out as a high ball was dropping towards him. It was a late tackle, a dirty tackle, and Rodney was badly concussed. Dr John O'Driscoll, our hugely competitive and abrasive number six, went berserk. He called the pack together, even though it may not have been his function to do so, and proceeded to dance something akin to the Haka. He was bouncing off the ground with temper. I have never seen a man so incensed. Harry Steele, my second row partner, looked at me, and I just looked at him. There was no need to say anything; it was game on.

Duggan was everywhere, at his contrary best. Fergus Slattery was superb as captain. Slatts was the best in the world in his position in those years. He was fast, skilful, hard, ruthless if provoked, and now he tackled as if his life depended on it. O'Driscoll, though, was the man of the moment. John is, of course, Brian O'Driscoll's cousin, another of that famous Irish rugby family. Black cat, black kitten, as they say in Knocknagoshel.

We played as if possessed and pulverised the Australian pack. The Australians knew what hit them because everything was done up front. We never lost control. Colin Patterson was incredible. The little Ulsterman had a devastating break and a quick rugby brain. He always brought the best out of Wardy when they played at half-back together, and took a lot of pressure off Ollie Campbell that day. He scored two tries while Ollie did the rest with a couple of penalties, two conversions and a drop goal. We came back from trailing three points down to hammer the Australians 27-12. I often replay that game in my head on black days when the windscreen wipers can't keep up with the rain and the memory of it always gives me a lift.

Rodney O'Donnell recovered but his career was to end

the following on the Lions tour to South Africa. Rodney was immensely popular among the Irish team. He was reliable under the high ball and never shirked a tackle. He was also very superstitious. He tied his shoelaces with his leg crossed. If his togs touched his legs as he pulled them on, he would start the process all over again. And he had to be the last man out of the dressing room. The problem was, so did Willie. A compromise was agreed whereby they walked out together, each watching the other to make sure neither strayed a step in front or a step behind. The antics continued on the pitch. When the ball went out of play, maybe for a 22 or some such, Rodney would throw the ball off the bar and catch it again, training it to hit the crossbar from the opposition's kick.

Rodney had it all figured out. He not only put the mockers on the opposition kicks, he made huge efforts to project a positive karma over ours. If we told Rodney we had met a red-haired woman, he would walk halfway around the world to meet another, because two were lucky and one was not. It was the same with magpies. We wound him up unmercifully about it but he was well able for the slagging. You had to be if you wanted to survive in the Irish squad. That was one of the most enjoyable things about playing rugby for Ireland, the humour. Rodney was one of the lads but the big thing about him was his bravery; when he was tackled he never took his eyes off the ball. We won that match for ourselves and for Ireland, but mostly we won it for Rodney. He would surely have gone on to win 50 caps if injury hadn't intervened.

We celebrated long into the night but I didn't overdo it. I knew I would be playing again on the Wednesday. My discipline paid off when I spotted the referee on his own in a corner of the room. I had waited all night for my chance, and went over to him after his minders had left. I decide to play the innocent country boy and asked him for a bit of advice, well aware he was due to referee the second Test in two weeks time.

'Can I ask you about the lineout, ref? What's the best way to go about jumping?' I looked at him again; he wasn't put off by the question. 'I'm a bit confused about the rules down here and everyone is giving out shit to me.'

The official explained that he only penalised going across at the lineout. In other words, if you jumped up on a player on the other side of the line, he would award a penalty; everything else was fair game.

The secret is to train for the referee and in the week before the second Test Phil Orr and myself practised the art of lineout lifting. At that time it was totally illegal. Our moment came in the second Test, at a lineout in the Australian 22. Fergus Slattery called it on Willie Duggan or John O'Driscoll at the back – normally a sound option. I shouted to Slatts to change and call it on me at number two at the front. Ciaran Fitzgerald threw, Phil Orr lifted, I tapped down to Colin Patterson who passed it out to Ollie Campbell, and Ollie dropped a goal. As the ball sailed high over the bar I said to Orr, 'You can let me down now, Philip.'

The Irish side was much more of a unit than the Lions had been, and unlike the marathon in New Zealand our six weeks in Australia was about the right length for a tour. Once again I used up all my annual leave in one go. There was no compensation for missing work, and though we were granted a tour allowance, you would not save up on it. We had a very good management team also, with Jack Coffey, a great Lansdowne man and an excellent organiser as manager, and Noel Murphy as coach. Murphy was a Lion himself and a Munster man, and knew what it took to play international rugby. He had us playing like a Munster pack. He was always up for a laugh but he was sincere in his beliefs. He gave the players a fair amount of responsibility and didn't over-coach his teams, and he expected this trust to be reciprocated. He was very conscious of his players' welfare; he even organised Mass in a hotel room the mornings of both Tests for those of us who wanted it. I attended both Masses and it meant a lot to me.

Off the pitch we enjoyed ourselves and found we got on well with our laid-back Aussie hosts, they're the nearest you can get to the Irish mindset in the Southern Hemisphere. There was sure to be a good laugh, a few beers, as much slagging as you could take and a healthy disregard for bullshit in any shape or form. They were generous as well. There was no penny pinching and we were all treated like adults. The players always came first. That's the secret of their success and if they said they'd do something, they did it. And they didn't make a compliment out of it. There was also the realisation that while winning was everything rugby was still a game. It was meant to be fun. The travelling was manageable too; the tour was mainly focused on Brisbane and Sydney and we had only one major flight from west to east. The weather was a big factor, too; we hardly saw a drop of rain in Australia. I love the sun, even if I seemed to go around for the most of that tour with a sunburned face and a big red nose.

An Aussie girl came up to me at training one time and asked for an autograph.

'But you're so pink,' she said.

'Ah sure that's the way it is back in Ireland,' I replied, 'everyone wants to go pink from the sun; no one has any interest in going brown. It's the most unfashionable skin colour of them all.'

'But what about Tony Ward?' she asked in a state of shock as she looked longingly in Wardy's direction, 'He's really brown.'

'Ah poor Wardy. The women wouldn't look twice at him back home. It's so sad. He just doesn't have that lobster look,' I said of the first sex symbol in world rugby.

She went over to Wardy next and I could see him breaking up with the laughter. And he needed a lift; he had just been told he wasn't in the team for the second Test.

The game was played in the famous Sydney Cricket Ground. One of the groundsmen came up to me before the game and asked me if we played cricket in Ireland.

'Oh yes,' I replied. 'In fact I won a Castle Island District League playing full-forward for Currow.'

I had Wardy going again.

That was the end of the fun, though. The Australians were embarrassed by their annihilation in the First Test, and they took us on up front, but we were more than able for them. Ciaran Fitzgerald took over from the irrepressible Pa Whelan, my old Munster friend, as hooker for both Tests – another close call, though not as controversial a decision as Ward and Campbell – in a game that marked the start of Fitzgerald's illustrious international career. The pack were beginning to get on extremely well together. I would have loved to face the All Blacks in Wellington with the Irish pack we had just then.

We didn't play as well in the second Test against Australia, but we did enough to win 9-3. The tour had been a huge success, and a highlight of my career, both on and off the pitch. We had beaten the best in the world and I was heading home knowing that I was getting married in a month's time.

The month flew, what with organising everything from Anne's dress and Anne's four sisters, Carmel, Michelle, Maree and Paula who were the bridesmaids. Then there was the sending out of the invitations, the baking of the wedding cake and the organising of the ceremony at the University Church in St Stephen's Green. All of which of course I had absolutely nothing at all to do with – Anne did the lot. Anne's brothers Gerry and Matt were by now good mates and advised me to sit back and leave everything to her. It took me a week to get over the Aussie tour and there was the Lansdowne stag, the Kerry stag, the Cork stag and the non-aligned stag. Before I knew it I was marching up the church in my best suit with my shoes polished (by Anne, in case I might forget) for the first time since my Holy Communion in Currow Church. Canon Matt did the honours and set the tone for the day with his good humour.

I was moved when it came to the marriage vows part of the ceremony. The 'love and honour' bit I had no bother with, but I knew I would struggle with the 'obey' part of the marriage promise. Father Matt kept up the tempo. 'Moss you may kiss the bride now but go easy; it isn't a rugby player you have in your hands now.'

There was a cheer more in keeping with the scoring of Christy Cantillon's try against the All Blacks in Thomond Park the previous October.

I'd been given the job of organising the venue for the reception. And where else would I have it only at Lansdowne Road? Lansdowne Rugby Club to be precise. We took the wedding photos in the middle of the pitch and the press was there in strength. A reporter from the *Indo* approached Anne and asked her what it was like to be married to an Irish rugby international?

'I haven't a clue,' she replied. 'I am only married to the man an hour. Ask me again in 20 years' time.'

As we walked in to the clubhouse we were serenaded with *The Rose of Tralee*. One of the boys, I think it was Mick Quinn shouted out, 'Mossy you're well tackled at last.'

It was that kind of a day and we loved every minute of it. There were double entendre jokes in the speeches, like Brian's pun about my being 'keen to get Anne Dunne.' Dunne is of course Anne's maiden name. My father made a speech in which he brought in all his skills as an actor with the Currow Drama Group. He reminded me he had won an All-Ireland at the drama, but I had never won an All-Ireland at anything. Anne's family made me welcome and our crowd got on famously with the Dunnes and the ever-friendly people of Laois and Offaly.

There was even a congratulatory telegram purporting to come from UCC Gaelic football club that went as follows:

> Moss when you played on the college teams, for a good many years, it seemed to us that we could never find your best position. We tried you at corner-back, full-back, full-forward and even left outside, during your suspensions. Your friends, colleagues and former teammates in the University College Cork football club sincerely hope you find your best position tonight. Have a great day Moss and a great life.

I was lucky enough to have a sympathetic boss and I was granted two weeks' special leave, without pay, for my honeymoon, as all my leave ran out on the tour.

We decided to go off to Cornwall. We were told, 'the weather would be lovely. Cornwall is very south and is absolutely beautiful. The seafood is delicious, fresh off the boats And the people,' continued our consultant, 'are so Celtic, big into rugby and very friendly.'

The travel expert got the rugby and the friendly bit one hundred per cent right. I cannot tell you if Cornwall is beautiful or not. I'm sure it is but we hardly ventured outside the door. And there was no fresh fish. The boats were all tied up to the harbour wall. The weather was appalling. There were gales that staggered me without so much as a drop of drink inside me and there was major structural damage all along the coast. The Fastnet yacht race had to be cancelled and there were several fatalities among the competitors. It never stopped raining.

I had an unfortunate experience in a kip of a hotel in Weston-super-Mare. Anne chose it because it had ye olde English Inn look. I said to Anne it had 'ye olde knock the shagging thing down look.'

Anne was as ever chatty and friendly and she told the receptionist we were on our honeymoon so we were shown to the bridal suite. Anne said it was lovely. I thought it was badly in need of a lick of emulsion or a lick of a wrecking ball.

That night Anne was dolling herself up for going out and I was taking a bit of a snooze in this rickety four poster bed, with a mattress as bony as donkey's arse and a tent overhead. Maybe the roof was leaking as well. Anyway, whatever way I turned over, the wood-wormed old bed broke in two.

We fled almost immediately, forfeiting the tariff we'd paid in advance. We were too embarrassed to face the receptionist and booked in to a modern hotel nearby, having first of all carried out a structural audit on the bed.

The people of Cornwall didn't know what to do for us. They were stone mad about rugby and we weren't allowed to buy a drink. But there was nothing they could do about the weather.

We stayed in a lot, and that wasn't so bad either.

ELEVEN

Scoring for Ireland

It was 1980, at the Ireland v Scotland game, Lansdowne Road when a strange event, as rare and wonderful as a cow that milks out ice cream in hot weather, took place.

There had been no signs of such a miraculous happening early on in the international season. Willie and Ginger were dropped after a 24-9 defeat to England. It could have been any one of us. We were dire but Donal Spring and Mick Fitzpatrick had come in for the boys and played very well.

We'd lost 19-18 to France after my old friend Alan Hosie disallowed what we considered to be a try. Wales were beaten 21-7. It was our first win over them since 1970. And my first Welsh triumph. There had been many days when I thought I would never see myself on a winning team against Wales.

And now we were facing Scotland on our home ground. We beat them too and guess who scored the winning try?

I intercepted the ball on my own line. Off I went at speed, with half the Scottish team chasing me down. I dummied Roy Laidlaw, shimmied past Andy Irvine and crossed the halfway line. The crowd was going crazy but there were still seven Scots in front of me. I wasn't going to make it so I steadied myself, took aim and let fly with a drop goal attempt from fully 50 yards, as they knocked me to the ground. I tossed them off my back and watched the ball sail into the gale force wind. But one of those infamous Lansdowne Road gusts took the ball slightly to the right of centre. I was up and running. I managed to get myself under the dropping rebound as it hit the posts and landed on the Scottish 22. I ran the rest of the way to the try line with Scots swinging off me. I didn't feel a thing – I was so intent on crossing the line.

I crashed over for the greatest try ever seen in Lansdowne Road and the crowd at the back of the goal cheered like mad.

In my dreams…

The truth was Donal Spring passed me the ball and I trotted for no more than six or seven yards before I crashed through one tackle and flopped down in the corner.

It was to be my one and only try for Ireland. You would swear I *did* score one of the greatest tries of all time. It was I suppose a proud moment. I'd had a few near misses in the past. Not many mind you but a few. I was a small bit embarrassed by the reaction of the crowd. Donal Spring sensed it and said, 'well done Mossy, what's seldom is wonderful'. I didn't feel too badly after that. I was afraid the boys might think I was losing the run of myself, what with all the cheering and clapping for a very ordinary try. Looking back on it I suppose I should have enjoyed it more. But that was just the way it was back then, you never scored for yourself. All the scores were communal and everyone took equal credit, irrespective of who had touched the ball down. That was the ethos of the game, what rugby was all about.

I was well-settled into married life by the end of the season but spent far too much time away from Anne. She was very good about it and when the season ended I made it up to her. That summer was spent in my little bit of bog above in the Dublin hills. Anne came up with me and we had some great days even though Anne remarked only a Kerryman would head for a bog when the rest of the city was off to the beach.

Friends would approach Anne and say, 'Anne you have a lovely colour, were you away out foreign somewhere?'

'No,' she would reply, 'I got it in the bog!'

By September it was back to school for brown Anne, and back to rugby for pink Moss.

Tommy Kiernan was the Irish coach for the new season. Players always worry when a new boss comes on the scene but I was delighted when Tommy was appointed – he was a canny, inspirational Munster coach and I knew he'd make a success of the Irish team. Tommy knew what had to be done and he just did it, simple as that. He understood that the primary duty of a rugby forward is to win the ball, and to do this you have to be prepared to get your hands dirty. He believed passionately in the Munster way of playing rugby. In other words, he liked hard forwards strangling the life out of the opposition. There would be no softies in a Kiernan pack. Kiernan was a former international full-back so he knew a thing or two about back play as well. He was not afraid to bring on young players either. I just knew when he took over that we would win something.

The amazing thing is that we were favourites to win the championship that year, though we only drew with Romania in an autumn international. Romania were a superb side – they hammered Munster out of sight in Thomond Park – and it was a great pity that the subsequent misfortunes of the country wrecked Romanian rugby.

It turned out to be a frustrating year. We nearly beat the Welsh in Cardiff – in fact, the game was the nearest we ever came to winning there. It was a boxing match, and on that score we would have been awarded a victory on points. Wardy was brought back on at out-half and Ollie played in the centre. Some of the back play was superb and we scored two tries, but even though we had the two best place-kickers in Europe, we failed to get a single kick on target. Wardy's radar was askew for once. We pulverised the Welsh pack and even stopped their fans singing for long periods of the match, but our losing run in Cardiff continued. I was never to win a game there.

England beat us by four points and Scotland beat us by a point after an intercept try, and to round off a miserable season we lost to France by a narrow margin. From heroes to zeroes.

In the event we had lost every match and duly got the wooden spoon. Well, you could say we were just getting ready for the following season. The team played reasonably well and were only narrowly beaten, losing by an aggregate of only 12 points over the four games.

I'd a good few games to play with Lansdowne that season as well. I'd been made captain and I knew I'd as hard a task ahead of me as in any of the Five Nations games. We'd won the Cup in '79 under Dick Spring's captaincy and 'Basher' Boylan had followed that with another win in 1980. He thought he had an impossible act to follow then but I was asking myself how I was supposed to compete with the two of them. My only way out was to win the double, the cup and the league, which we did. It was three-in-a-row for Lansdowne and a nice compensation for me, after a poor international season.

All through the season I worried about whether or not to go on the 1981 tour to South Africa that summer. Would I go or would I would I follow my conscience? On the one hand I wanted to go on the tour. I had been to Australia and New Zealand; South Africa was the last great rugby-playing nation left to visit. But on the other hand South Africa was still in the grip of the apartheid regime, a place where it was

Five Nations Championship 1981, Ireland v England. Maurice Colclough and myself – my left arm is working miracles on his shoulder! *(© INPHO/Billy Stickland)*

Five Nations '81 again – Ireland v France this time. Willie Duggan always liked to have the odds on his side and here he is cleaning out a French prop-forward! John O'Driscoll and Slatts were ready and waiting to move in.
(© INPHO/Billy Stickland)

1982, Lansdowne – the bread and butter of the game.
We were going for four-in-a-row in the Leinster Cup that year.
(© Ray McManus/Sportsfile)

Our Grand Slam bid, Ireland v France 1982 – France meant business that day.
They brought back all the old hands so they wouldn't end up getting the
wooden spoon and it worked. *(© INPHO/Billy Stickland)*

February 20, 1982, Five Nations, Ireland v Scotland – the Triple Crown decider.
Duggan was probably thinking to himself, Keane has gone off on
another mystery tour!
(© Ray McManus/Sportsfile)

Sean Kilfeather, Donal Lenihan and myself with some of the supporters in
O'Donoghues after winning the Triple Crown. It was a memorable night!

March 5, 1983, Ireland v Wales, John O'Driscoll, myself and Gerry 'Ginger' McLoughlin. It was the only game we lost in '83. You'd think we were facing the firing squad or something. The question is which one of the three of us gave away the bloody penalty! *(© Ray McManus/Sportsfile)*

1984, training at Lansdowne Road – I was obviously on the way down from the lineout! *(© Ray McManus/Sportsfile)*

Munster beat the All Blacks in '78 and won the Grand Slam in the provincial rugby as well. Then we headed off to Connaught in '79, expecting to win by about 50 points but we were beaten 13-9. *(© Billy Stickland/INPHO)*

TODAY'S WEATHER

Irish Independent

Vol. 90, No. 265   C   MONDAY, NOVEMBER 9, 1981   Price 22p

Has Moss played his last game for Ireland?

Leo Lynch, President of Lansdowne FC makes a presentation to mark my 50th Cap in 1984.

The William Webb Ellis Trophy, World Cup South Island, New Zealand 1987. It was the first time it was unveiled. Jointly held by the two Mosses – I hope I'm not going to be the only Irish player to ever hold the thing!

A small Giant! Signing an autograph for seven-year-old Kieran Smith at the International friendly for former Irish and Welsh players in 1992.
(© INPHO)

Kerry Greats – Jack O'Shea, Micheál Ó Muircheartaigh, myself, MickO'Connell and John B Keane in Lansdowne when Kerry invaded for the day.
(© Photostyle, Dublin)

Portarlington Golf Club – Michael Moore is presenting his trophy, the Moore Cup, to Jim Dempsey, our late, great manager. We won the Cup, out of about 48 clubs, and to date it's our only victory. I never thought golf would be twice as hard as rugby!

At John O'Shea of GOAL's 60th birthday party, in Blackrock
College Rugby Club, a number of years ago!

Giving Seve Ballesteros some golfing tips at the opening of
The Heritage Golf Club, Killenard, Co Laois!
(© The Carlow Nationalist)

Anne Marie, Anne, myself and Sarah on the occasion of their
Granny's 80th birthday party last year.

a fact of life that men and women were denied access to sport and segregated because of the colour of their skin. I knew the itinerary had been arranged so that a number of coloured and black players would appear against us; some said that was just window-dressing, others thought the South Africans were at least making an effort to make the game multiracial. Behind it all there was still the unacceptable reality that black people in South Africa were denied basic human rights. I was in a quandary.

My good friend and fellow Kerryman, Donal Spring, refused to go. I asked his brother Dick for his opinion and he just said, 'Moss, if I was picked I *would not go* … .' I trusted Dick's judgement. He could be a great laugh in the clubhouse or a witty companion on an evening out, but he was a serious man too and I knew he was prepared to go to the wire on this one. And when Spring took as firm a stand as this, he had to be right. At the same time, he never put any pressure on me to stay off the tour.

On the flip side, Tommy Kiernan was another man of the highest integrity and he had decided to go. Even though he was very much opposed to apartheid, Tommy took the view that isolation would only make matters worse. He had insisted, along with the IRFU, that Ireland would have to play games against coloured players for the tour to go ahead. We needed to bring South Africa along with us, and the best way to implement change was through dialogue; that was how he saw it. And subsequent events showed the soundness of that view, when Errol Tobias was capped against Ireland and became the first coloured player to play an international for the Springboks.

In the end I thought that the reality was that the IRFU should not have taken on the tour in the midst of international political controversy. To their credit, though, the IRFU put absolutely no pressure on us to travel. There were no phone-calls from Tommy or Slatts, who was tour captain.

My decision was made easier when the Government decided to impose an embargo on all public servants forbidding them from travelling on the South African tour. This, of course, included me. I was not as influenced by the possible loss of my job as one might think. Things were bad in Ireland then – the economy was in recession and our biggest exports in those years were our emigrants – but I had been offered other jobs with different companies and knew I could find alternative employment. I had an offer to manage a building society; I was even offered a job as a sales rep that I politely turned down. Rugby opened doors, but I liked my job and while no one ever got rich working for the State, one had security of tenure, in those days anyway. Most of all, though, I hated the idea of not working in agriculture, and it bothered me too when I thought of all the money it took to educate me to become a dairy scientist.

In the end I didn't go. I thought of the men and women who fought and died to win us freedom from the apartheid regime that existed in Ireland prior to Independence, and came to my decision. But I would be a hypocrite if I said I was absolutely sure of my position, because I was not.

I had good friends who went on that trip, and good friends who did not. I had good friends who lost their jobs because they decided to go. John Robbie was refused permission by this employer to travel so he resigned his position. He never returned to Ireland and is now one of the most popular radio presenters in South Africa. The South Africa tour caused terrible conflict in the world of rugby. I didn't speak out back then and maybe I should have, but whatever way the winds of politics blow, I have never turned my back on a friend. I respected and understood their decisions, and they in turn respected mine.

Ireland performed very well in South Africa, losing both Tests narrowly, and I was afraid I might not regain my place when the new season started. There was a break for five or six weeks and then Tommy Kiernan called the squad together for a team talk in the Shelbourne Hotel in late September 1981. I sat at the back with Duggan, like two schoolboys, trying to make ourselves look as a small as possible in case Tommy started asking some hard questions.

Kiernan began to talk about the season that lay ahead, and as he spoke he implied that a few of the team were getting on a bit and that he wouldn't hesitate to make changes if he had to. The coach outlined our responsibilities as players and told us we would have to train harder. He didn't mention any individuals but everyone there knew his remarks were aimed at the members of Dad's Army Mark 2. Duggan, one of our senior members, turned to me and whispered out of the corner of his mouth: 'We'll see that man out Moss.'

Kiernan knew which buttons to press. We took him at his word and put in a huge effort to meet his demands, Willie more than anyone. I was in the form of my life. When Munster went to play Ulster at Ravenhill on the Saturday of the Hallowe'en weekend, I was never in better shape. I had trained hard all summer for a change and upped the tempo in the autumn after Kiernan's comments. This may well be my last season, I thought, and I better make bloody certain it's a good one.

The game was going well when I tried to turn sharply to grab a tricky Ulster winger. My upper body swung around but my ankle refused to budge. I knew straight away I was in trouble. I was loaded up on a stretcher. Players from both sides came up to offer sympathy, and the Ulster fans, fiercely partisan though they were, applauded me off the pitch.

As we made our way to the sideline, one of the first aid crew, a small Belfast man, turned back to the pallbearer bringing up the rear and remarked, 'My back is bollixed.'

'Mine too, and I think I strained my shoulder,' said the other one.

'How is it the wee boys never get injured, just the big fat ones,' returned the porter in front.

'Lads,' I cut in, 'why don't ye hop up on the feckin' stretcher and I'll carry the two of ye.'

They had to put the stretcher down by the side of the pitch for a couple of minutes to get over their fit of laughing.

It wasn't so funny when we got to the Royal Victoria Hospital in Belfast. The diagnosis was badly torn ligaments. Ireland were to play Australia two weeks later in an autumn international and I had no chance whatsoever of making the game. The long-term prognosis was even worse: I was told I would not be fit enough to take my place in the first two games of the international championship. I was 33 years of age and it looked as if my international career was over. Even if I was ready to come back and play for the second half of the international season, I would be totally unfit, and facing into two hard games without any training. It was highly unlikely the selectors would take a gamble on me. I had never missed a Five Nations' game up until then, but I was beginning to burn oil.

'Has Moss played his last game for Ireland?' was the front-page headline in the *Irish Independent*. It was the end of the road for 'a loyal servant, the captain of Dad's Army,' wrote another scribe. It was like reading your own obituary.

If I was going to quit, I decided, it would be on my own terms.

Anne and myself went for a drive in the Dublin Mountains. 'Mossy,' she said, 'are you going to retire?' I told her I would shoot the selectors and anyone else who stood in my way before I would give in.

'If it means that much to you, Mossy,' Anne said, 'keep

at it or I will shoot you myself.' Anne was from a rugby background and understood how much I put into the game.

I had no problem with the concept of retirement, I knew it was inevitable, but I still felt I had a few good years left in me. Except for my ankle. When it did not respond to conventional treatment, there was only one thing for it, and I hit the road for the Druid of Dunboyne, Sean Boylan. I drove up to Meath on one leg, even though I had been warned off driving, but I was in the kind of mood where I would listen to no one.

Sean sent me back down to Dublin with a specific rehabilitation treatment: I was to take up paddling. Cold seawater was the best cure for an ankle injury, he said. I did what I was told. I had great faith in him since his help in curing the touch of hepatitis I had suffered after the Lions' tour. Sean looked at the whole man, from the head down, and he was also used to dealing with athletes at different stages of their careers. He knew how to treat me. Even though he was a quietly spoken, almost shy man, he had great presence and was a hugely calming influence on me. I would trust him with my life.

I paddled every day in Dollymount Strand, for half-an-hour, even though the cold was unbearable that November. I rolled my tracksuit bottoms up above the knee and just walked in. I was afraid I would be recognised, so I put a woolly hat over my head and pulled it down over my eyes. My hands went deep into my pockets and I twisted an old woollen, green-and-gold scarf around my neck. If I saw anyone heading in my direction I pulled it up over my face like a mask. I was afraid that if someone saw me paddling in mid-winter they would think I was going mad.

I was even more afraid of the sea than being spotted. I have always had too much respect for the water and after my most recent attempt to learn to swim in Fiji, when I nearly drowned, I was more afraid than ever. Even when my mother brought us to the beautiful beach in Ballybunion for the week's holidays every year I never ventured in above my knees. The waves in Ballybunion are full-blooded Atlantic waves but the ripple in the Irish Sea is no more truculent than a fart in the bath. Irrational as it might seem, if there had been big waves in Dollymount I would never have been able to go through with it and my rugby career might have been over.

One day I decided to walk down near the rocks on Dollymount. It was further away from the car park and a bit more secluded. Before I knew it I'd stumbled on a courting couple who were doing a bit a more than courting. The two ran off as fast as they could when they saw me standing there, laughing.

I visited Sean regularly, and he would massage my leg and apply a poultice, the recipe for which was handed down to him by his father. The leg was not improving but I kept at the paddling and never missed a day. I also made sure I didn't drink any alcohol or eat too much, and in fact I lost a few pounds.

While I was at the thalassatherapy, Munster beat the Australians in the 1981 match, thus maintaining our proud record against touring sides. Foley and new boy Donal Lenihan were outstanding in the second row and were quite rightly picked to play for Ireland. Both played exceptionally well in the international. Even though Ireland were beaten by Australia, I thought it more significant that we owned the ball and our pack had the better of the opposition. We were very unlucky not to win, losing 16–12. It was Donal's first Cap and the beginning of a long and illustrious career in the green of Ireland and the red of the Lions.

It wasn't looking good for me either, but I had it in my head that if I could make it back for the final trial in late

December I would at least show the selectors I was over the worst of my injury. I would then have about two weeks to get myself into shape for the first game against Wales in early January '82. Not an ideal preparation, by any means, but it was all I could hope for. I took a risk and played for Lansdowne the week before the final trial teams were to be picked, even though I hadn't trained in nearly two months. Gibbo remarked that he would carry me around the pitch if necessary. The Lansdowne lads covered up for my lack of fitness. To impress the Irish selector watching from the stands a few of the boys in the pack would shout, 'Well played, Moss,' every time we won a ruck, even though I might have had nothing to do with retrieving the ball. I just about got through the game even though the ankle was still very painful. Immediately after the match I headed for Sandymount Strand, no more than five minutes drive from Lansdowne Road, and stood like a heron in the gathering dark, with the hat pulled down over my eyes. I cursed and thanked Boylan at the same time. The leg was definitely improving, but not fast enough for me.

That night I picked up the newspapers and discovered I was picked for the Possibles, or the second team, in the following Saturday's trial. I took back what I had said about Boylan, and said a prayer of thanks for Sean and Lansdowne.

I played well in the trial, too. The ankle wasn't 100 per cent right but I was getting there. Ciaran Fitzgerald captained the Possibles and we won. I had been careful not to do anything wrong during the game, but the question was had I done enough to make the team? Back to Sandymount for another freezing paddle. More cursing Boylan as I shivered and pondered my future while the lights of the electricity station winked at me in the dark.

Tommy Kiernan phoned the following morning. Usually when you received a phone-call from the coach it meant you were dropped. My heart sank to my socks when I heard his voice on the other end of the phone.

'Congrats, Moss. You're back,' he said in his refined Cork accent. 'I know you won't let me down.'

'You can be sure of that, Tommy.'

But doubt set in after the initial elation had worn off.

I went to the New Year's Eve party in Lansdowne that year and the place was packed. At midnight we all linked hands and sang *Auld Lang Syne*. I was wondering if they might be singing it for the end of my rugby career. I was still not happy with my fitness. And Ireland had an awful record against our next opponents – the Welsh.

TWELVE

The Triple Crown 1982

I knew I'd been lucky to get on the team for the Welsh game. I always got on well with Kiernan and of course we had that bond from the Munster win over the All Blacks, not to mention the game we drew against the same opposition in 1973 when Tommy was captain and full-back. I had it in my head to tell him I might not be able to last 80 minutes of international rugby – the last thing I wanted to do was let him down. Kiernan was always straight with his players and he expected the same back in return.

I found myself in the Carmelite Church in Clarendon Street, off Grafton Street, where I lit a candle and said a few prayers to think it over. I had trained hard but it was a crash course in getting fit. I might have managed to get by with such a training binge ten years before but the mileage clock had gone around a good few times since. It was the Monday before the Welsh game and it was make-up-your-mind-time.

By the time I got back to my workplace, just down the road at Harcourt Terrace, my prayers had been answered. My colleagues in the lab I was supervising at the time told me there was a blizzard forecast, the kind of snowstorm that only hits Dublin once every 20 or 30 years. When the snow kept falling, the game was called off, rescheduled for a week later. Hallelujah! The extra few days made all the difference.

I had been about to phone Tommy and tell him I wasn't up to it. It was that close.

The weather was so bad I could barely train, and sprinting was impossible – so no change there – but the delay gave me the extra time needed for the ankle to heal. I went out every day and did as much as I could. It was eerie training in Lansdowne in the snow. There was no traffic but it still took me two hours crawling to get across the city. The country was brought to a standstill. Shops, offices and schools were closed. Squad training was cancelled. After about four or five days there was a thaw, and I drove down to Kerry for a funeral.

'Where are you going with that bucket?' my father asked as I left our farm in Currow for Dublin.

'Banna,' I replied. All through the worst of the weather I had kept up the paddling.

Banna Strand was about half an hour's drive from Currow. I filled up my bucket with seawater – there were big waves and I didn't like the look of them – and stood on the shore with one leg in the bucket. A man approached me.

'How are you, Moss?'

I didn't know him but from his accent I knew he was a local. 'Are you a doctor?' I replied.

We discussed the effects of the Gulf Stream on the Kerry microclimate and how it had helped the county escape the worst of the ice and snow. The rugby match came up for mention, and as he took his leave the man wished me 'the very best of luck' on Saturday against the Welsh. He never said a word about what I might be doing standing on Banna Strand with my leg in a bucket of seawater.

We needed all the luck we could get for that Welsh match. The man I met at Banna was no different from anyone else in the country when he told me he didn't fancy our chances. We were written off, for the most part, in the newspapers.

That suited us fine – Irish rugby specialised in ambushes.

Ciaran Fitzgerald, an Irish Army man, was named as captain. Ollie Campbell was out-half – Tony Ward had done well against Australia the autumn before but Ollie got the nod before him. Mossy Finn came in on the wing with Trevor Ringland on the other side.

Trevor was a relatively new boy. He was on his second Cap and there were certain induction formalities to be upheld. We organised the set-up at a squad session, after which I was put sitting beside him at dinner. He was a small bit in awe of us all. Only a year or two before he had been watching from the schoolboys' section of Lansdowne Road. He was only about 20 at the time of his first Cap and studying first law at Queen's University, Belfast. Fitzy gave me my orders.

'You are going to have to do this well, Moss,' he said. 'This fella is a bright boy, a top student, honours all the way.'

The moment we sat down at the table, I gave Trevor his first full-frontal experience of a Kerry accent in full flow, and went on to talk rubbish at top speed for a full five minutes. 'And what do you think of that yourself?' I put it to him when I'd finished.

'You're dead right, Moss, dead right,' he said, wondering how he'd get away from me. He was ribbed unmercifully for that, but he knew he was now one of the boys. There were great spirits in the camp, and we also shared a little secret no one else in the world of rugby was privy to – we knew in our hearts we were good enough to beat the Welsh if we performed to the best of our abilities.

One thing I noticed in the last squad session before the game was that the backs were flyers. Without pace in a back line, you have nothing. You can coach everything except speed, and we had a few naturals who turned the game: Moss

Finn, a schools' sprint champion, scored two tries, and Ringland, unstoppable from 20 yards out, scored another. Ollie Campbell was brilliant as usual – the only bad game he ever played for Ireland was in his first cap, and that was due to inexperience. He made both tries and kicked like a Kerryman. I played reasonably well and lasted right through until the end, despite the ankle.

I was kind of humming to keep myself going. The Welsh thought I was a bit crazy and maybe it suited me to let them think I was, as they left me alone. If they thought I was teasing them they would have let me know soon enough. It was like one of those films we used to go to in the Astor cinema in Castle Island long ago, where the mad lunatic of a singing cowboy is allowed to ride his mule unmolested through Apache country.

Fitzy left me alone too; he knew the humming was keeping me on the field. And I didn't want to leave it. We had got our arses kicked so often in Cardiff, it was sweet to beat my old tormentors by 20 points to 12. The minute the final whistle went I was totally exhausted, but I hadn't allowed myself to feel tired until then.

I was so worn out after the game I couldn't walk into the shower. I just sat on the bench, my legs weak under me. Ginger McLoughlin dragged me up and helped me into the shower area.

'Jesus, Moss, I'm lifting you up in the lineout all day and now I have to lift you into the shower,' he said.

It was in fact young Donal Lenihan who had won the aerial battle in the lineout, while I rode shotgun for him. We struck up an immediate understanding on the pitch. Donal was half Kerry; his father, Gerard, was a Listowel man and a former Irish boxing champion, as well as a noted GAA player. I said to *The Kerryman* newspaper afterwards that 75 per cent of the second row was from Kerry and that was the winning of the game.

I was only just out of the shower when the news came through that David Irwin, who had been carried off early, had broken his ankle. It was a terrible blow. My old roommate in the 1979 tour of Australia was playing the greatest rugby of his career. He was replaced by Tommy Kiernan's nephew, Michael, who came on for his first cap. Michael was a different type of player to David, but he had incredible pace and was to prove equally effective. Michael had won the Irish senior 200 metres championship the year before and would have made the Olympics had he kept at running. Even so, Paul Dean was as fast as him over 20 yards. Deano was the fastest man I ever saw to go from 0 to 60 from a standing start and he had the hands of a magician.

The celebrations went on long into the Dublin night, but I took it easy. I knew we had a chance of achieving something special that year, and anyway I was knackered. When I took off my shoes before going to bed the bad ankle was swollen to twice the size of the good one. I had two weeks to go before the next game, England at Twickenham on February 6, 1982. I couldn't train very much but, against England, I could run on empty for miles.

There was, as ever, an incredible atmosphere around the ground. You have to remember that Twickenham isn't really like an away game. It's more like another home game. There are nearly as many Irish in Twickenham as English. Thousands travel over.

Our pack was well on top and we took the game with a forward's inter-passing try deep into the second half. It was scored by Ginger McLoughlin, the only man I know who has three names: his mother christened him Gerry, the press christened him Ginger and Shannon RFC called him Locky. He was as good as three men in any event, and after scoring that famous try he told us that he not only carried the English

pack on his back but the Irish one as well. There was no
doubt he scored the try but the truth was that the referee
couldn't see the touchdown, so technically he should not
have awarded a try. Nowadays the referee would have referred
the decision to the video referee and the try would not have
been awarded. But when it's your year, it's your year. As the
ball went over the line we all jumped in the air with delight
and ran back to the half-line as if there was no doubt that
Ginger had managed to touch down.

We had scored a comprehensive victory by one point.

Twenty-five years on, I found myself sitting next to him
at a reunion, and I asked him if he really did touch down the
ball that day. There was only the two of us there just then.
'It doesn't matter, Moss, whether I did or not, once the referee
thought I did,' he said. It came as no great surprise to me
when he won a seat on Limerick City Council in recent
years.

Hugo MacNeill, another of the new boys, in just his
second season, scored a great try too that day. I don't think
he ever dropped a ball for Ireland and he never missed a
tackle. I was a bit worried the first time I met him when he
told me he was acting in a Beckett play in Trinity, but I
knew he was sound the minute he took to the field.

And Ciaran Fitzgerald was a great captain. I got to know
him well because we lived near each other and trained
together nearly every night, once my ankle started to come
good. He knew how to get the best out the troops. By then
I could motivate myself, but Fitzy could drag out that bit
extra. He never bullied; he encouraged and cajoled, and
reserved the effing and blinding for times of special need.
Then he would go ballistic. We all looked up to him, even
though he was the smallest man in the pack and only in his
second full season at international rugby.

All through the game against England he kept repeating

two instructions: 'concentration', which was fair enough, and 'fuck us', which I found a bit strange. I couldn't figure it out – Fitzy was always so positive. As a senior player I felt it was my solemn duty to raise the matter with him. Fitzy got a fit laughing when I asked him what was wrong. 'Focus! That's what I was saying,' he told me. It was the new buzzword. Naturally I hadn't heard it.

Fitzy also hammered home to us that some of the journalists were describing us as a Dad's Army and our reputations were on the line. If you were to believe the press Slatts, Phil Orr, Willie and myself were all drawing the pension. For some reason John O'Driscoll was included in this group too, even though he was a few years younger. Guilt by association, I suppose. In fact, Philly had matured into the best man in his position in the world of rugby. Despite the critics' contention that it was harder to get off the Irish team than on it, I can say with my hand on my heart that no team in the world would have taken us that day. England, remember had won the international championship two years previously and came close to repeating their victory the following year.

I went down to Camden Town later on that night for a few pints. I stood out a bit in my dress suit, with my nicely developing shiner, courtesy of a retaliatory strike that was much deserved. Rugby was never the game of choice of the Irish builders in England, many of whom would see it as a foreign game played by public school boys. I wasn't surprised when a ganger-man came up to me and said, 'Moss, it's an awful shame to see a big lump of a man like you wasted playing that oul' rugby. You'd be a great man at feedin' a cement mixer.' Then he bought me a drink. I didn't have to buy another all night. I had met emigrants from Kerry in 'The Crown' in Cricklewood, when I was over before, decent, hard-working people who had to leave home because there was no work and no hope of work for them there. I always thought of them when I was up against England, and knew how much it meant to them when we won. Every man and woman I met watched the game on television.

I missed almost all of the official dinner thanks to my jaunt to Camden that night but my timing was impeccable – the speeches were just over when I arrived.

The build-up to the final leg of the Triple Crown was something I had never experienced before, not even in New Zealand. We were swamped with requests for tickets. The Scots were going to be tough opponents – they had drawn with England and had a good record against us. One great point in our favour was that the game was to be played at Lansdowne Road. Dublin was rightly regarded as the best city for a Five Nations' game at the time. A new generation of younger fans had latched onto the team and they were the loudest supporters in the land. You could come into the ground half an hour before the game and no one would be present, then five minutes before kick-off the place would be full, and all the fans singing. It was as good as a six-point start to us.

A general election was held around the same time as the match, but the game took up more newspaper columns. The publicity and the hype never bothered me – in fact I thrived on it. I enjoyed when people come up to chat about the match in a positive and supportive manner. It was especially nice now, because we had taken a good deal of abuse from pub experts in previous years. As I said all you could do was finish up your pint and move off, but I won't say I didn't take any notice, because I did. It hurt all of us in the team, which was bad enough, but our families felt it as well. Most people were good even when we were in defeat, but as is often the case, it's the gobshites you remember.

Billy Beaumont, my good pal, was out of the game

through injury, and in fact he would never play again. One day before the game he rang me to wish me luck.

'Moss, this is it,' he said. 'You have to win this one.'

He knew how to do it, too.

'You have to wear them down in the tight, Moss. Wrestle for every ball. If you let them play a loose, fluid game they will be very hard to beat. Keep on your feet as much as possible or they will foot-ruck you to bits on the floor.'

He paused to see if this advice was sinking in.

'We only pass this way once, Moss. If you win they'll build a statue of you in Cork.'

'Billy, you bollix,' I pointed out, 'I'm a Kerryman.'

I genuinely believed the whole rugby world was behind us. The only problem was that we were now favourites for the Triple Crown and Irish teams usually kept their best performances for days when everyone had written us off. But we had a nice mix on the team. The new boys were all sound, intelligent men and the rest of us had been through every kind of carry-on, both on and off the pitch. In the days before the Scotland game, Slatts and O'Driscoll, Willie, Philip and myself talked a lot about the Dad's Army tag and the gobshites who upset us in pubs. There was no doubt that it annoyed us intensely. I can never figure out why sports' people are described in the newspapers as 'veterans' when they're only in their early 30s. I'm in my 50s now and I reckon it will be a good few years yet before I can be called a veteran. Fitzy, of course, kept the pot boiling. He might drop a comment casually in conversation and then leave us to ourselves.

Tommy Kiernan was as solid as ever. He exuded a quiet confidence. He never raised his voice and when he spoke he didn't say too much. Every man was pulled aside for a short private chat. Kiernan was fantastic in the week leading up to the game, always saying the right things and quietly

motivating each and every one of us. On the weekend before
the game a huge crowd showed up to watch us train. We
desperately needed a bit of privacy to practise back moves
and lineout calls. Kiernan sensed also that we were being
overwhelmed by the supporters' fervour. He organised some
secret sessions away from the hype. He was always sensitive
to our needs as opposed to our whims, and he trusted us as
players. The night before the match I went up to Sean Lynch's
pub in Aungier Street, about ten minutes' walk from the
hotel, for a few quiet pints. I assured Kiernan I would be
home early; I just wanted a sociable pint to get me off to
sleep.

Sean Lynch knew the score, and spoke about anything
and everything except rugby.

I stopped at Paul Andreucetti's family chipper for a one-
and-one on the way back. Paul was a fine centre for St Mary's
and Leinster in his day and was part of the squad for the
1979 tour of Australia. There was no charge for the fish and
chips. I signed autographs on greaseproof paper for a few
fans in the chipper and was back in bed in the Shelbourne
for 12 o'clock as promised. But for the first time since my
first cap in Paris all those years before, I failed to get myself
to sleep. I thought of the great players before me who had
never won a Triple Crown. I thought of my family at home.
I thought of the goodwill in the chipper and the
unquestioning support of the fans. The worry of letting any
of them down kept me awake for a long time that night.

The Triple Crown decider against Scotland is a bit of a
blur. To this day I can hardly bear to watch the game on
video in case I see myself making a mess out of something. I
remember the Scots came at us and scored a try. I know
Ollie scored 21 points and one of those was a drop goal
from a move the backs had been practising since January
but kept secret until the Scottish game. We should have

scored a try, but the three points from the drop goal kept us ticking over. I'm certain we won the battle of the packs. We did as Beaumont and Kiernan counselled and kept the Scots from running all over the place. Ollie kept them pinned in their own half with his astute tactical kicking. He could control a match better than anyone else I know – the Scottish pack must have had a collective crick in the neck from turning to see where the ball was heading.

We went six up, but Roy Laidlaw, who often tortured us in the past and would again in the future, made a break and set up John Rutherford to score a try. Andy Irvine kicked the conversion. We didn't panic, though; we were around too long for that. We just stuck to the plan.

Luck went our way when the Scots missed a few penalties – I gave away one of them. Much as they pressed to get back in the game, we kept it tight. We ground them down. The key was to hold the Scots in the rucks as long as possible by tearing, scraping and rooting. It was one of the things I did best. I kept pulling at opponents' arms and legs – it's very hard to attack a back line if someone has your arms and legs in the stocks. One of the Scottish forwards grew a bit agitated as a result of my tactics. 'Moss,' he pleaded, 'will you let ma arm go, I'm no a bloody chicken you're eating.'

We were just too physically strong for them. O'Driscoll was ferocious in the tight and in the loose. He was my man of the match, after Ollie. Slattery was everywhere that day. We let him loose and he caused mayhem wherever he went. Willie was – well, Willie. All I can say is that I was just glad he was playing for us. And Lenihan cleaned up in the lineout. It was a huge relief for me to have him there – I was more of a disruptive lineout jumper – and I left the artistic stuff to Lenihan and the back row. I saw something in him that day; Donal went on to captain Ireland and both play for, and manage, the Lions.

And Fitzy led. Scotland landed a penalty mid-way through the second half. The score was 15-9 and the Scots were beginning to get up a head of steam. I ended up on the ground. I had a sore lower back going into the game and it was beginning to stiffen up. I got up as quickly as I could, afraid that the inaction would make the back injury even worse. Fitzy, who was several inches smaller than me, pulled my head down towards his and put his forehead right on mine, pressing it in to my head as if he was trying to transfer his thoughts to me by some form of cerebral osmosis.

'Moss the lads are bollixed and so are you. Keep going. You have to. And don't be in any hurry getting going again, we badly need a breather.'

The thing about Fitzy was he had a private word with every one of us along the same lines. It wasn't that he was telling lies. It was the truth; we were tiring. But his words of encouragement were exactly the right thing to say at that time in the game, against a good, young Scottish team. Every one of us depended on each other. Journalist Val Dorgan later described the meeting of foreheads and minds between Fitzy and myself in the *Irish Examiner*:

'The brief tableau had an intense quality, as though suddenly reflecting all Ireland's hopes and fears for the long sought after Crown.'

The final score was 21–12. Ollie scored the whole damn lot – six penalties and a drop goal. It was a world-record points tally.

When the referee blew the final whistle all hell broke loose. Thirty-three years of waiting was over. We discovered afterwards that the ground was full, well beyond its capacity – police estimated 10,000 people gained entry on forged tickets – and the fans came swarming onto the pitch.

I was just happy we won and that I was part of it. I knew I was lucky to have won a Triple Crown but the emotion of the whole occasion left me drained. There was almost a sense of anti-climax about it. I thanked Tommy Kiernan and just sat in the dressing room not quite believing what had happened. The boys kept coming up to me, asking if I was alright. I shook hands with them – I couldn't talk. I was thinking of absent friends and how much I was looking forward to going back to Currow. I called Fitzy over.

'Hey, Fitzy. I'm the oldest so I'm taking the cup to Currow next weekend. No more about it – my mind is made up.'

'But, Moss, there is no trophy. The Triple Crown is a mythical trophy.'

'Is there a medal?' I asked.

'No, Moss.'

'You mean to say we went to all that trouble and they won't even give us a shagging medal?' I was genuinely disgusted. I'd a vision of myself standing up on the trailer of a tractor, holding the Triple Crown trophy aloft, while bonfires blazed all over the village. The Sergeant would allow the pubs to stay open all night and I would give a short, modest speech from a specially decorated creamery lorry. When I was back to form the following day the whole squad had a good laugh at me.

The country went mad – after all, it was Ireland's first Triple Crown for 33 years – but so did we. We had a month to the next game in Paris so we felt we had time to celebrate. There was a lot to distract us. One of the oddest was when some of us were invited to the Embankment in Tallaght when Russell Harty screened an episode of his English TV show in the pub. The show was basically a tribute to the family of the late Brendan Behan, and I still can't understand where we came in; in any case, it added nothing to our preparations for Paris.

Before we knew it the four weeks were up and we were togged out in Parc des Princes. The Grand Slam was there for the taking, but we played absolute shite – it was a bridge too far. France had lost all of their Five Nations' matches up to that point and they brought back all the old heads to avoid the humiliation of a whitewash. They played well, and we were hammered 22–9. To make matters worse, Willie was injured, even though his replacement, Ronan Kearney, also from Kilkenny, played as well as any one on the day.

I think we had mentally settled for the Triple Crown win. We had also won the International Championship for the first time since 1974. Back then the Grand Slam wasn't the main focus in Irish rugby; we felt it would be nice to win it, but the Triple Crown was always our real aim.

It was, I suppose, a very good year for me. Fitzy paid me a nice tribute some years later in an interview with John Scally in his book, *The Giants of Irish Rugby*:

> There were a lot of myths about Willie and Moss Keane at the time in terms of drinking and lack of training. That's rubbish. I was living beside Moss and was training every other night with him. I'm not exaggerating one bit when I say I was going flat-out just to keep up with him.

Stories about my drinking were greatly exaggerated. My favourite is the one where I was in a pint-drinking competition, where the aim was to drink eight pints in five minutes. I was supposed to have slipped off for a short while before coming back to drink the eight pints in world record time. When I was asked where I had gone, I'm said to have replied, 'I went out to the pub next door for a practice run, to check to see if I could drink a gallon in five minutes.'

I enjoyed a good night out, but that was that. I probably draw a bit too much attention to myself because of my size. It's very hard to have a few quiet drinks when you're six feet five inches tall – scrumhalves and wingers get away with murder. And admittedly I did go crazy in the last few weeks of the Lions tour in 1977. But that was 1977 and I began to look after myself from there on. I would never have lasted eleven years without missing a match in the Five Nations otherwise.

Fitzy said one other very nice thing in that interview, 'At the time, the young players looked up to Moss Keane like he was God.' Well, that was an exaggeration, but I like to think they had some respect for me.

There was a sad side to the year when Billy Beaumont retired. I missed him. The former English captain was the bane of my life on the pitch but we were great friends off it. His last words to me on a rugby pitch were, 'Keane, do you want to wake up with a crowd around you?' I had stood on his toe while he was jumping for a lineout ball – one of my favourite tricks.

Billy could take it as well as dish it out though, and we certainly gave it to him when nine of the Triple Crown team travelled to Fylde, Billy's home-town, for his retirement match. He was slagged by one and all, but none more so than Tony Neary, at the after-match dinner. A few years before that, Erica Roe, a fine buxom girl, had run across Twickenham topless in the course of an England game when Beaumont was captain and her picture had hit the front page of every tabloid in Britain. Billy had put on a bit of weight around his nether regions since we had last seen him and was well quartered, as they say of cattle and horses back home. Neary couldn't let the moment go, and reminded us all of the day he saw a woman running across Twickenham with Billy Beaumont's arse on her chest.

The year wasn't over yet. I was invited to play in Queensland during their centenary celebrations, an invitation I accepted without a moment's hesitation. I had hit it off very well with the Queensland boys when we toured in 1979 and did not need much excuse to go back to Australia. They came back again and asked me if I would captain a World XV to play against Queensland. To be asked to captain a team containing players such as Graham Mourie was a great honour. I headed for Australia with Ronan Kearney, who was the only other Irish representative on the trip. Ronan was about 23 at the time and he was in for a rapid matriculation.

We flew from Dublin to Heathrow and from there to Zurich, where a group of Spanish tourists joined us. Next stop on the itinerary was Jeddah, then on to Bangkok. I was going out of my mind with all the flying. I had a bottle of duty free whiskey in my bag and I uncorked it to shorten the journey. Ronan was slow to accept my hospitality but he accepted after I applied some pressure; I hated drinking on my own. The courier in charge of the tourists had pretty good English and I asked him to join us for a drink too.

Ronan and myself helped to cart him off the plane in Bangkok.

The trip to Oz was, as ever, enjoyable both on and off the pitch. I captained the World XV against Queensland. Fujiwara the Japanese winger came up to me and said, 'Moss I understand every word of your team talk but what do you mean by sheet or get off the pot.' It was a wonderful couple of weeks and a great lift to receive such respect from the best sporting nation in the world.

There was another trip later on that summer, this time to Barcelona for a rugby tournament just before the soccer World Cup. Anne and I headed over early to take a few days for ourselves, before the start of the tournament. We stayed in Salou, a seaside resort, and took the train from there to Barcelona. As we sat waiting for the train to leave I saw a man I knew walking up the carriage, even though I had never before been in Spain. It was the courier. He looked at me. I looked at him. He waved his hands in the air and shouted, 'No drink, no drink!' and ran off down the carriage. And that was the last I ever saw of him.

But just when everything was going well, I received some bitterly disappointing new. I was in Romania with Munster in the autumn of '82 when I received some bitterly disappointing news. We were working our way through our nightly repast of pork, tomatoes and beans – it was rough tack, that's for sure – when Edmund 'Ned' van Esbeck dropped a note by my plate and left in a hurry.

Written on the piece of paper was the score of the 1982 All-Ireland football final. Offaly had sneaked a goal by Seamus Darby in the last minute to deny Kerry the honour of becoming the first team in GAA history to win five All-Ireland titles in a row.

I looked around. It was time to shoot the messenger, but Ned had disappeared. Anne, being an Offaly woman, offered no consolation and I knew when I got home I was never going to be allowed forget it, which is true to this day.

THIRTEEN

Moving On

We knew coming into the 1983 season we would be favourites for everything from the Triple Crown to the Five Nations to the Irish Greyhound Derby. Ireland, it was said, never performed well when burdened with the weight of expectation, but I was delighted we were on top. After all, Kerry were favourites every other year for the All-Ireland Gaelic football championship and it never seemed to bother anyone in the county in the slightest. Coming off the winning year we had just had, I felt it would take a hell of a lot to beat us. The Triple Crown instilled confidence in the side. We knew Ireland were a match for anyone.

Our first game was against Scotland. They were improving all the time, and would go on to hammer us out of sight a year later to win the Triple Crown in Lansdowne Road themselves, but we won by two points. Our win was largely thanks to our back row of O'Driscoll, Slattery and Duggan. Slattery was the big man for us that day. I think he easily gave the greatest display I have ever seen by an open-side-flanker. The three lads played together for four seasons or thereabouts, lasting longer as a unit than any breakaway combination in world rugby. They were uncompromisingly hard but treated opponents fairly, provided this fairness was reciprocated; if anyone wanted to mix it, though, they would meet no harder men.

We took on the French in the second game. Moss Finn had had a marvellous game against Wales the previous year. He'd scored two tries, yet he has no recollection of either – he was concussed accidentally in a tackle and I made the situation worse when I clattered into him later on. He scored two great tries again against France that day.

We went for almost all the French forward pack that day. It was revenge for the battle in Paris the year before. I really enjoyed a rough game, and had one of my better performances against France, almost increasing my try scoring record by 100 per cent. I was mooching around at the back of a ruck, just yards from the French line, when I ripped the ball from a Frenchman and went for glory. John O'Driscoll, who had the shit kicked out of him in the very same ruck, was at my shoulder. I was about to fall over the line and score when John ripped the ball from me. The ball was slapped to the ground and bounced forward. Knock on. Scrum to France. I was livid.

'John,' I asked, 'do you mind my asking, old friend, why it was you decided to take the ball from my grasp just as I was about to double my try tally for Ireland?'

O'Driscoll's reply I can quote verbatim.

'Ah, sorry, Mossy. I was hit so hard I thought we were on the 22 and I wanted to get the ball further up the field before you fell over it.'

I could only laugh. I told O'Driscoll afterwards he should get the shit knocked out of him more often – he had one of his best ever games in a green shirt. And as for the third member of the back row, Willie Duggan, he was his usual powerful self.

In fairness to this French side, they never stood back. It was tough stuff but great sport. I spoke to several of them after the match, as I always did. Jean Pierre Rives was a close friend of long standing. We often had long talks and never had any bother understanding each other. How is it that the English, Welsh and Scots claimed they couldn't make out anything I said whereas the French could understand nearly every word?

We won the match 22–16; our first win over the French in eight years. But our next game, against Wales at Cardiff, was an unqualified disaster. We started well but we kept giving away penalties. We were too fired up. We had not won in Cardiff for years and the desire to win clouded our judgement. That said, we were very disappointed with the refereeing. There had been a big commotion after the French game and the ref never took his eyes off us. Wales were the better team on the day, eventually winning 23–9.

Kiernan was furious with us after the Welsh game. He believed in the Irish way of playing rugby, but he'd insisted that passion had to be tempered with control. 'Keep your head in the fridge and your heart in the fire,' he told us.

As the England game approached Kiernan and Fitzy hammered home the need to keep our discipline and not give away any penalties against England. We were down after our Welsh defeat, but they kept saying that even though the Slam and the Triple Crown were gone, we could still win the Championship.

At one team meeting, Kiernan said we were straying offside far too often. I put up my hand. 'Tommy,' I asked, 'how do you expect us to beat the English if we don't play offside?'

Ginger McLoughlin answered on Tommy's behalf. 'We'll take them by surprise, Moss, with new tactics. They won't have a clue what to do if we play according to the rules.'

There had been calls for changes to the team for the game against the English at Lansdowne, but though the selectors were very disappointed with our performance against Wales they fielded an unchanged side.

Ollie kicked 21 points against England before he went off injured. In came Wardy, and I remember the look on the English faces when he came on – talk about out of the frying pan and into the fire. England paid for our frustration at the Cardiff defeat – we won by 25-15, even though we gave away five converted penalties. It was a much improved performance.

I had a strange feeling coming off the pitch. I knew that this was about as good as it was going to get. I said to myself, retire now, Moss, while you're on top. It would have been a good way to go, all the more so as we shared the Championship with France that year. And we'd beaten them so we were the moral victors. And when Tommy Kiernan announced he was retiring as coach, having given Irish rugby the most successful couple of years any of us had ever known, I would have been going in good company.

The Lions toured New Zealand in the summer of '83 but I wasn't picked for the tour and didn't expect to be. It was a shorter tour than in 1977 and part of me would like to have gone, just to take one last crack at the All Blacks. Of course they had the finest, driest winter on record for that tour. Instead I was given the consolation prize of a trip to the South of France with the Welsh touring side Crawshays, a type of Welsh Barbarians. Moss Finn, who should have been off with the Lions, was picked to go along with me. We were the first non-Welsh players to travel with Crawshays, and we felt quite honoured.

When we arrived to play in some small place near Lourdes, I suggested to the Welsh heathens that we should all go see the town where Our Lady appeared. They were respectful and deeply impressed, as was I; I filled my kitbag with bottles of holy water to take home. The spiritual impact of the shrine didn't last long, though.

Next day when we played the local team, and a supple, athletic young lad was simply cleaning me out in the lineout. I barged into him a couple of times to try to knock him off his stride. It was nothing nasty, but very annoying for a clever player who liked to keep on the move. I had played often enough against the French to realise what was going to happen next. The young lad threw a haymaker. I saw it coming and ducked. He connected with Lawrence Delaney, the Welsh international prop instead.

The Welsh and the French never got on too well and that ill-feeling had been simmering beneath the surface up until now. Once the French struck, a mass brawl broke out. I took a step back. They beat into each other but I stayed well away from the front lines.

Moss Finn was most aggrieved that I hadn't got stuck in. 'You cowardly fecker you why did you keep out of the mill. Where were ya, ya langer ya?' he pointed out in a most aggrieved Cork tone. Moss himself was sporting the makings of a shiner.

'Moss, my friend,' I responded, 'it's one thing to die for Ireland, but I have absolutely no intention of dying for Wales.'

As the year went on I started to get the feeling that I'd had the best of the year already, after sharing the Championship and having a great summer. When Willie John McBride, my old second row partner and one of the finest players ever to wear the green of Ireland and the red of the Lions, was appointed Ireland coach at the start of the new season he had an impossible act to follow. He was taking over the team in the wake of Tommy Kiernan, the best coach I ever played under. I knew Willie John would find it difficult to drop me; we had been through so much together. I should have made the decision for him; I should have retired. Instead I decided to hang on. After all, I had never been dropped or

missed a Five Nations' game through injury and I felt I was
worth one more season. It was a major error of judgement.

Some of us had thought Mick Doyle might have been
picked for the job – he was in charge of a hugely successful
Leinster side at the time. When I ran into my old neighbour
from Currow one day in town and I asked him if it was true
he was in contention as Ireland's coach.

'I am, Moss. It's down to me and Willie John.'

'Young Mick,' I said, poking him in the chest, 'just in
case you're thinking of putting me out to grass, don't forget
my mother used buy day-old chicks off of your oul' fella.'

My mother had a great rapport with old Mick Doyle,
Mick's father, and bought chicks from him which she reared
in our garden.

In the end Willie John won the vote, if he can be said to
have won anything. We were an ageing team and this extra
season would do for us. I was in good shape. I had trained
hard that summer and enjoyed a short tour with the Welsh
lads, but eight of the others had gone on the Lions tour to
New Zealand and it took a lot out of them. Tony Ward and
Ginger, who should have been on the team to begin with,
had gone out as replacements. The tour hadn't gone well.
Fitzy was the victim of an unfair campaign to have Colin
Deans of Scotland installed as hooker and captain in his
place. Fitzy had been undermined from the start and wasn't
the same man on his return and Ollie Campbell had started
to get hamstring trouble. Willie John was dealt an impossible
hand.

The international season got off to a terrible start in 1984
when France beat us easily in Paris that January. It was a
strange encounter with our Gallic rivals; there weren't too
many punches thrown that day. We had agreed to a truce in
the bar of The Shelbourne Hotel the night of the previous
year's match. The French had by then proven themselves to

be just as tough away from home as they were in Paris. I think they came to the realisation that once the final whistle went in Paris we would be counting the minutes to our revenge in Lansdowne the following year, where retribution would follow as surely as night follows day. In one sense I was disappointed because when the French started fighting they lost concentration.

Slattery was dropped and replaced by Willie Duncan, a good young player, but it left the boys of the old brigade one down. Slatts never played for Ireland after that. I suppose it could be said we won't ever see his like again. He was one of the greatest players I ever played with. It saddened me so much to see him dropped. I thought our army would last forever. There was a lesson there somewhere. Jump before your pushed, maybe.

Then Wales beat us. Fitzy was hurt and Harry Harbison of Bective came in for him. Harry didn't weaken the team in any way; in fact, he was a superb player and a fine lad but I missed Fitzy all the same and he missed the rest of the season. Then Ollie went off – his hamstrings were troubling him again – and that was the last time he ever played for Ireland. Another cornerstone gone as the house came tumbling down around us. I was beginning to realise it was all coming to an end.

It was a disappointing day and the night was worse. I was standing around disconsolately in the foyer of the Shelbourne Hotel when I saw Richard Moriarty, the Welsh second row come in the revolving door, dressed in full dinner jacket and dickie bow. He was grinning. Not smirking; just grinning, happy he had won that day. I was frustrated and in bad form, and I had some unfinished business with Richard – nothing personal, just a balancing up from the field of play. Something just snapped inside me. You let nothing go, that was my first lesson with Munster and I had a feeling I would never play against Richard again. I can't even remember what it was that I was so sore over. In that instant I made up my mind. I let fly. Richard side-stepped but Eddie Butler, the Welsh number eight, did not – he was downed by friendly fire.

I just couldn't believe it when it happened. How could I have done such a thing? Eddie was not only the thinking man's number eight but one of the nicest man you could ever meet. He was tough on the field but never mean-spirited. He was always the first man to come over to shake hands and buy a beer.

Now he was standing in the middle of the foyer of the Shelbourne Hotel with blood pouring from his mouth. I asked Eddie if he was all right. He was badly shaken, not so much from the force of the blow, but due to the fact that it was me who had hit him.

'I'm fine, Moss. But what did I do?'

'Nothing, Eddie,' I answered, 'it was Moriarty I was after.'

Eddie just nodded and I left the hotel.

I should not have thrown that punch. There was really no excuse for it. Fair enough if it was on the pitch but it wasn't. I am still embarrassed as I think back on it. Neither Richard or Eddie has ever mentioned the incident in public, but as the punch was in public, I feel the apology should be in public.

The following Monday I phoned Eddie. I learned over the weekend that he had damaged his front teeth and wondered if he would even speak to me. I apologised, of course, and offered to pay the dental bills.

'No need for that, Moss,' Eddie said. 'Just buy me a pint the next time we meet. I live near Cheltenham and you can stay with me any time you want to go to the racing festival.'

I haven't seen Richard since. Maybe I owed him the belt from his early days in international rugby. He had long since matured, though, and I was left wondering if maybe I hadn't.

It seemed that I was not going to find giving up, not just the game but the whole rugby way of life, as easy as I had thought. I knew in my heart I was past it, and yet I was beginning to have second thoughts about retiring at the end of the year.

I pushed it to the back of my mind again as we went to play the English at Twickenham, with Willie Duggan as captain for the first time. He handed me the ball as we lined up in the tunnel. It was my 50th cap. Did I ever think I would see that day when I was shivering on the sideline as a sub back in St Brendan's? But you tend not to dwell on such matters when you are still actually playing. There was a match to be played and, in international rugby, you are only as good as your last game.

'Off you go, Moss,' he said, 'and don't go too fast or you'll be worn out for the game.'

'No, you take it. It's your first day as captain.' But Willie handed the ball back to me. I handed it back to him. He refused to budge and both teams were held up. The television cameras were beginning to zoom in, wondering what was delaying the teams' entry onto the pitch.

'What's this?' asked Lenihan, who was standing just behind me, 'a game of pass the feckin' parcel?'

Willie put the ball back in my hands, and it struck me he would not give way even if it meant that the match was cancelled. It was more than just friendship – he had his old superstition that unless he was the last player out on the pitch, disaster would follow. I was seething. I hated being put in the spotlight, but I carried the ball onto the field all the same.

I will never forget the reception I received, not only from the Irish fans but from the English as well. It touched my heart, so much so that it was well into the first half before I could really find the necessary malice and badness to get properly stuck into the game. I was so sure we would win.

Whenever we were going really badly, we could be relied upon to beat England. This time, though, they got the better of us by a penalty.

We'd lost to France, Wales and now England. Scotland was my only hope of a victory in my last season.

Before the game I was having a chat with Willie. He said we'd won the toss and we got talking about which way we should play. There was a gale force wind blowing and Scotland were going for the Grand Slam.

'It will take the Scots 20 minutes to settle down and they'll lose half the advantage of playing with the wind,' I remarked.

Willie wasn't sure but I talked him into playing against the wind in that first half.

We went in, 22-0 down at halftime – sound advice how are you!

The Scots were up for it; not even the vagaries of the wind could stop them, and certainly not us. They gave us a hammering in my last international at Lansdowne Road and took the Grand Slam and Triple Crown in the process. I didn't begrudge them in the least. We always got on well, even if they were ferocious at times, and this was a great Scottish team, the best they ever had. It would have been a disaster for them if they had lost.

Eleven seasons playing for my country ended in serial defeat.

I would love to have gone out with a win, but if we had, I might just have kept on going. It's like when an atrocious golfer hits one good shot near the end, and it persuades him into thinking that maybe he will be the first 50 plus handicapper to win the Irish Open. My head still knew the direction, but my legs just wouldn't take me where I wanted them to go. I was even turned over in possession for one of the few times in my career. The Scots did Irish rugby and me a big favour; the following season a new Irish team won the Triple Crown under Mick Doyle's coaching.

I made my way alone through the thousands of Scottish supporters who had invaded the Lansdowne pitch. One man in a kilt came over to me and said, 'Thanks for the memories, Moss.' I was trying to get my jersey off to give it to him but he was swept away in the rush of his compatriots. A small boy asked me for my autograph. I signed it and tried a second time to take the jersey off to give it away, but the crowd just swept us apart. I walked into the phalanx of Scots players lining the route in time-honoured fashion to clap us off the pitch.

There were a few beers that night. Rugby wasn't mentioned and neither was retirement. I said something about waking up and smelling the roses – Willie threw his eyes to Heaven at that.

I announced my retirement later on, when I was safe in bed. I woke up at about five in the morning. Anne wasn't used to being roused on international nights, what with the effort of the match and the few beers and all that, and I kicked her gently when she didn't wake at the first time of asking.

'What's up with you, Moss?'

'I'm retiring, Anne.'

'Not again, Moss,' Anne replied, and went back to sleep.

Fergus Slattery, Willie Duggan, Robbie McGrath, John O'Driscoll, Ginger and myself all retired at the end of that season, without any discussion or common agreement. It was just in the nature of things. Dad's Army Mark 2 had finally been decommissioned.

There was one last tour before the end though. The Scottish Co-optimists – Barbarians in Scottish guise – brought Mike Gibson (Gibbo) of Lansdowne and myself along as guests on their tour of Zimbabwe in 1985. It was my second time in the country. In 1980 I'd spent a few weeks there on what could be best described as a rugby holiday. I was nearly the cause of drowning some of the finest rugby playing talent in the world when I arranged with the boat driver to announce that the brakes in our boat had failed and we were going to topple over the edge of Victoria Falls. We had a good few drinks on board – in fact, the bar ran dry – and I had to physically stop one man from jumping over the side in panic. I had kept a low profile for the rest of the night.

In 1985 I was delighted to have Gibbo with me as a back-up man. We were, of course, clubmates and the best of friends, international buddies as well. Tony Doyle from Greystones was another welcome addition to our group. Jonathan Davies of Wales was the only other outsider the Scots had brought along with them.

One second into the first match of the tour Gibbo and I collided while going for the kick-off. I was heavier so he got the worst of it. One word borrowed another and before we knew it we were trading blows. Jonathan Davies called us aside. 'Would you mind starting again, boys,' he said. 'I missed some of that.' Our hosts were astounded at our carry-on, and even more amazed when they saw we were inseparable during the rest of that trip.

There was another incident later on in the tour, in a hotel bar, when a Scottish international came up behind the referee and decked him. I was called to testify to the disciplinary hearing that followed. I had seen who struck the blow, though the tour manager had not. I told the inquiry I had seen nothing.

'But you were there! I saw you!' the manager exploded. But he didn't see who threw the punch.

'I was lost in my own thoughts,' I said, and so I was.

I was only home a few weeks when I received a call at work purporting to come from a man who identified himself to our receptionist as Ian Smith, the former Prime Minster of what was then Rhodesia but which is, of course, now known as Zimbabwe.

'Ian Smith here Moss.'

'And I'm Charlie Chaplin.'

I was sure it was a wind up. I was busy at work and didn't really have the patience for any messing that day.

'Ian Smith,' he said. 'I really am.'

'Ah fuck off,' I replied and put down the phone.

Ten minutes later he called back again.

'I only have a few minutes,' he said. 'I am under house arrest. I just managed to slip out for a little while and I'm calling from a payphone as my home number is bugged.'

I knew it really was Ian Smith when he said that. Robert Mugabe had taken over the country a few years previously and Ian Smith had been placed under house arrest ever since. Ian was a big rugby fan and I'd met him at the games I played in, on both visits. I'd told him Anne and myself were interested in spending some time in Zimbabwe as aid workers. I fell in love with the country and the people and I'd always wanted to do something that might help a little in Africa. Ian had promised to look into the situation and now he had a message for me: 'Moss you must not bring your family here. It is far too dangerous right now. I must go.'

I didn't even have time to thank him.

I eased myself out of rugby gradually. I retired from representative rugby, Ireland and the Lions, but I played one more season with Lansdowne after that. And when that was over, I didn't really miss playing all that much. I did my best, but I was beginning to recognise my own mortality. My body was beginning to give in. My shoulders were shagged, my lower back was crocked; I also had a bit of knee trouble. I had only about 70 per cent rotation in my neck and it stiffened up if I had to reverse the car for more than a few metres. The herpes, of course, paid its regular autumnal visit and a broken nose didn't help my sinuses – other than that I was in great shape.

When you begin to worry about your physical well-being, it's time to give up. I was a family man now. We had two lovely little girls – Sarah was four and Anne Marie was two. I loved spending time at home but I was away far too often. Anne was always up front and to the point.

'Moss,' she said one night, 'I think you should spend more time at home.'

I sat up on the sofa where I had been lying down exhausted for most of the evening, after a hard week's rugby.

'You're right, Anne', I said.

Point taken; but I knew myself by then what I wanted to do. If I was badly injured I would be anxious for my family. Up until then the rougher and tougher the game the better I liked it, but now I was just a different man, and the many stories of terrible rugby injuries troubled me.

Time had moved on and so had I.

FOURTEEN

Mugged

No one is perfect. After my last Lansdowne season I became an alickadoo, a word which is now part of rugby's vernacular. It describes a senior club member who wears a blazer and enjoys a couple of drinks in the company of his peers after watching a match and criticises all and sundry. By the end of the 1985–86 season I was a fully paid up member.

But it wasn't all about socialising. It was payback time as well. We all felt we owed the club so much. A few of us decided to take over the coaching of the Lansdowne under-19 team. The selectors were former Ireland star Mickey Quinn, Ray Hennessy, a superb full-back, Munster captain and final trialist, who definitely was good enough to play for Ireland, John Kelleher, who had a gift for logistics, and Moss Keane, esquire, retired. We set our sights on the McCorry Cup, the big competition at this level. University College Dublin and Blackrock College dominated it. UCD had a huge range of students to select from, while Blackrock could call on the past pupils of Ireland's greatest rugby nursery but we thought we'd a chance.

We four selectors had the added advantage of being friends – we never fell out on any issue that year and, following Con Murphy's example, we never missed a training session while we were in charge. The four of us shared a common vision, and we were all Lansdowne, through and through.

I drilled the forwards as best I could. We had a very small pack so I poached a winger, Killian Kavanagh, who was six feet four inches tall and built accordingly. I shifted him to number eight.

'But Moss,' he said, 'I never played number eight before.'

'My dear man,' I replied, 'I never even played rugby until I was 22 years of age. I didn't even go to a rugby playing school. So stop talking shite and do what you are told.'

We decided to concentrate on the basics, and were soon doing 70 or 80 scrums at each session. That wasn't down to me – the lads asked for the extra punishment. The emphasis in the lineout was on disrupting the opposition's throws. I might not have had the take-off skills of fellow Lansdowne man Gibbo – I had too big a payload – but I could mess up the best of them. I passed on the benefit of years playing destructive rugby to the lads.

One night we were practising 'a peel', a lineout move where the number eight tapped the ball down to the second row, Gary Ryan, who was then to circumnavigate the back of the lineout and swing around into the straits towards the out half position. My fellow coach was off with the backs practising ballet dancing, so I stood in as out-half just to give Gary a target. The plan was that he would 'turn and feed' the next player up, but Gary was so primed for action he went through me for a short-cut and left me sitting on my arse. The upshot of this manoeuvre was that I burst my knee and eventually ended up in the Blackrock Clinic. And, as if things weren't bad enough, I had only third party, fire and theft health insurance and had to fork out a small fortune to get the cartilage fixed up.

The slagging was nearly as bad as the pain. There was no mercy in Lansdowne for serial mickey-takers like me. Gibbo, who had bounced for many a ball I hopped in front of him over the years, gloried in my fall to earth.

'You mean to say an under-19 did what the All Blacks could never do?' he'd never tire of asking me.'

One Saturday morning not long after the operation, our entire squad was loaded into five cars, clad in full-playing gear. My driver, Ray Hennessy and myself refused to disclose our destination. I threw my crutches into the back of the car, glad to be off my feet. Hefting myself around on crutches was a frustration I could do without.

We drove off to the Dublin Mountains for a day in the bog. My bog, which I should have been tending all this time. Whoever coined that phrase, 'you can take the boy out of the bog, but you can't take the bog out of the boy,' wasn't far wrong. In Dublin it was a term of derision to be called 'a bogger' but I regarded it as a badge of honour.

Lansdowne held the most unusual training session in the history of the club in my bog that day. The under-19s, still dressed in full battle kit, loaded up the turf in relays, brought it home to my house in Rathfarnham and filled my turf shed to the roof. Then we went back to the clubhouse for a traditional Kerry post-turf feast – ham sandwiches and tea.

It is widely accepted that the day in the bog was the day we won the McCorry Cup. It was a great 'bondage' exercise, as a neighbour at home said when he heard that Kerry manager Páidí Ó Sé was bringing the team to Playa del Ingles in the Canaries for 'winter training'. We went on to beat Blackrock in the semi-final, and after an epic encounter got the better of a highly-rated University College Dublin team in the final. That under-19 win gave me as much satisfaction as any of the Gaelic football or rugby triumphs I enjoyed during my own playing days.

We kept at the training for three more years, but, though Lansdowne went close, we never won the McCorry again. In our last year in charge, we went 12-0 up against UCD, but the university side scored two second half tries and pipped us 13-12. It was heartbreaking on the sideline, as well as on the pitch, but our lads had given it their all and were a credit to the club. Conor O'Shea, the Irish international to be, was our best player but even Conor couldn't swing it for us.

I would have liked to win the Cup again. That was the way it was with rugby – you just moved on. I enjoyed coaching, but if I moved up another level or two it would mean I would miss out on time with the family. And I still had trouble figuring out the laws.

I always knew there would be another series of changes, with twists and turns. I am a great believer in fate and in the notion that sometimes what seems like chance has rhyme and reason to it. There have been many instances of this in my life.

Not that many years ago I was in a lift in Edinburgh after an Ireland v Scotland game, when a man asked, 'Do you know me Moss?'

'You have me at a disadvantage,' I replied.

'Well you should know me Moss. I was the referee who should have sent you off against France in 1975, in Lansdowne Road, when you punched that Frenchman in the eye. I was about to send you to the dressing room but something just clicked in my head and I said, "ah to hell with it I'll give him a chance."'

If I had been sent off I would have missed out on the rest of the season and maybe I might have been seen as an expensive luxury on subsequent Irish teams. And all this was a follow on from the fraction of a second when I was stamped on in Paris on the occasion of my first cap for Ireland. So much happens that there is no accounting for it at the time but when you look back on it years later you see there must have been a greater force at work.

There has to be.

I believe that same trail of fate took me to India when I visited Calcutta with GOAL, the sports charity that provides aid to under-developed countries. The time I spent there changed my outlook on life, just as much as any of the games in my rugby career had done.

My travelling companion was Conor Sparks, who played out-half with Blackrock, UCD and Leinster, and who was taking time out from his job to work with GOAL. We slept on the floor of Edith Wilkins's flat in the centre of Calcutta, near where she had helped establish a school for the street children of the city. Many of these kids, girls especially, were used in the sex trade, which was heartbreaking to see. Yet it was a profound, humbling and almost religious experience to watch Edith, a young girl from Cork, devote her life to these children's welfare.

I am very proud to have been able to help in some way. I'd been involved in GOAL from the beginning when John O'Shea set it up. John has Kerry roots and we became friends the first time we met. He can be blunt and abrasive when it comes to fighting for the interests of the disadvantaged, but if you peel away the outer skin you'll find he's all heart inside. He is one of the most remarkable men I have ever met and the organisation he founded has grown to the stage where it now operates on an international basis, providing support systems for the sick and suffering in the world's poorer countries.

John was a fine rugby player, but not quite as good as he thought he was, a very good tennis player and a sportswriter for the *Irish Press*. He is as opinionated about the game as he is about poverty and development aid. Ciaran Fitzgerald used to wave his articles about in the build-up to the big games – John was always sure to write something controversial, though he wasn't as good a judge of the game as he liked to think. There were a few men in Irish dressing rooms who would be ready to wallop him because of some over-the-top comment, but they always answered the call to help out with GOAL.

I met the most selfless people in Calcutta. Mick 'Bomber' Browne, a hooker for Blackrock and a hard man on the field, was there also, performing eye surgery. In many cases he was restoring sight to men and women who would otherwise have gone through life in darkness.

Everywhere we went we were pursued by beggars – small kids as young as five years went around on their own in the middle of the bustle of the city, begging for food or money. Their bones came out through their backs, as they hurried along on their stick legs with the begging bowls held out in front of them with their skinny hands. It was nearly too much to take. I was overwhelmed by the whole experience.

For all the good work done by GOAL there were times in Calcutta when I felt like my great-grandfather must have done when he was throwing the heads of cabbage from the back of his donkey and car to the poor and starving of my home place in 1847. But GOAL do make a difference, they really do. I've seen it for myself. It was good for me too. My involvement with GOAL and other charities eased that sense of conscience I think everybody feels at times.

The people of Calcutta had something going for them though, too, and that was their good humour and intelligence. They were the most beautiful people I ever met in my life. And anything you did for them was repaid by a smile that would melt your heart. The GOAL volunteers, or the Goalies as they are known, are not a bunch of do-gooders living in plush surroundings. They live right slap-bang in the middle of the city, among the people, and the money people contribute really makes a difference. Administration costs are shaved down to a minimum and the organisation is extremely efficient. Remember all this was going on long before the incredible miracles of Live Aid and Live 8. O'Shea was the first man to exploit the goodwill that exists towards sports' people for the benefit of the poorest of the poor and I'll always do as much as I can for GOAL.

John O'Shea was hassling the Government to increase Ireland's contribution to Third World aid long before anyone else and as far back as 30 years ago he could be very critical of corrupt regimes, sometimes at great personal risk to himself. He's no saint though. He likes a few pints and would drive you to distraction with some of his rugby comments. That's what's nice about him; he's human – but he does saintly things. But there's more to GOAL than John O. It's a whole worldwide network of, mostly young, people who give up a good chunk of their lives to work for GOAL. As I'm at it, if you have a few Euro to spare send it on to GOAL. You'll have great luck for it.

I wasn't long back from Calcutta when I went off to see my uncle, Canon Matt. He wanted to hear all about the India trip. We got talking about their beliefs and one of the things that came up was water divining. Some of the people I'd met in Calcutta believed in it, as did Canon Matt who is a water diviner himself; the sally rod twitches in his hands when he crosses water. I had known for many years that he had this gift. He had me at the water divining as well, when I was just a small lad. I could find water, though I used two metal rods. When I got near water the rods crossed over, without any help from me. About one in fifty people have this gift.

The water divining got me interested in the whole notion of magnetic fields and geopathic stress. I can walk around a house and tell by the twitching of the rods if there are underground streams running beneath the building. There can sometimes be a number of streams and if two streams cross it can cause a very negative effect on the people in the house, particularly when the streams flow under the bedroom. If today was yesterday I think I would have gone into this whole area of study in my science degree.

Uncle Matt reminded me of the stories about my Grand-uncle Nicholas or Uncle Nicholas as we used to call him. He was the seventh son and I believe he also had some kind of telepathic connection – he could sense that certain things were going to happen.

I will always remember one story Uncle Nicholas told me. He was working around the farm when my grandmother went into labour. He was in his early forties at the time and he was still living in the house. Everything seemed to be fine but Uncle Nicholas was almost at the highest point on the farm when he started to shake.

'I ran down to our house from the high fields. I was sure and certain your grandmother was dead. And the little baby too, Moss. Do not ask me how I knew because I cannot tell you. All I can say is that I knew for sure and certain they were dead. Imagine that. It was a terrible thing. When I got down to the house my brother Maurice, your grandfather, was a pale as milk. He was in shock and could hardly speak. I knew my premonition was true. Eventually he got it out: "Herself and the little baby died just a few minutes ago." And then he brought me into the room to say goodbye. She left two small children and the sadness of it would go through you. I never forgot that or the fact that I foresaw it, in a kind of a dream. Your father and Matt were only small fellas and had no memory of their mother. I just could not put it out of my head. And I still can't.'

That whole story had a profound effect on me, not just from the viewpoint that Uncle Nicholas had that terrible foreboding, but it also brought it home to me that such tragedies are still happening, all over the world. Even now, it's happening in lands where medical knowledge is far less accessible and facilities are even worse than they were here when my grandmother and her baby died, nearly 90 years ago.

* * *

A few years later Anne and I moved to Portarlington, County Laois, Anne's hometown. We were happy in Dublin but it was time to move on. Anne Marie and Sarah had always loved visiting Portarlington, and all their cousins and family. We soon settled in and we had the back up of Anne's family. I was a country boy again.

I set about building them a swing in our new garden. It took me half the summer to put it up but when it was finished I decided it was too dangerous. I'd noticed that the trees I'd used for support were riddled with Dutch Elm disease. Years later the girls remarked that they'd spent the whole summer looking longingly at the swing and wondering if the doctor had any cure for the Dutch disease. The girls were into sports and I did my best to encourage them.

As time went on we built an extension to the house which my daughters call 'a Kerry extension' as we started out with four bedrooms and finished up with three. But the house and the countryside around were just perfect. Though I would never be much good at household chores and child husbandry. Sarah and Anne Marie often remind me of the morning I chased them around the house with a fork. Anne was on a shopping trip to the city and I couldn't find a brush for their lovely, tangled long hair, so I went for the next best thing – a fork.

I was happy in Portarlington and in my job in the Department. I got on well with my colleagues and I always tried to put myself in the shoes of the people I was dealing with – except when I was on the rugby pitch. There you just had to concentrate on winning and you had to be ruthless, not just for your own sake but for your team. I often tackled a man very hard but you just could not allow yourself to feel any sympathy until after the game. Otherwise you wouldn't be able to do what you were supposed to do. But that attitude only extended to the field of play. I hold no grudges from my playing days and I have no enemies that I know of.

I never lost my temper in work though – if tensions or difficulties crop up in the workplace. I try to defuse the situation with some humour, even a touch of play-acting. One day a colleague was getting agitated over some work-related issue, and perhaps rightly so, though she might have overdone the complaining. I swept her up and put her sitting on top of the highest cabinet in the office. She couldn't get down – it was too high – and I left her there for a full ten minutes. By the time I took her down, she was not only calm, but also back to her usual good-humoured self.

Every day I took the hour-long train journey from Portarlington to Heuston Station in Dublin. Every evening I walked from work in Kildare Street back to the station and took the evening train home. I had become a commuter. It was a boring routine, a safe existence, and I loved it – the certainty of coming and going, the same thing every day. I would retreat into my own world as I sat on the train or walked to and from the station. Sometimes people would come up to me and ask if I was Moss Keane. And then I could spend a half an hour talking to complete strangers and finish up missing my train. Generally I just walked along uninterrupted, left to my own thoughts.

But there have always been outside forces at work in my life. Most were for the good, like my fortuitous introduction to rugby in University College Cork, and the detective work by Anne on the occasion of our first date, but some have been profoundly negative.

On a Wednesday afternoon in early September 1993, Ireland played Lithuania in a soccer international at Lansdowne Road. I was to go to the game, but changed my mind when I realised I wouldn't make it back to Heuston in time for the train home. Instead, I headed for a pub owned by Anne's brother-in-law Mel Timmons. Mel's was a pub I loved, but due to the limits imposed by the railway schedules, I didn't get to call in as often as I would have liked. The bar was busy with people watching the match and I stayed on for most of the game. Ireland played reasonably well; we went a goal up early on and by the time I left we had added another. I had a few beers, nothing more.

I asked Mel to cash a cheque for me before I left. I had won £200 in a draw and was going to use it as 'Moss money', a few quid the existence of which was known only to me and was kept solely for my own personal use and pleasure. Back in 1993, £200 was a nice tank; nowadays you'd hardly get a good feed for two in a high-class restaurant for it.

One of the good things about being a big man is messers usually never bother you – muggers and thieves tend to pick out the people they see as the weak and vulnerable. My apparent invincibility made me careless; I left the money up on the counter for a minute or two before I put the wad of notes in my trouser pocket. I think it was Mick Doyle who told me always to keep your cash in the front pocket. Doyler's theory was that if anyone sticks a hand in there, he or she would inevitably make contact with a sensitive area, and alert you to the danger.

I left before the end of the match. It had grown boring – Ireland was well in control and the Lithuanians were happy just to keep the score down. As I got up to go I remarked to a lad with a close-cropped haircut that he looked just like Roy Keane. I meant it as a compliment. I always tried to be extra friendly when I was in Mel's. He was not only Anne's brother-in-law but also a man who ran a good shop. But I knew by the surly expression of the Roy Keane lookalike that he didn't think much of Roy, nor of me for that matter. Maybe he had something against Keanes.

I slipped on my coat, put my hands in my pockets, and hit for Heuston and the 5.35 pm to Portarlington. It was dry and bright. I was early but I planned to watch the end of the match in the station bar. I'm not sure why I turned around. Maybe it was a sudden movement in my side vision or just pure chance. I turned and without warning was hit by a slingshot – a white plastic bag filled with a cement brick. The brick exploded in the bone in my right eye, just below the temple. For a second I thought I had been hit by a car. I staggered and almost fell. My legs felt weak, my vision was blurred and the sky was growing very dark. All they had to do was get at me and I was finished. I felt a hand go for my back pocket – the muggers obviously never played under Doyler – and I managed to let out a roar. It was a bluff. I thought I was finished; that the game was over, ball burst. Moss Keane RIP. But the roar did the trick. They ran off. I think I may have given one of them something to remember me by as they left, but I can't be sure. I am certain though, that they thought the blow would knock me out, and if I had not turned around it would have done it, or even smashed my skull.

I barely made it into the station. One of the staff came to my aid, and then the sky closed over me. I woke up in St James's Hospital.

'By any chance would I be in heaven?' I asked one of the nurses.

She was from Kerry and told me that if I thought working 12-hour shifts in an under-staffed accident and emergency department was heaven, the attack was even worse than the doctors had diagnosed. Her attitude reassured me. And it was good to know I was being cared for by one of the Kerry exiles, who always looked out for each other in the city.

I lapsed in and out of consciousness as I was taken to my next port of call, the Eye and Ear Hospital in Adelaide Road. There is no doubt that concussion does strange things to the head. The notion of heaven was stuck in my mind. I asked a nurse if she was an angel. 'No, Moss,' she said, 'I can be a right bitch at times.'

I had to be watched over for a night or two because I kept trying to get out of bed and go down the fields to give my father a hand driving the cows home for milking.

I came across wonderful people in both hospitals. I was minded like a baby. The nurses were great sport and never stopped slagging me over the fact that a big lump like me had been downed. Whatever nurses are being paid, it ought to be doubled.

I was out of danger after a few days but the vision still hadn't returned to my right eye. I recovered sufficiently however, to check my pockets and the money was still there. That gave me a great lift. The money itself had nothing to do with it; it was the thought that the muggers could have been enjoying it while I was lying on a hospital bed that bothered me most.

Anne and our daughters came in and the worry and love they had for me gave me another lift. That was a kind of a heaven all in itself, even if Anne succeeded where the muggers had failed. She put my blood-stained trousers in a plastic bag and the £200 in her handbag and mugged me without ever throwing a punch. The 'Moss money' that nearly cost me my life was spent on buying curtains.

The specialist, Mr Moriarty, came to see me not long afterwards.

'How are you, Moss?' he asked.

'Never better,' I replied.

Mr Moriarty advised me that, because of the trauma to the eye, he would have to wait a year at least before he could implant a new lens. Until then I would have to put up with blurred vision and headaches, but he told me not to worry. He said that in his professional opinion, from what he could gather from our many chats, I suffered from those same symptoms many Sunday mornings.

In the finish, I was more exhausted from the amount of visitors who called in to see me in the hospital than from the force of the blows. The nurses even had to send people away, but it was nice to know I had so many friends.

There were two important visitors from the Gardaí, two detectives, I think, and they were fairly sure they knew who had attacked me. But the whole thing had happened so quickly I just could not be sure about identifying anyone and there were no witnesses. I knew the fella with the close-cropped hair was there, but there were thousands of young lads with that hairstyle then, and I was afraid that my evidence might convict an innocent man. The police had picked up a few suspects in and around Heuston station, all of whom had form, but by that stage I'd had enough of the whole incident and wanted to let the matter drop. I also knew I might be walking to Heuston for a good few years yet. I was in my mid-40s now and had no illusions as to my own mortality. And Dublin was changing. I still loved the city but it was getting more violent. Criminals were using guns and there was a serious drug problem on the streets. Many of the city's Gardaí were incensed by the assault and wanted to do something about it but I could do no more. I just wasn't sure who did it.

'Did you know it was smashed to pieces Moss?' the detective remarked as he was leaving the hospital ward.

'What was smashed to pieces?'

'The cement brick. You must have a hard head, Moss.'

About ten days after the attack, Anne came to take me home. She was driving down the Naas dual carriageway when the back wheel came off an articulated lorry and raced straight for our car. Anne swerved; the wheel jumped a ditch and galloped off into a field by the roadside. There was no doubt about it; my number wasn't up just yet but we were both in shock. As we slowly drove home I reminded her we were all still alive and we would be the stronger for the experience. I was always fairly religious, but the mugging and the subsequent attempt on our lives by a runaway wheel persuaded me someone up there was looking after me. I hate to have to say it, especially for the perpetrators, but it took me a long time to get over the mugging.

Goosey Goosey Gander had upset me when I was a small boy threatened by Tom Bradley's gander and now the mugging spoiled a biblical tale for me. The girls were channel-hopping on a wet Sunday afternoon when the film David and Goliath came on the screen.

'Turn that thing off!' I ordered with notions of the slingshot in Heuston going through my head. They didn't have to be told twice. It wasn't that I was suffering from post-traumatic stress or anything like that. The thought that the muggers had got away without any retribution burned me up.

In September 1994 I had a new lens fitted in my eye by Mr Moriarty. He did a magnificent job and if he ever decides to pack it in as a surgeon he'll do very nicely as a comedian.

I'd decided to have the operation done under local anaesthetic. I was never too put out by a drop of blood and I have more stitches inserted in me than Frankenstein caught on the wrong side of a ruck against the All Blacks. I could feel the surgeon probing around the eye but I didn't take too much notice; part of me actually appreciated the experience, and I asked a lot of questions, probably too many.

'Will there be much blood, doctor?' I enquired, as he poked at the back of my eyeball.

'Don't worry, Moss,' he replied. 'I have my wellingtons on.'

My sight was soon back to normal and I have little if any trouble from the bad eye now, apart from a little weeping from time to time and the occasional blurring of distant objects. Things go a small bit out of focus sometimes because I have long-range vision with one eye and short vision with the other, and sometimes people think I am crying when I'm not, which can be a problem too. I went to a funeral lately, out of a sense of respect to a colleague whose mother had passed away. I didn't know the deceased lady and had never seen her until I said a prayer at her coffin in the funeral home. My eye was weeping a little and I took out a hankie to wipe away the tears. A colleague at the department turned to me and remarked, 'Moss, you're taking it very bad. I never knew yourself and the old lady were so close.'

It took me a while to get over the mental trauma of being attacked all the same. It upset me to realise that people would do such a thing to me. Mr Moriarty had assured me I could take a few drinks if I wanted to and there would be 'no side-effects other than a hangover'. I had suffered several concussions by then – there was the mugging, the concussion in New Zealand with the Lions, and an earlier con-cussion with Lansdowne in Vancouver, when I thought the scenery was moving when actually I was in the revolving restaurant of the Post Office Tower. They still slag me about that one in Lansdowne. But I was worried about my health. I decided, notwithstanding my surgeon's advice, to give up all alcohol for a period. I had another motive. I just wanted to prove to myself that I could do it.

I was always fond of a few pints but I simply decided it was time to take a break. I wasn't an alcoholic. I did like a drink and I still do but I'm one of the lucky ones – I can go off it whenever I want, though there are times when, to quote Doyler, I 'give it a lash'.

The weeks gathered into months and I stayed off the booze for seven years altogether. I was never more popular as a driver; the phone was constantly ringing.

'Moss, any chance of a lift?'

I went out to socialise, and stayed on in the pub enjoying the company. But when the foot-dragging and horseshit began late at night, I would issue my companions an ultimatum: 'Home now or I'll leave ye there.'

And sometimes I did. As one stranded friend said to me at the time: 'There's none so pure as the reformed whore.'

FIFTEEN

Parties, Presidents and Doyler

On July 27, 1998 I was the victim of a surprise party, an ambush organised jointly by Anne and my friend Mick Kearney. It was a set-up. I played golf that day at Druid's Glen with Ray McLoughlin, Dr Al Moroney and Gerry Culliton, all former internationals. The round was a treat. Miraculously, I won the money. After our game, as we were driving home Gerry Culliton told me he had to drop by Lansdowne to collect his son Ronnie, who was attending a club function. I went with him, but said I wouldn't go into the clubhouse; instead I hung around outside. I just didn't feel like attending a function for a young gang less than half my age. Three times I was invited in and three times I refused, and in the end Culliton came and said it would be a personal favour if I went up for just a minute.

'But, Gerry,' I complained, 'I don't know them, and most of them have never even heard of me.'

'Ah, Moss,' Gerry replied, 'you'd be doing me a big favour if you came in.'

In the end I gave way and went in with Gerry. We walked into a darkened room. On went the lights and at once there were some 400 people in front of me. I was going to run, but every man, woman and child in Lansdowne rugby club surrounded me. I had no way of escaping. Suddenly there were so many people, some I hadn't seen for years, that I didn't know where I was for a full minute.

Anne had rounded up people from every part of Ireland, including a huge wagonload from Currow.

My 50th birthday was one of the greatest nights of my life.

Gibbo came up to me at the end of the night, put his arm round my shoulder looked me straight in the eye and said: 'Moss, men find it very hard to talk about how they feel about other men in a platonic way of course.'

'Of course Gibbo,' I agreed. I had never heard Gibbo talk such shite before.

'Well I just want to say Moss, from the bottom of my heart, that you are without a shred of doubt… ' and he stopped for a moment as if to regain his composure. Then he continued, ' … Moss you are without a shred of doubt the worst lineout jumper who ever played in this stadium.' And off he walked delighted at having set me up for the seventeen thousandth time. I always said there was a cure for egos in Lansdowne.

Like Lansdowne my school will never really go out of my life. I often meet my old schoolmates from St Brendan's. The memories come flooding back every time you meet a man who was at school with you and the friendships made all those years ago are sustained and renewed. Tony Behan, who played for Brendan's in that Colleges' Final against St Mel's was principal of St Brendan's back in 1999.

'Moss is their any chance you could do me a favour?'

'Of course,' I replied, before I even heard what it was. I was and always will be a Brendan's man. Furthermore Behan was always nice. I had a few rough old days in St Brendan's, particularly in the early years when I was lonely for Currow but the good days gradually won the count.

I was a bit surprised though when he asked me to perform

the official closing ceremony of the boarding school section of St Brendan's in 1999. The school is still vibrant, with several hundred boys attending as day students, but there were only a few boarders left. I opened my speech by saying I still felt the pangs of hunger thirty-four years later as I entered the refectory, where the closing down ceremony was held.

I chatted with the students afterwards and they all spoke well of the school. It felt a bit strange though. A bookmaker would have given you huge odds that the small boy who was petrified of even getting up out of his seat to answer the knocks on the study hall door would now be bringing down the curtains on 138 years of educational history.

Jim Coghlan who followed me on to UCC from Brendan's remarked, 'Moss the reason you were asked back was that you ate more than anyone else.'

My boyhood friends from St Brendan's got a fair old kick out of that.

I have a few other good friends from way back. Sometimes I visit an old friend's house in Dublin, a big place with the biggest garden in the city. I lived in the same building as the *fear an tí*, the man of the house, years ago. Martin's a dentist now. Back in 1971, when I first got to know him, he played for Queens University Belfast against University College Cork in the Sigerson Cup final.

It was a strange Sigerson. We were beaten twice in the same weekend in a knockout competition, but after the first defeat, by UCD, we qualified for the final while UCD were thrown out of the tournament when they were found guilty of fielding an illegal player. But we knew nothing about the objection. All we knew was that we were out of the Sigerson, and so we decided to go on the rip. We finished late that night and started again early next morning, straight after Mass. Then, just a couple of hours before the match, word came through we were back in the tournament and playing in the final. We finished our pints, rushed back to our hotel to get our football gear, and went out to do our best against Queens. We almost beat them, but they won by just a point at the finish. If we had been better prepared things might have been different, though it must be said some of the lads commented that the few pints had helped to relax them for the game.

Martin played corner-forward for Queens. He was quick and smart and you couldn't mark him; he equalised for Queens with five minutes to go. It was the best score of the game, from way out on the wing. They scored another point to win 0-7 to 0-6.

When Martin subsequently qualified and moved to Dublin he was an occasional caller in our luxury apartment in Garville Avenue, Rathgar. The poor man wondered how we could live in such a place. He was a tidy, neat man – he even hung his pants on hangers and I think he might have owned an iron – but he had no chance with us. These days Dublin Corporation would close our flat down for contravening the laws on illegal dumping.

Martin eventually left our area for more salubrious surroundings. He lived near by and we used to meet up every so often. We always got on very well. He was a gentleman, the kind of fellow you could rely on. When his girlfriend, Mary, came down from Belfast one weekend, he brought her over to visit us in Garville Avenue. We offered her tea in our good cup. It was a cup I had borrowed from the Shelbourne Hotel around the time of my first game in Lansdowne Road – a souvenir of that great occasion. Mary rinsed the cup for five minutes and then scalded off any remaining germs with boiling water from the kettle. She was a bit shocked at the state of the place but we got on very well even so; she had a great sense of humour. We fell to discussing some cultural event going on in Dublin just then.

'Moss,' she said, pointing to the purple-yellow hairy fungus growing in the bottles decorating the window-sill, 'the only culture you'll find in this place is in the bottom of those milk-bottles.'

Mary called again after that first visit, and was as nice then as she is now.

She was still the same Mary when she was made President of Ireland.

In 2001, on the 30th anniversary of the match in Galway, Mary and Martin threw a big dinner for the Sigerson Cup squads in their house in the Phoenix Park. President McAleese and Martin greeted all of us at the door.

'It's a bit of change from that flat you used to have in Rathgar,' she said by way of welcoming us to Áras an Uachtaráin.

The dinner was a great success. Old friendships were renewed. Our captain back in 1971, Jim Coghlan, got up to say a few words: 'As I was saying back in the dressing room in Galway 30 years ago – do ye remember my rousing speech to ye that day? Do ye remember what I said before we ran out on the pitch?'

None of us had the slightest recollection.

'I said: "Lads, we can't leave the Sigerson after us. If the President has a reunion in the Áras in 30 years time do you want to be known as the losing team?"'

I have been back to their home many times since. On one occasion the President introduced me to Ronnie Flanagan, who was then Chief Constable of the Royal Ulster Constabulary. The President has done as much as anyone to foster better relations between north and south. I suppose, in spite of my background, I always got on particularly well with the northern boys. I patted his balding pate and said, 'Mary, there was a lot more hair on that the last time I stood on it.'

She was taken aback for a second until the Chief Constable explained the remark – Ronnie had played for CIYMS and Ulster and many is the hard battle we had.

Mary McAleese's presidency knows no boundaries. She is a GAA fanatic, but she can discuss any sport. There's no airs or graces either – what you see is what you get – and I believe the President wants more than anything to bring the people of this island closer together.

I haven't told her yet that I'm a President myself these days – of the Monasterevin/Portarlington Lions' Club here in Portarlington. The Lions do a lot of valuable work for local charities and for GOAL. I act as bouncer at our fund-raising dances. The only time I ever had any bother was when two female pensioners fought over a man. He didn't look fit enough to break eggs, but it took me all I could do to keep them from leathering each other while lover boy sat up at the bar sipping his half pint of shandy.

Some wit said I made history in that I was the first Lion to become President of a Lions' club and that my most successful Lions' outing was our golf day to Portarlington Golf Club. I manage to get out to the golf club most Saturdays, except, of course, during the rugby season. There can be little doubt that it is one of the most rewarding and at the same time infuriating of games. I will never master it, but there are still the occasional moments of glory, such as the day I sank a long putt and won the major of the agricultural world, the County Laois Ags Society (CLAS) Captain's Prize. Later, in the clubhouse, I was asked about the putt.

'Lads,' I replied, 'it was so far away from the hole that I lit up a tipped cigar and by the time the ball went down into the hole I had half of it smoked.'

Sport still plays a major part in my life, I go to as many rugby matches as I can manage, and, if I can't go, I watch the game on television. I hardly ever miss a Kerry All-Ireland Championship game, and I hate it when we lose. There's always a next year with Kerry, though.

I was lucky enough with injuries. There were many good friends who needed surgery on hips and knees. I think it was the potions that kept me right.

I suppose I have my own way of looking at most things. I always tried to think for myself. While I conform when I agree with conformity, beyond that I try to look at every angle of every aspect of my life. And I have always had a good regard for my health and healthy scepticism towards conventional medicine.

Having said that there are times when conventional medicine is the answer. Dr John Craig, my Lansdowne teammate, was very good to me when I had the hepatitis back in 1977. Mr Moriarty gave me a new lens after the mugging. There are serious illnesses such as cancer and the like that need full-on treatment but personally I seldom if ever take pharmaceuticals. The medical establishment has viewed medicine in different ways down through the centuries and of course they were always right. Then comes thalidomide, for example, and I can think of several families, who grew up just after me, who suffered because they took a 'safe drug'. Most ailments can be sorted out with alternative medicine or a mix of both complementary medicine and conventional remedies. I have my own remedies for a good many maladies.

I take a gulp of cod liver oil the odd morning to guard against arthritis. My left shoulder has never been the best since I played against doctor's advice on the occasion of my third cap, Ireland against England. I was afraid I would be dropped if I missed a game, so foolishly I played. I was young and I didn't have enough self-confidence to cry off. At the time Willie John McBride had copped that something was wrong and asked me if I was okay but I'd just nodded. I remember it took me a while to get going but when the shoulder warmed up I was able to raise my arm over my head, and I was so fired up, I just ignored the injury and played through the pain. It was very bad at times but I think I must have been a very driven man back then. I actually played fairly well that day. I've paid for it since, though. The shoulder comes against me from time to time.

I still call to see Sean Boylan in Dunboyne. Boylan now has a big practice, with a suite of offices and several employees. When I knew him first he operated out of his front room. Sean makes up this gallon of liquid made out of herbs and plant extracts. I take a good swig out of it every so often. It's for the liver and boosts the immune system.

But I have my own potion as well. Boylan will not disclose the contents of his – the Boylan formulas have been handed down from generation to generation and he guards their secrets as closely as the Coca-Cola formula – but I'm going to give you the ingredients of Keane's bottle free of charge. But don't blame me if you hate it – you're trying it at your own risk. I believe it can be a cure for many forms of rheumatism, arthritis or any kind of pain in the joints. You throw a spoon of crude blackstrap molasses into a mug with a bit of boiling water in it, then you add a dollop of honey and about a big spoonful of cider vinegar. Stir it with a spoon until it's well-mixed.

I tried to get Donal Lenihan to take a drop of it the first time we roomed together in the Shelbourne Hotel, the night before the Welsh game in 1982, the Triple Crown year. He politely declined. Yet he never stopped addling me that first night with his, 'What's in the bottle, Moss?' I explained it was a mix of Aloe Vera juice and Noni extract, but still he wouldn't take it. I offered him garlic tablets instead. Again he refused.

I still take these on occasions, but raw garlic is better. There's wild garlic growing around the farm at home and right by my house in Portarlington, and that's the best of all. How often did I hear an opponent in a scrum complain about the smell! When the next ruck would come I would breathe all over him. Almost kiss him. It drove fellows mad, even the French.

I have a rub as well made up out of poteen into which I add hot mustard, wintergreen and ammonia. It really gets the skin tingling. Be careful with the ammonia – as they say in the circus, don't try this at home.

A few years ago I met Joan O'Flynn from Tarbert, County Kerry, who specialises in energy healing, and I firmly believe in the benefit it brings as a back-up to other forms of treatment. Joan and her husband, John, imported a machine that alleviates the effects of geopathic stress, and when we tried it out we found that, when the machine was switched, the rods stopped twitching in my hand.

I try to fit in a bit of meditation every so often. I have adapted it to suit my own needs. I attended courses in meditation over the years and have developed my own mantra. I cannot disclose the mantra; it's considered bad luck.

Now all this stuff may not be for you, but it works for me. That's all I'm saying. I still go for check-ups. And a few quiet pints at the end of a long day can be the most therapeutic treatment of all – if I'm not driving that is. My job is based in Kilkenny now and I'm on the road most of the time. I'm involved in carrying out audits to ensure EU policy and regulations are complied among other things with but my job's changing now and rapidly. The accession of the new member states to the EU means that there are more demands on our common budget. We are all eating out of the same pot, which obviously means less for everyone. The small farmers with eight or nine cows, the people who made up the fabric of society in Currow and places like it when I was young, are a thing of the past. A holding that was considered a big farm even ten years ago would now be considered uneconomic. Farm-size is expanding to try to keep up. These changes are a serious challenge for all of us involved in the industry, and will have far-reaching consequences for rural Ireland. There is a very real danger our cities and towns will get bigger and bigger and the countryside will be left to the animals and the ramblers. I worry about the future of farming and the consequences for the farming community, but farmers are ever resourceful and hopefully we can keep the industry at the forefront of Irish life.

My mother and father were part of that older style of country life. They died some years ago, having lived a simple life right through to old age. In their later years they finally travelled a bit – to Medugorje, Rome, Lourdes and Fatima, which had a profound effect on them – and enjoyed the first holidays they had ever really had together. They were well deserved; when we were children my father could hardly take time away from the land to enjoy a few days by the seaside. My folks worked hard in tough times, as did most of their generation, and passed on a value system I have always tried to maintain, especially my religion, which is very important to me.

My brothers, Matt and Brian, are good and close friends. I am as welcome in their homes as they are in mine. We never fell out over anything, and we never will. We haven't had a scrap since the days when we used to clatter each other playing football back home in Currow, when we were young lads.

I suppose you could say I'm a happy man. There are days I still regret not making the most of the business opportunities I was offered in my heyday. Maybe I was better off. I might have turned into a ruthless man, and I've never had much time for those kinds of people. And as for any mid-life trauma, a visit to Calcutta wouldn't be long curing you, and that's for sure.

Anne and I get on very well together almost all the time – not all the time; that would be very boring. Her family has taken me on as one of their own and I am well settled in Portarlington. Anne works as a teacher. We have a Kerry expression to describe a woman who has a nicely paid job of her own, 'a laying hen'. 'That's fine', advised my mother 'as long as the hen doesn't eat all her own eggs.' We're not millionaires, far from it, but you could say we're 'comfortable'. And we pool our resources.

We have always been close, very close. We have two lovely girls, both of whom went to college and are now doing masters' degrees. Sarah and Anne Marie are well able to account for themselves. They can tell their own stories in due course. If I was lucky on the field, I was even luckier off it, and I wouldn't swap my three girls for the world. And that's the thing about family. It's the cornerstone. I pass by Sarah's and Anne Marie's empty bedrooms, but it doesn't get me down. Yes, I miss them, but our girls are making their own way out in the world. It gives me a great lift when I think of them. That's a natural thing and the way it should be. They come home as often as they can.

And there will always be rugby. It's still a huge part of my life. I love to see all the provinces prosper but Munster is the team nearest to my heart. My greatest wish is to see Munster win a European Cup. Even if they don't, they have given us more hours of pleasure than any mortal deserves. I missed out on playing for Munster in the European Cup, though I doubt if I would have won a place with Donncha O'Callaghan and Paul O'Connell to contend with.

I look forward to Munster matches and when the tannoy plays *Stand up and Fight* as Munster run onto the field my heart soars. The Munster wit comes to the fore in Thomond Park and the supporters always play due respect to the opposition – something quite rare in sport today.

There will always be a Munster. I love the fans and the camaraderie, especially when we play in France, with the odds stacked against us and referees missing blatant opposition fouls. What is with referees and Munster? We have suffered so much from incompetent refereeing. It's us against the world, at times. It broke my heart when we were beaten in two European Cup finals when we should have won both.

Galwey was sin-binned after the referee missed an earlier knock on in the same play by the opposition in the final against Northampton in 2000. Mick tapped down a pass near the opposition line. Northampton had no chance of scoring but Mick was sin-binned all the same. It was a very, very harsh decision. Then John O'Neill scored a valid try, which television evidence subsequently proved should not have been disallowed in a semi-final against Stade Francais in 2001. Neil Back put his hand where he shouldn't when we looked as if we could have scored against Leicester in Cardiff in 2002. The referee and touch judges amazingly missed the incident. Those Munster defeats and the injustice of them took as much out of me emotionally as any of the losses I suffered in a green, or green-and-gold, jersey.

I'd love to have played with my fellow Currow man, Mick Galwey. I togged out with a 75 per cent Kerry second row when I played with Donal Lenihan, a 100 per cent Kerry second row with Donal Spring, but it would have been lovely to have played in an all-Currow second row for Ireland. Wishful thinking, seeing as Galwey is 18 years younger than this old soldier.

I was so proud of Mick when he led out Munster. It was even better than the thrill I felt when he equalled the Currow try-scoring record for Ireland, jointly held by Mick Doyle and one Maurice Ignatius Keane. Galwey scored in the same corner of Lansdowne Road where I had managed to score against Scotland in 1980 and Doyler had also touched down in that spot long before I started to play the game. I sometimes think I should ask the IRFU for a few sods from that holy place before they knock the old stadium down and dig up the hallowed turf. Maybe they could erect a little plaque and name it 'Currow Corner'.

Mick Galwey brought his rugby expertise to Shannon, when he took over as coach, and in his first season in charge he managed the club to an All-Ireland League title.

Poor Doyler – I retired the year he took over as Ireland's coach. He and Ciaran Fitzgerald called to see me and asked if I would stay on, but I did him a big favour, one I should have done for Willie John – I stayed retired. Doyler would have started me in his first season, and maybe I could have hung on to win a second Triple Crown, but I doubt it. His was a new young team and I would have been out of step with the rest of the lads. In fact, I was yards slower, years older and a married man with children. But I appreciated the compliment.

Doyler's teams played rugby in his own image. They were fast, intelligent and imaginative. He loved the game. I think he had that Kerry thing about playing the game, not just to win, but to honour the glory of sport itself.

We grew very close as the years went on. We met at rugby internationals and dinners, and I'll never forget the day we spent on the banks of the Brown Flesk River, making a documentary about Mick Galwey, with producer Eamon Keane. The sun was splitting the stones so we all went for a paddle and I pointed out the exact spot where Doyler's Uncle

Bill used to launch his cattle raids into our land. Doyler was unabashed. 'But for the high quality manure they spread,' he shot back, 'your place would have been a desert.'

It was good to be back in Currow, a village with more rugby internationals than pubs. Mick Doyle and his brother Tommy, Mick Galwey and myself all pulled on the green jersey. Only three of us wore the green-and-gold of Kerry, though. Doyler missed out on that one, something I never tired of reminding him.

Galwey remarked that 'the Keanes were in the Killiney end of the village, looking down on the rest.' I suppose that was fair enough, seeing as we lived on a hill. Later he was asked how many rugby internationals came from Currow. 'Four,' Galwey replied, 'but only three of us played for the Lions.' He was proud of that, though too modest to point out that he was the one Currow man to captain Ireland, play for the Lions, and win an All-Ireland senior medal with Kerry. It was a remarkable record of achievement. By the way Tommy Doyle, the man who wasn't a Lion, gained ample compensation. He won an All-Ireland minor medal for Kerry in 1962.

In 2004 we attended a lunch in honour of Con Houlihan, the most poetic of all sportswriters. Con came from just down the road in Castle Island. Jimmy Deenihan and Bobby O' Connell and the people of Castle Island erected a statue of Con in the Main Street. Doyler was full of his fun, recalling the days when he played in a Castle Island back row with Con and writer John B Keane:

> 'Con refused to wear boots in case he inadvertently hurt the opposition and John B was a tearaway wing-forward. My teammates discussed every aspect of literature, from Maupassant and his facility for economy in his

> writing, to Dickens' ability to make the
> extraordinary seem normal. And this was in the
> middle of the game.'

His speech brought the house down. We made a night of it. Many of our friends were there.

'Hey, guys,' Doyler said, calling Mick and myself over. 'I am very proud to come from Currow and very proud of you guys.' There were tears in his eyes.

'Doyler,' I said, 'will you stop the bullshit. Can you not call us lads? What's this "guys" thing?'

Doyler ignored me. He had more important matters to announce. 'Some day,' he predicted, 'Mick Galwey will go on to coach Munster and Ireland.'

'Yeah,' I said, 'and then some bollix in a pub quiz will ask how many of us coached Ireland and Mick will stand up and say: "Only two of us!"'

The slagging went on all night long, with Doyler coming back to the company to tell us some new joke or recall an old story about one of our neighbours. The strangest story of all, though, was the one about the four international rugby players who came from a village with no rugby team. But the Castle Island boys claimed him as one of theirs. I said, 'lads we have a few wasters we can give you if you want but Doyler is ours.'

We eventfully agreed joint sovereignty and awarded Doyler dual citizenship.

Hopefully the tradition will go on. We had encouraged and supported one another, and now, whenever I'm at home, I keep an eye out for a big, strong, young lad who migh have the makings of a rugby player – a young lad too big fo Gaelic football. If I recruited a lad who was good enough play for Kerry I would never be allowed home again. F behind our laughing and joking that night, we were pr of our village and the fame and glory we brought to our own place. And Doyler, because he had spent so much time away from home, felt that most of all.

That was the last time we were together. A few months after that lunch in Castle Island, Doyler was killed in a car accident. It was a sad day, a dreadful shock; it hit me hard. I was very, very fond of Mick Doyle and his death upset me no end. He beat all kinds of health problems, made a miraculous recovery from a stroke and then he went and got killed in a car crash. I thought he was indestructible.

I lost not only a friend but also a wise man who always gave the right advice, even if it might not have been what you wanted to hear. I remember one time, after I was long retired from Lansdowne when Mick Kearney suggested I should speak at a much-needed fundraiser for the club. I was apprehensive. Kearney, the then President of Lansdowne, was a pal and in any case you don't refuse him when it comes to doing something for Lansdowne. I phoned Doyler for advice. The function was to be a lunch held before an international game at the ground and Mick Doyle could talk at will – he never showed any sign of nerves.

'To thine own self be true, Mossy,' was what he told me, and he gave me a tip too.

The big function room in Lansdowne pavilion was packed as the guests sat down to their meal. If I could, I would have hidden under the table. Doyler had reminded me of a story I told him years before and which I had long forgotten, so I had that much to start with at least. I'll tell it again in his honour. He'd like that.

'I'm often asked how it was we are so big in Currow. Well, it's all down to the feeding. We ate for Ireland as well as played for Ireland. On one occasion, my mother asked a neighbour to go to the butcher's in Castle Island to buy a pig's head for the dinner.

"Where will I cut it from?" asked the butcher, pointing to a full pig stretched out on the big wooden block in front of him.

The neighbour thought of the hungry gang of Keanes back home in Currow before she answered.

"I suppose," she instructed, "you better cut it as close to his arse as possible.'"

* * *

Club rugby is very much in decline in Ireland at present, a fact of which the IRFU is only too well aware. And it's such a shame. Rugby is more than a game. The club is more than just a sports facility. There are structures for young people to help them develop, support for any who may hit a bit of trouble. Friendships are made there that last forever. Friendships I made in the game have carried me through life. Des Fitzgerald of Lansdowne and the Lions and a great mate always said the true test is not the caps you win but how many show up at your funeral. One of my greatest honours was to be chosen for the most prestigious Lansdowne team of all, when I was one of six who carried Con Murphy's coffin on his last outing in the club colours. Like other clubs, Lansdowne looks after its own to the last.

I still look forward to the rugby season every year. I hardly ever miss an Irish home game and I was the happiest man in Lansdowne Road when we beat Scotland to win the Triple Crown in 2004.

It bothers me, though, that there seems to be very little time for players to recover from the rigours of the game nowadays. There are summer tours, autumn internationals, Heineken Cups, domestic leagues – today's rugby players are in everything bar the crib at Christmas. I know it's great to work at something you truly love: up every morning training, eating just the right food to build up muscle, doing weights and working in the gym; then going to bed early to be ready for tomorrow's schedule. But as a man back home with five cows in his shed asked when a farmer with ten cows was being discussed: 'is he happy?'

The game was always just that for me – a game, not an obsession. I loved it and enjoyed most of the time I spent playing rugby football. I trained hard, too. There were times when it wore me out, particularly when I played two games in the one day – Gaelic football and rugby – for University College Cork, but that was what I wanted to do just then; no one was telling me I had to do it. I trained even harder when I joined Lansdowne and became an international, but I was more experienced by then, and I learned a lot from my teammates. I learned so much from Willie Duggan, who knew how to pace himself when it came to the physical stuff, so I worked to be fully fit when I needed to be, and not before. We took long summer holidays from the game, too – unless we were going on tour and that didn't happen too often. I couldn't even look at a rugby ball most summers.

We only played seven or eight serious games a year, and only about five of those were internationals. Players today play far more rugby and the hits are more ferocious. When anyone plays a game as tough as rugby football they know there will be consequences. We knew it back when I played, and none of us expected to walk away unscathed. But though there were some terrible injuries, the game overall was hard but fair. It's when I look at my few aches and pains that I wonder, how will today's players fare? I pray the players of today will come through so they're in reasonable shape by the time they get to my age.

Rugby was always hard, but I suppose the boys are stronger now, bigger and faster than we were. I worry about them in the years ahead though. I know that Eddie

O'Sullivan, the current Irish coach, is equally concerned, and the IRFU has ensured that Irish players at least will be given support and assistance. Ireland has one of the best player welfare structures in world rugby but, even so, the dangers are obvious. The powers-that-be in world rugby must ensure our players have a good quality of life when their playing days are over.

I think I would have given it a miss. Though in many ways I don't think I would have had much of a choice, as a person coming from my background would have definitely missed the boat. With professionalism, everything is now geared towards rugby academies, under-age structures and the like – a system that will likely see Ireland miss out on some great talent.

* * *

In the early morning I often walk down by the wood next to my house. Sometimes I come across a herd of deer. I love the peace of the wood. I don't have to be anyone or do anything. There's no place like it, except my old home in Currow.

I'm 57 now and have never felt happier with life. I'm not one that thinks of how I'd like to be remembered or shite like that. I've had many great days and I've been lucky in life. I played rugby 51 times for Ireland and made lasting friendships out of the game. What I achieved was certainly against the odds but sport can throw these things up – that's the beauty of it.

I'd like to think that success never went to my head and that if someone, somewhere, was asked they might say, 'Moss Keane? – Ah sure he did his best.'

He did his best.

That would do me nicely.